*Handwritten:* To: Jacob - Christain Love August 14, 2016 Malcolm Edge Glencoe High School Retired Teacher 1959-1996

# Life Is So Simple When

# WE CHOOSE TO LOVE GOD'S WAY

**(Because we are all about His love)**

*by*
Captain Herman L. Hinton

(A man of God who happens to be
an officer of the law)

Unless otherwise indicated, all Scripture quotations are taken from A Regency Bible, *The Holy Bible, King James Version*, Copyright © 1990, Thomas Nelson Publishers.

All Scripture quotations marked NIV are taken from the *NIV Study Bible,* Tenth Anniversary Edition, copyright © 1995, Zondervan Publishing Edition.

All definitions are from:

*The Layman's Bible Dictionary*, George W. Knight & Rayburn W. Ray, Eds., Barbour Publishing, Inc.
or
*Merriam Webster's Collegiate Dictionary,* Tenth Ed., 1996.


*Life Is So Simple When*
WE CHOOSE TO LOVE GOD'S WAY
ISBN 0-88144-222-4
Copyright © 2005 by
Herman L. Hinton
P. O. Box 59194
Homewood, Alabama 35259

Published by
Christian Publishing Services
P. O. Box 701434
Tulsa, Oklahoma 74170 U.S.A.

Text Design: Lisa Simpson

Printed in the United States of America. All rights reserved under International Copyright Law. Contents and/or cover may not be reproduced in whole or in part in any form without the express written consent of the Publisher.

# Contents

Introduction

| | | |
|---|---|---|
| Chapter 1 | Know God's Love (Simply Love) ............9 | |
| Chapter 2 | Choose God Today Above All Else (Simply Choose) ........................47 | |
| Chapter 3 | Know the Benefits of God's Love (Simply Benefit) ........................67 | |
| Chapter 4 | What Does the Bible Say About Love? (Simply Study) .........................89 | |
| Chapter 5 | How Do I Improve My Love Walk? (Simply Improve) ......................109 | |
| Chapter 6 | Recognize the Importance of Forgiveness (Simply Forgive) ........................143 | |
| Chapter 7 | Consider the Consequences of Disobedience (Simply Obey) ..........................165 | |
| Chapter 8 | Choose To Be Happy (Happiness Is a Choice) ................187 | |
| Chapter 9 | Always Give Thanks (Simply Thank God) ...................207 | |
| Chapter 10 | Know Your Role in Society (Simply Win Souls for Jesus) ...........225 | |

About the Author ................................251

# Introduction

On October 6, 2003, I received a timeout in my life as police lieutenant of the Homicide Unit in Birmingham, Alabama. I experienced a serious accidental gunshot wound that severed one of three main arteries in my lower right leg while breaking my tibia and fibula. The prognosis was that I would be idle between nine months to a year and possibly even lose my leg. There were no guarantees that I would ever regain my normal walk, let alone return to work. However, because of God's favor and with weeks of arduous therapy, I was back at work six months later with no restrictions, very little pain, and no abnormalities in my walk.

Three weeks before returning to work on March 7, 2004, the Holy Spirit revealed to me that I was to write a book to address the need to renew our minds, stop the senseless killings, and turn our attention to God's perfect love, which is available to each of us. All God asks is that we love Him first, love each other with the same intensity that we love ourselves, and always seek to do what is right just because it is right! Once God's way of love is permanently embedded in our life, we will experience the best of God's perfect love.

In this book, I reveal several hindrances and blockages that we build and launch each day when we refuse to follow God's recipe for love. These blockages will not go away if we do not adhere to the living Word of God or if we are in denial, refusing to acknowledge that He exists. God's love and His Word are food for our soul, and like any food that is good for nourishment, we will never get enough during one setting to last a lifetime.

In this book, I also expatiate some very simple things you can do to overcome the blockages. You will have an opportunity to mirror your life and see for yourself where you are and what you need to do to get where God wants you to be. No one will ever completely master God's Word, but once we learn to put

## Life Is So Simple When
## WE CHOOSE TO LOVE GOD'S WAY

our trust in God and in what He says in His Word, it will become second nature to work our way past mental and physical blockages.

These blockages will hinder our forgiveness, preclude our blessings, and put chinks in our path to receive the perfect love that God has for those of us who believe and follow the instructions laid out in His living Word. First John 4:21 NIV says, **"Whoever loves God must also love his brother."**

For more than twenty-one years I have worked as a devout Christian in the criminal justice system, the last five years as commander in the Homicide Unit. I have witnessed hundreds of cases where victims were brutally murdered simply because the perpetrator's love for God was replaced by a false sense of honor. Having reviewed more than four hundred violent crime scenes over the last five years alone, I have an inspiring message of encouragement from our heavenly Father about His great love for each of us and the beautiful returns He guarantees when we *Choose to Love His Way*. It is based on the Holy Spirit's guidance, my Christian and worldly experiences, and the unimpeachable Word of God.

God loves us dearly, and in John 15:12 He gives us a simple command: **"That ye love one another, as I have loved you."** All of the great things we may do in life have their place, but nothing precedes the love of God, which was demonstrated to us through Jesus' death, burial, and resurrection.

The things God requires us to do in this life to live successfully are so simple, yet we continue to look for deep-rooted philosophical answers that do not exist. All we need to do is *simply love God's way* by choosing Jesus and staying on the path that He has chosen for our life.

I often wonder how many of us have given serious thought as to how this world would fare if we would totally submit to God and encourage one another to *simply love His way*. We can't simply love God's way until we get it right, but we must love His way until we can't get it wrong! Can you imagine what

## Introduction

the world would be like if we were totally persuaded by the love of God and made a valiant effort to extend our cadre by at least one person a day? Do you love God's way? What is there in your life that precludes you from receiving the absolute best that God has to offer?

For me it started with a self-assessment. Shortly after experiencing the gunshot wound, I made up my mind to give my life totally to God and never renege on giving Him even the smallest of my concerns. Much to my delight, this simple act of obedience has far exceeded anything I could ever fathom. Now it's your turn. Remember, God is no respecter of persons. Begin to trust Him right now and permit Him to guide you in every compartment of your life.

This book is for the Christian who is just beginning his or her journey, no longer a babe in Christ. It is also for those God is waiting on to find their way back to His ark of safety. You will find practical guidance with scriptural backup as to how simple life can be when you are rooted in the Word of God and when you make godly decisions by following His plan for your life. Simply love Him first, then extend your love to others.

Herman L. Hinton

# Chapter 1

# Know God's Love (Simply Love)

*I* believe love is the most powerful action in the world. There is no price tag on it and its value is beyond estimation, yet many people reject it. The greatest gift that anyone will ever receive or ever want was born in a manger, wrapped in swaddling clothes, and later laid down His life for us on Calvary. The life of Jesus is offered for all mankind as the "gift of salvation." Over two thousand years later, we are still privileged to have the opportunity to receive this gift through a simple belief in His precious blood.

This gift of salvation, which delivers us from sin and reconciles us to God, is a gift of love from God that could never be earned. Through this transition of love from God, through Jesus to us, the blood of Jesus washed away all of our sins, shortcomings, sicknesses, and personal failures. He was nailed to the cross, bearing the weight of the entire world on His shoulders. God loved us so much according to Romans 5:8 **"that, while we were yet sinners, Christ died for us."**

Who can fathom sacrificing the life of an only child — a child of royalty — for a world of people who have never stopped doing the very things that prompted God to make this sacrifice in the first place? That's the kind of love that only God can give.

The cornerstone of our belief, however, is that Jesus not only died for our sins, He was supernaturally resurrected by the power of God. Romans 10:9 says, **"That if thou shalt confess with thy mouth the Lord Jesus, and shalt believe in thine heart that God hath raised him from the**

**dead, thou shalt be saved."** There must be an inward belief and an outward confession that Jesus gained complete mastery over the grave for us.

So through our belief in His death, burial, and resurrection, we too are able to get up, rebound from our shortcomings or any other area of personal failure, and move forward in the right direction, manning our positions in His perfect will. God has made the process to receive His unmerited favor so simple, even to those who feel that they are in a quagmire, with no semblance of hope.

In Luke 15:7 Jesus said, **"I say unto you, that likewise joy shall be in heaven over one sinner that repenteth, more than over ninety and nine just persons, which need no repentance."** This indeed is one of several biblical validation statements, making it undeniably clear that God is concerned about every one of His precious creations, and that the gift of salvation is free to all.

Regardless of how much God loves us and wants us to abide in His perfect will, we must choose of our own volition whether or not we will serve Him. God does not deploy deceptive devices or scare tactics. His love will never force us to receive His unmerited favor. He simply guarantees us the benefits of a right to eternal life through the death, burial, and resurrection of Jesus if we will:

- Confess and believe.
- Repent and receive.
- Remain obedient to His Word.

It is not enough to know that Jesus died for us. Jesus came to earth out of perfect obedience and love so we might have life. He demonstrated His love in a more profound way than it could ever be expressed by you or me. Ephesians 5:1-2 says:

> **Be ye therefore followers of God, as dear children; and walk in love, as Christ also hath loved**

**us, and hath given himself for us an offering and a sacrifice to God for a sweet-smelling savour.**

Jesus followed His Father's plan to the letter. Moreover, He pleased God the Father. We should follow Jesus' example in life with the same vigor as He followed His Father and exemplified His love for us.

When we were young, most of us probably admired someone in a special relationship out of love and respect, whether it was our mother, father, grandparents, or someone else. At some point, perhaps we tried our best to mimic them. Children are commanded to be loyal and honor their parents.

As followers of God, we are to proceed with the love walk with Jesus, displaying the same fervor as He did in following His Father. Jesus said in John 14:10, **"The words that I speak unto you I speak not of myself: but the Father that dwelleth in me, he doeth the works."** Just as He was obedient and submissive to the authority of His Father, always showing love and compassion for us even when we didn't deserve it, we are expected to live and love each other with the same veracity, intensity, and consistency, mimicking our heavenly Father in every imaginable way.

The love that Christ displayed during His earthly love walk is the same love that should guide us in showing compassion, forgiveness, and in lifting people as we attempt to meet their needs and lead them to Jesus. As saints of God, we are charged with being imitators of Jesus.

In John 15:10 Jesus said, **"If ye keep my commandments, ye shall abide in my love; even as I have kept my Father's commandments, and abide in his love."** To keep our heavenly Father's commandments is not a hit-and-miss deal or a one-time verbal agreement. His commandments are to be adhered to at all times. Not just when we feel like it, predicated on what we need at that moment, or who we are with at the time.

Our omnipotent God says in Jeremiah 23:23-24:

**Am I a God at hand, saith the Lord, and not a God afar off? Can any hide himself in secret places that I shall not see him? saith the Lord. Do not I fill heaven and earth? saith the Lord.**

Just as God's love follows us and keeps us from harm, His eyes also see everything that we do! God's love and His presence are universal. No crime goes unnoticed, and every wrong will be addressed. The Word of God, if applied to your life, will help serve as a barometer for your character. It will make you feel uncomfortable in any setting that is not conducive to the lifestyle of an ambassador for His Kingdom.

God knows your character when you are seen in the light with others, and He knows your character whenever you think that others do not see you. Christ is present with two or three witnesses or with a multitude of people, and God's power is also our companion in the form of the Holy Spirit or Comforter who abides with us forever. We are constantly reminded from His Word to be obedient to the Word.

To consistently do as God has instructed us has been our Achilles' heel since the beginning of time with Adam and Eve. However, there was never any doubt about the obedience of Jesus or His love for His Father. There was never a debate, or "let's talk it over," or "let me think about that." They demonstrated more than a prototypical Father-Son relationship. Their relationship was a model of excellence, one that could never be duplicated, the type of loving relationship that men and women today should satiate their families with. We can never overstate the importance of obedience if we are to emulate the love walk of Jesus.

First John 4:8 says, **"He that loveth not knoweth not God; for God is love."** Love is the very nature of God. God's love for us is indescribable as stated by the Apostle Paul in Romans 8:38-39:

# Know God's Love
## (Simply Love)

**For I am persuaded, that neither death, nor life, nor angels, nor principalities, nor powers, nor things present, nor things to come, nor height, nor depth, nor any other creature, shall be able to separate us from the love of God, which is in Christ Jesus our Lord.**

Neither life nor death nor anything in between can keep us apart from the love of God that was revealed to us through Jesus. God's love is always present and it will always do exactly what He said in His Word. A love of this scope, with this kind of warranty, most certainly deserves our best efforts at all times in everything that we do to exemplify it.

This is more than just "deep love." The faculties of no earthly mind can grasp the magnitude of God's love for us. Outside of the Trinity (God, Jesus, and the Holy Spirit) I can think of no other person more qualified to make this categorical claim regarding God's love for mankind than the Apostle Paul who was transformed from a persecutor of Christians to a Christian living exclusively for Christ.

The Apostle Paul says in First Corinthians 13:13, **"And now abideth faith, hope, charity, these three; but the greatest of these is charity** [or love]." Love is essential to man's relationship to God as well as man's relationship to others. The God-kind of love will last forever. What does it mean to be the greatest? It means to be preeminent over others or remarkable in magnitude. God's love is the greatest, and if we desire to love with the love of God, then *choosing to love God's way* should be our number one goal.

We consistently say, "It is more blessed to give than to receive," and all of us desire to have the best of God's blessings, yet we do not consistently give the God-kind of love that all of God's children should practically exude. Is it because these are trite statements that we flippantly repeat? Or is it that they are simply words that we use as catch phrases? I believe that most people really desire to love God's way. I believe that the vast majority of people in the world are genuinely concerned and are searching for truth and for answers to the social ills that confront us today, albeit in the wrong places.

As a nation we have been known to search for things that were stretched out before our very own eyes. It might literally blow you away to know that the answer lies within each of us, and it is quite simple once you have given some serious thought to this matter. Say this with me: *I must first love myself.*

**We cannot give
What we do not have,
But if we study the Word,
Pray, and confess,
By the grace of God's love
We will possess.**

I want you to ponder this. Every time anger or unkind words or actions manifest in our conversations or behavior, it is simply a reflection by an outward expression of how we really feel inside; namely, about ourselves. Our renowned Teacher and Savior Jesus Christ said in Matthew 19:19, **"Love thy neighbour as thyself."** He knew that in order for us to successfully administer love to others we had to first *love ourselves.*

When I say, "You must first love yourself," I am not committing to external extremities such as fine clothing, jewelry, shoes, and fragrances. These nuances are important and they do have their place. God wants us to have them and more. David said in Psalm 37:4, **"Delight thyself also in the Lord; and he shall give thee the *desires* of thine heart."** God not only wants us to have our needs met, but He also wants us to have the things that we desire. He wants to bless us exceedingly so that we can be a blessing to others and they can see His great works through us.

But what happens when your mind begins to match wits with unkind words that someone says to you, and your eyes are no longer attracted to or affected by the outward appearance of that person? In other words, your focus has changed. The script has flipped. What happened is known as a paradigm change. The real you suddenly appeared. Your behavior is actually a microcosm of the way that you feel about yourself on the inside.

When Jesus says, "Love your neighbor" He is not talking solely about "next door." He means your fellowman. That includes everyone regardless of race, sex, creed, or any other differences. It makes no difference what they have done or said about you. To "love your neighbor" means to have compassion for people, to recognize their needs, and to render assistance as the Spirit leads.

People need to know that the Kingdom of God does exist and they need to see it clearly demonstrated through you. Throughout the four Gospels — Matthew, Mark, Luke, and John — Jesus constantly showed love and compassion for people, whether it was turning water into wine (John 2:1-11); calming a storm (Mark 4:35-41); feeding four thousand plus people (Matthew 15:32-39); or cleansing ten lepers at one time (Luke 17:11-19). Likewise, we should feel a sense of obligation to rescue people.

Every person you come in contact with is your neighbor, even if you never see him or her again. This is why it is so important that whenever we meet people we should always be concerned with leaving a lasting impression — the right impression, which is the impression of Jesus, a worthy impression. The world needs to know that the love of Jesus exists everywhere, and as ambassadors for Him, it should be evident in you and me.

Have you ever had a run-in or an unfortunate incident happen between you and a stranger and you felt that it never really got resolved? When you left that scene, you were convinced beyond a shadow of a doubt that you got the short end of the stick. Months later, you go to talk to someone in company management about a late charge that you feel you unjustly received on your last month's bill. You arrive at the business and guess who is eagerly waiting to greet you at the customer service desk? This would be an uncomfortable situation.

## Life Is So Simple When
## WE CHOOSE TO LOVE GOD'S WAY

Most people do not like any sign of conflict or confrontation, but both will always exist in this world whether we are prepared to handle them or not. However, Jesus reminds us in John 16:33, **"Be of good cheer; I have overcome the world."**

Whatever you are confronted with, learn how to deal with it through the "fruit of the Spirit," which resides in every born-again saint of God. Whenever you have a chance to take a winning shot for Jesus, do it. Don't pass the ball on to someone else.

According to Galatians 5:22-23, those of us who live in Christ possess the fruit of the Spirit — **"love, joy, peace, longsuffering, gentleness, goodness, faith, meekness, temperance: against such there is no law."**

If the Holy Spirit dwells in you, then you already have the fruit. One meaning of "fruit" is a product. We often equate fruit with success, and why not? We are expected to bear, share, and enjoy good success in our life. Remember, for trees to bear fruit, it requires a process. Jesus tells us in Mark 4:28, **"For the earth bringeth forth fruit of herself; first the blade, then the ear, after that the full corn in the ear."** The fruit of the Spirit are already processed and readily available in you. Once we are saved, we receive these features of God to help us make it in life and to handle confrontation. All we need to do is activate them through prayer.

I find it amazing that the first fruit of the Spirit listed is *love.* We are talking about agape love, the unconditional love that Jesus possessed and expressed, as He showed compassion for the well-being of others while often denying Himself.

Any Christian who does not choose to activate the fruit of love is fruitless. There are no statutes or laws on the books that will cause an arrest or conviction if you are armed with the fruit of the Spirit. As Christians we need to be able to successfully tap into every spiritual weapon that God permits in our quest to make a statement to the world that through Christ we have whatever we need in every possible situation.

# Know God's Love
## (Simply Love)

The fruit of the Spirit assists us in walking in the righteousness of God through our faith in Christ. We simply cannot do it by ourselves. We need the help of God and the guidance of the Holy Spirit.

There are many people who do not know the love of God, and even some Christians who profess to know God who continue to walk with a short fuse ready to explode at a moment's notice. Sometimes it seems as though the more we try to avoid certain people, the more we actually come in contact with them or the more we need their service. Believe me, this is by design. As children of God, we represent God's Customer Service Department, and if we are going to be His ambassadors, winning souls for Jesus, our motto should be *to treat everyone right the first time we see them and every time we see them.*

This is just another reason why it is so important for saints to get a revelation of the importance of a God-fearing love walk each day. Confrontation is a golden opportunity for us to exhibit the God-qualities that are found in the love of Jesus that should be evident in all Christians. We ought not let anyone lower us into using words or anti-Christ behavior that is not representative of the Kingdom of God. Once the world manages to get us on par with their rationale, they absolutely pin us down with their worldly experience. Anger and using the wrong words grieve the Holy Spirit.

In this world, we will be confronted with implacable people whom we should simply walk away from. But even at that, the way we respond should be in a manner such that if a third party was observing, they might be blessed and led to the knowledge of God through our action. You never know who is watching or listening. Regardless, we should always strive to be kind and to do well on purpose. We should examine ourselves each morning to ensure that we have fueled up with the Word of God and are fully charged with His Spirit as we prepare to spread His love wherever we go.

Now that we have set the tone for loving God's way, let's take a closer look at our foundational word **"love."** For some people, love entails an attachment or relationship, and most of us base this attachment on affection, a blood relationship, a want, a genuine concern, a sexual desire, or simply a personal adoration. However, God's love commands that we love everyone with the love of Jesus, even if they do not love us.

Jesus said in Matthew 5:46, **"For if ye love them which love you, what reward have ye?"** The expansion of God's Kingdom is predicated on people, God's most important creation. So we must be about God's business of winning them to Jesus. I know there are a myriad of motives or reasons that we could come up with as to why we choose to love or not love another person or even a certain group of people. But once you get revelation knowledge of how the love of God works in God's grand scheme of things, and what Jesus did for all of us when He died on the cross, you will never again accept any reason not to love everyone.

There is beauty in all of God's creation, but there is an inexpressible beauty in God's creation of human beings. The first chapter of Genesis reveals how God spoke the world into existence. Genesis 1:31 says, **"God saw every thing that he had made, and, behold, it was very good. . . ."** After speaking the world into existence, He made man in His own image.

First John 4:19 says, **"We love him, because he first loved us."** To be made in the very image of God, the Creator of the universe, and to be loved first by Him, is the quintessential model of love. The human body is a creation of beauty that requires an insatiable amount of love from birth to death just to survive. We know that there are other God-given essentials that this sculpture of beauty called the body requires, but for the long-range success of any human being to walk in whatever their beliefs might be, he or she must have love. We must have love because God is love. A person is confused in their theology if they profess to be a child of God but they do not exude the love of God towards everyone they meet and greet in their *daily* love walk.

# Know God's Love
## (Simply Love)

Each person is precious to God. He loves us so much that He gave the life of His only Son Jesus. First John 4:10 NIV states, **"This is love: not that we loved God, but that he loved us and sent his Son as an atoning sacrifice for our sins."** He gave His life so that we might receive life. Colossians 1:22-23 NIV says, **"But now he has reconciled you by Christ's physical body through death to present you holy in his sight, without blemish and free from accusation — if you continue in your faith, established and firm, not moved from the hope held out in the gospel. . . ."**

Through the redemptive blood of Jesus, we are made above reproach in God's sight and full of His love. After the resurrection, Jesus ascended to the Father. However, He did not leave us alone. We have been afforded the luxury of a Comforter, the Holy Spirit, a present help 24/7. The Holy Spirit is always moving and present, but He does not begin to operate or hover over our life until we give Him something to work with. We must begin to confess the Word of God on a daily basis.

Unless we have received the love of God through His Son Jesus, we cannot give the love of God to others. If we have an earnest desire to improve our love walk, we should get to know Him. The only way to make this a reality is to study and meditate in His Word every day. A consistent work-study process in the Word of God is the foundation for building a masterful love relationship with God.

When you build your relationship with God through Jesus, it is a gradual construction that eventually develops into a wholesome relationship, and it will continue to enlarge if you nourish it daily. Your relationship with God will continue to invigorate as you become more knowledgeable through His Word and His spiritual guidance.

The Apostle Paul reminds us in Second Timothy 2:15, **"Study to shew thyself approved unto God. . . ."** To study involves work. You must form a habitual relationship with Him, winning His approval as you apply His Word to your life.

## Life Is So Simple When
## WE CHOOSE TO LOVE GOD'S WAY

As you know, we inherit some of our habits and traits genetically while some are formed environmentally. A renewing of the mind must take place to erase all of the bad data that we have mentally collected during our life span. Think what it would be like to feed defective software into your computer's hard drive. If you continue to do this, you will in all likelihood harm your computer, perhaps causing irreversible damage. So it is with our minds. The mind is a wonderful, powerful computer, personally designed and given by God. We can cause any action we want by simply feeding a thought into our mind. That's why in order to meet God's specifications we need to replace the world's defective software that has been downloaded into our minds for years, with software from the Word of God.

The Apostle Paul emphatically reminds us that only then can your new and improved God-quality lifestyle begin to take shape. This is not a complicated process, but it does require some action on our part. All components of love involve action. He first loved us, and He demonstrated His love by creating us and by giving us dominion over His perfectly designed earth. Even after Adam had damaged His original plan, God continued to show His great love for us by establishing a plan of redemption through His Son Jesus that we might, through our belief in Jesus, receive eternal life.

God loves you, Jesus loves you, and the Holy Spirit is readily available. Why do you think that Jesus Himself, the Greatest Teacher, said in Matthew 22:37, **"Thou shalt love the Lord thy God with all thy heart, and with all thy soul, and with all thy mind"**? This happens to be God's greatest commandment, while also giving us His commandment in John 15:12, **"That ye love one another, as I have loved you."**

Why is love emphasized and so widely promulgated throughout His teaching? Because He knew that if we did not get revelation knowledge of how to simply love God's way, we were destined to flounder. God's love is an awesome power and is an absolute requirement for our spiritual growth, our mental and physical endurance, and our long-term success in this world and in the world to come. God is concerned about the total welfare of all His special creations, and He wants us to trust His Word totally, which leads us to all paths of least resistance in pursuance of His perfect will for our life.

## The Acronym "L-O-V-E"

### "L" — Love

We talked briefly about a definition for "love," but sometimes an illustration or a physical description can be a very helpful concomitant in painting a picture to bring about clarity. Think about the acronym: ***L-O-V-E.*** There is something symbolic about these four letters of the alphabet. Take the "L" in love, which I believe represents *listening.* When you listen, it means you pay attention with not only your ears, but with your eyes as well. You have been alerted and you are showing concern for the welfare of another.

Remember, love is an action word and to listen requires effort. To listen effectively, you must stay focused, paying strict attention to what is being said as well as to reactions, without interruptions, so as not to miss out on any instructions, details, or signs that could prove significant.

During the crucifixion of Jesus, many things were spoken, if we would only listen. Think about the magnitude of this inhumane and unjust punishment. I mean, really think about it. With all of the pain, agony, and suffering that Jesus endured and with the hue and cry and all of the wailing and commotion that was going on around Him, He still had the wherewithal to focus, listen, and respond to one of the two thieves. This thief stated, **"Lord, remember me when thou comest into thy kingdom"** (Luke 23:42). As He listened carefully to what was said, Jesus gave this unbelieving man a favorable response by rewarding him with a promise: **"To day shalt thou be with me in paradise"** (v. 43).

## Life Is So Simple When
## WE CHOOSE TO LOVE GOD'S WAY

It is absolutely unimaginable for any human being to hang from a cross, die such a horrendous death, yet be compassionate enough to listen carefully to anyone, let alone a thief, and respond to him by giving him the ultimate gift of life. But then, this was Jesus, Son of the living God, the Father and founder of love — the only One who is able to listen to all of our cares, concerns, and petitions and answer our prayers.

When you and I put our selfishness and differences aside and look at the death of Jesus, our model for life, we realize that the paucity of energy required for us to listen attentively to each other on a daily basis, rendering assistance whenever needed, is not really cumbersome at all. Jesus responded to a need, even as He Himself was dying on the cross. He simply continued to deny Himself as He had done throughout His earthly ministry, listening carefully with a compassionate spirit, showing great love until the very end.

When we listen to the concerns of others, we should give them our undivided attention, regardless of how we feel, and not try to read their minds or finish their sentences. It is imperative that we deny ourselves of whatever we are going through, retaining our thoughts and opinions, though just for the moment, in order to surrender center stage to another. This requires respect for others as well as a compassionate spirit.

Proverbs 18:21 says, **"Death and life are in the power of the tongue...."** At some point we are going to have to impress clearly in our minds that the negative words that come from our mouth each day are constantly framing our world. A negative brick here and a negative brick there over the years will invariably guarantee you an airtight world framed with the reality of failure and unhappiness. Why don't you start today not only to listen more carefully and guard what you say, but also to listen attentively to others and guard what they are saying to you? To know that a person can cause his or her or even your demise by what they say is enough to make all of us want to become better listeners and carefully choose what we feed our spirit.

# Know God's Love
## (Simply Love)

You can increase your abundance with your very own words, and with the same mouth you can abolish the likelihood of ever receiving your breakthrough. If you don't start to listen carefully to what is being said, you will continue to miss it. Are you listening to that soft voice of the Spirit that whispers advice and instructions to you daily as you travel down life's highway? I am quite sure that you have heard His voice before. He talks to us often, whether we listen or not. It's that soft voice that might say, "Call your mother." He may be simply giving you advice because He knows that the two of you had a disagreement and have uncharacteristically not spoken to each other in over a month. Does this prompt your memory? In case you forgot, she's that special lady who took care of you and nurtured you when you could not take care of yourself. Exodus 20:12 says, **"Honour thy father and thy mother: that thy days may be long upon the land which the Lord thy God giveth thee."**

God gives us precise instructions in His first commandment with promise. He guarantees us something extra if we stop our obstinate ways, and as children and adults alike, simply honor authority figures in our life. None of us are always right, except God, so it's okay to disagree with your mother. But remember, respect and honor to your mother, father, or any person(s) in authority, are always in order. Parents are to be venerated for the authority figure they represent, not necessarily for what they did or did not do.

Wisdom from heaven is available within you to give you godly directions, but you cannot know how to take full advantage of this benefit if you do not study the Word of God and learn to recognize the voice of the Holy Spirit. This is imperative in your quest to please God and obtain all that He has to offer. Do not allow a minor disagreement to sever a beautiful relationship between you and anyone, let alone your mother or father. God values relationships. The voice of the Spirit can and will aid you in every area of your life if you will simply listen. He will tell you things like, "This is a good car, but it is not the one that you should purchase." Or His soft voice may say, "Do not buy this house, just hold out a little longer." He may even insist, "Walk away from an argument. It's not worth it." He is not boisterous or redundant and He does not waste words.

Jesus said in John 10:27-28, **"My sheep hear my voice, and I know them, and they follow me: And I give unto them eternal life; and they shall never perish, neither shall any man pluck them out of my hand."** Whose voice are you listening to? It would behoove you to learn the voice of the Holy Spirit. God is available to all of us, regardless of where we are or who else may be calling us. When you pray, ask God to help you develop your spiritual ears. He made every part of you, and He certainly knows where you need to be polished. Be specific when you talk to your heavenly Father. He is not aloof, condescending, or haughty. The more time you spend worshiping and getting to know Him, the more you will understand how to simply love His way.

John 4:23 says, **"But the hour cometh, and now is, when the true worshippers shall worship the Father in spirit and in truth: for the Father seeketh such to worship him."** God is a Spirit, and you are a spirit who lives in a body. To please Him with your worship, it must be in spirit and in truth. Jesus said that the time is *now* when all true worshippers must worship God in the Spirit.

The very nature of God is Spirit. As individuals, we are a spirit with a body, not just a body that has a spirit. God's Word says that we *must* worship Him **"in spirit and in truth."** The word "must" denotes that something is required, imperative, or essential. God is patiently waiting for His special creations, from all walks of life, who will worship Him.

First John 5:3 states, **"For this is the love of God, that we keep his commandments: and his commandments are not grievous."** No order from God is designed to be burdensome or onerous. Jesus said in Matthew 11:30, **"For my yoke is easy, and my burden is light."**

# Know God's Love
## (Simply Love)

Work together with Jesus, hook up with Him, and let Him show you the way. You can rest assured that His load is not designed to be too much for you to bear. All of your seemingly insurmountable burdens can be handled through the Word of God. The sooner you get a revelation of this, the more lucid it becomes. So it would only make good sense for us to start thinking with our spiritual minds and using our spiritual faculties.

Look at it this way. All of us have a strong hand that we use most of the time. Either you are left-handed or right-handed. Very few of us are ambidextrous or can use both hands evenly. So in order for you to develop your weak hand or your lesser-used hand, you will have to start consciously utilizing it more. If you begin using your weaker hand on purpose, results will not come overnight, but if you are consistent in your desire to use it, you will see incremental progress. The more you use your weak hand, the easier it becomes to use and the more comfortable you will feel whenever you choose to use it.

Likewise, the more you stay in God's Word and learn to listen inwardly, the more conversant you will become with the voice of His Spirit. Listening and heeding the voice of the Holy Spirit are simply benefits that are provided in God's total love package. When people talk to us, do we really listen to what they are saying, or do we just pretend? Even when we make eye contact, are we giving total attention, or are our minds partially somewhere else?

I do not know about you, but I find it a little difficult concentrating on two things at the same time. Some people may be better at doing this than others. All I know is that when I try to listen and think at the same time, one of the two will almost always come up short.

Think of how powerful a computer is and the volumes of information it can store, yet it can only run one application at a time. How often do you find yourself on the offensive, preparing to take umbrage, or attempting to respond before you allow a person to finish telling you or asking you a question? The problem is that you are so prepared to present your opinion that you simply do not listen to all of their concerns.

We continuously permit ourselves to become so cantankerous that we end up making irreversible remarks. And in some instances, we commit indefeasible acts of violence that we most assuredly can never take back. If only we would patiently listen and not react impetuously out of frustration, we could save a lot of face. By simply shifting our focus towards our perception faculty to view the perspectives of others, we could eliminate a lot of ill will and perhaps salvage some relationships too, all while increasing our capacity to mature.

If we are fully committed, the love of God will certainly work in mending our broken relationships, regardless of any past differences or disagreements. The next time you are engaged in a verbal confrontation or a dispute between parties, allow others an opportunity to be heard without interruption.

Deuteronomy 1:17 says, **"Ye shall not respect persons in judgment; but ye shall hear the small as well as the great; ye shall not be afraid of the face of man; for the judgment is God's. . . ."**

Be fair with people and always hear them out, and by all means, listen to all parties involved, not assuming anything. Do not be concerned about which person is right or wrong, or how they will respond to your godly decisions. You are an ambassador of heaven and whether people respect your decision or not, they do expect you to be fair and to at least listen to their point of view.

You will be absolutely amazed at how it makes people feel so much better when you listen to their concerns, regardless of how polished you may be in conflict resolution. Just the fact that you listen to them kindly will make them feel better, while at the same time it will increase your capacity to develop a spiritual proclivity to perceive things from another perspective.

Jesus said in Matthew 7:24-25:

# Know God's Love
## (Simply Love)

> **Therefore whosoever heareth these sayings of mine, and doeth them, I will liken him unto a wise man, which built his house upon a rock:**
>
> **And the rain descended, and the floods came, and the winds blew, and beat upon that house; and it fell not: for it was founded upon a rock.**

The sayings of Jesus, or the Word of God, is our rock. Adhering to the Word of God will provide you with a rock solid foundation, but only if you are a doer of the Word as well as a hearer. This includes heeding all of God's Word, not just the passages of scripture that you prefer, the ones you learned when you were a child, or the most notable or quotable ones.

We have the potential to miss out on a blessing and perhaps cause someone else to miss theirs by pretending to listen or by not knowing what to listen for, and as a result, giving out ill-advised information. Pray and ask God to help you become a better listener.

The Holy Spirit relishes the opportunity to guide us in every area of our life. Once you become adept at listening to your inner voice, a whole new world will open up to you. The Spirit will begin to show you opportunistic doors that you never knew existed. But if you continue to refuse the opportunity to strengthen this area of your life, you will not only miss out on potential blessings, but more importantly, you will miss an opportunity to lead someone to Christ.

Our Creator gave us two ears and one mouth, so obviously, He intended for us to listen more and talk less. Without a doubt, listening will play an important role in our life when we choose to love God's way. We do not always know the answer to another person's problem, but if we are careful listeners and our spiritual ears are focused, we can use that opportunity to give them the Word and channel them in the right direction.

Situations may arise where the only thing you need to do is to listen. Often, people only need a little encouragement to make an intelligent decision on their own. But you have to listen intently to know whether a person is capable of making a quality decision with or without advice from you.

## "O" — Opposite

Now, let's turn our attention to the letter "O" in the acronym *L-O-V-E*.

In further viewing our working definition of "love," I firmly believe that "O" symbolizes **opposite.** Do you react or respond whenever your feelings are hurt? How do you deal with opposition? Are you easily angered? Whenever you are rubbed the wrong way, doing the opposite of what people expect you to do is one of the most powerful tools that you can deploy.

Listen to what the world's greatest Teacher, Jesus Christ, emphasizes in Matthew 5:44: **"Love your enemies, bless them that curse you, do good to them that hate you, and pray for them which despitefully use you, and persecute you."**

In Satan's world, this principle is unthinkable, and I am sure his loyalists would conclude, "highly impractical." But that's not all. Jesus demonstrated the classic example of turning the other cheek as He was betrayed and denied by His own disciples. He was insulted, whipped, beaten, mocked, and crucified for the sins of the world, yet He never sinned and never complained. No one can accurately verbalize the inhumane humiliation that He suffered for a myriad of crimes that He never committed. Yet the first words that He uttered while dying on the cross were, **"Father, forgive them; for they know not what they do"** (Luke 23:34). These words are in direct contrast to what any dying human would have possibly said, given the exact set of circumstances. Jesus Christ is truly a Paragon, and the only One we should ever attempt to emulate in every area of life.

Regardless of how strange this principle may sound or how difficult it may be for others to grasp, we have to trust in God, take Him at His Word, and give His Word a chance to work in our life.

Proverbs 15:1 NIV says, **"A gentle answer turns away wrath, but a harsh word stirs up anger."** More often than not, you will surprise people when you don't follow up with harsh words after someone has just given you a bucket full of them. This may be incomprehensible to some Christians, especially those who are just beginning their walk with God. However, a lack of faith does not and will not deteriorate or lessen the value of any of the examples or principles that have been written in the Word of God.

In Matthew, chapter 17, the unbelief of Jesus' disciples did not stop Him from healing a young man who was possessed with a demon. As a matter of fact, Jesus tells His disciples in verse 20 that the reason they failed to cast the devil out was **"because of [their] unbelief."** We must learn to pray and ask God to help our unbelief. There are no limits to what God can do, and through Jesus there are no limits to what you and I can do.

I am not advocating that Christians are to be credulous or simpleminded, but simply followers of Christ, attempting to make this world a better place to live by modeling the God-kind of love with the compassion of Jesus.

Speaking of opposites, look at how all of the controversy surrounding the movie "The Passion of the Christ" actually drew people to the theaters to see the movie and perhaps even exposed some of the naysayers to the knowledge of our Savior and Lord, Jesus Christ. Every soul that is won to Jesus is a victory for the Kingdom of God. However, we know that this movie will neither save the world nor is it the Savior of the world. Take the movie for what it is worth and learn the Word of God for yourself.

Hollywood or anyone else could never come up with enough money, personnel, or ideas to accurately depict what happened on Calvary. The truth lies in the Word of God and in the hearts of His people. The only thing in this world that is going to last is the true and living Word of God. There is still much work that must be done for the Kingdom of God by the likes of you and me.

I recall my wife coming home from work, filling me in on all the things that had gone wrong that day. When I thought she was just about finished, she began to tell me about another incident she experienced that left her quite upset. I could tell from the tone of her voice that she was heavy laden and perhaps needed some encouragement from the Word of God. Outside of lending her my ear, there was nothing else I could really do. But remember what I said earlier: *Know when the only thing you can do is listen and lend godly support and encouragement.* The next day her demeanor was somewhat tacit. This went on for about two days, so I gave her the space she needed. She and I both knew that she had to succumb and the sooner the better.

My wife approached me the next day and said, "Do you know that the Holy Spirit wants me to pray for that person?" Then she said in a soft voice, "I do not believe this." She didn't feel like it or even want to pray for that person, but she knew she had to pray and stay in God's perfect will for her life. In order to walk in the fullness of God's love, we must sometimes do the opposite of what people expect or even the opposite of what we may be accustomed to doing.

Maybe there have been times in your life when you felt you were used, abused, or even treated cruelly. Remember, the best way to handle a situation when we have been wronged is to do what Jesus did at the cross: *Talk to the Father and ask Him to forgive them.* If we profess to be born-again Christians, then the Word of God must be our guide.

People do not always respond to God's love. Sometimes after we have been berated we may get a little frustrated and suddenly doubt starts to creep in to keep us from showing His love to strangers or even to people we know.

# Know God's Love
## (Simply Love)

Matthew 10:22 says, **"And ye shall be hated of all men for my name's sake: but he that endureth to the end shall be saved."** This is why it is so important that we continue to stay in the Word and in prayer and ask God to continue to give us guidance through His Spirit to keep His commandment of love, especially when we have an unnatural feeling about doing what is right.

First John 5:3 says, **"For this is the love of God, that we keep his commandments: and his commandments are not grievous."** Keeping God's Word is confirmation that we love Him. This is not an arduous task, and when we remain obedient it will never cause us unbearable pain or sorrow. Second Corinthians 7:10 says, **"For godly sorrow worketh repentance to salvation not to be repented of: but the sorrow of the world worketh death."** Whatever God does is for our good. He is not the author of pain, sorrow, or suffering.

Jesus came that we might have life and have it more abundantly (see John 10:10). This extension of life is in direct contrast to the pain and sorrow that Satan desires for us to experience. If we are willing, God allows our grief, regrets, or disappointments caused by Satan to become training, consequently preparing our hearts to become stronger. We must then make up our minds to abolish our sinful ways and return to Him. Satan is so blind and ignorant that he does not realize that he is being used primarily as our sparring partner. Not only is Satan being used as a spar, but he also provides all of the equipment and personnel for our training.

God makes provision in His Word for us to repent and get back on track. Proverbs 28:13 NIV states, **"He who conceals his sins does not prosper, but whoever confesses and renounces them finds mercy."** Upon completion of the training session and traps launched by Satan that caused you a setback and sent you reeling into his gym, God will afford you yet another opportunity to have a change of heart, to repent, and turn completely around to face Him. Wow! What a provision!

## Life Is So Simple When
## WE CHOOSE TO LOVE GOD'S WAY

When we fail but quickly repent with a sincere heart and finally see things God's way, we can change our mind-set to take full advantage of His redemption plan and focus on His Word. Proverbs 3:6 says, **"In all thy ways acknowledge him, and he shall direct thy paths."** What a mighty and exceedingly great God we serve!

I can tell you from past experience that God will indeed take a pernicious incident that Satan meant for bad and work it for your good. Most pain is short-lived, but the long-term effect that it can cause, prompting your attention to return to God, will outweigh any pain and suffering that your earthly tabernacle could ever endure. Of course, this is predicated on your time spent in God's gymnasium working out in His Word. All it takes is a willing heart. Jesus has already completed the work.

One of the things that I did for my family was to write out a daily confession that we read one or two times a day. Our confession acknowledges God alone for who He is. We go to Him boldly, giving Him praise and thanking Him as we expect Him to answer us favorably. Hebrews 4:16 says, **"Let us therefore come boldly unto the throne of grace, that we may obtain mercy, and find grace to help in time of need."**

At some point in your life you are going to need the mercy of God. It is good to know that we can boldly approach our heavenly Father. However, you will never really feel comfortable approaching Him in a bold manner, reminding Him of what He said in His Word, until you have developed a personal relationship with Him and know precisely what His Word says about your situation. This will only happen when you decide to spend more time in His Word.

If you prefer, you can also tape record your daily confession for convenience. Make sure that when you record it, you word it as though you have already received your blessing or resolutions to whatever cares you give to Him. Thank Him in advance, for through your faith it has already been resolved. Matthew 21:22 says, **"And all things, whatsoever ye shall**

**ask in prayer, believing, ye shall receive."** Know that it is already done!

My mother and father had eleven children. My baby brother Johnny died in September 1968 when he was only five years old, resulting from a fire that occurred several weeks earlier. Over 85 percent of his body was burned. This incident happened around 5:00 p.m. on a vacant lot about a hundred yards northwest of where we lived. My father was at work and Mother was in the house when she was alerted. My mother, with the assistance of the next-door neighbor, Mr. P. H. Dukes, rushed my little brother to the hospital where he later died from complications from his burns.

Without getting into what actually happened, there was plenty of blame for my mother and father to pass to the responsible parties, but they chose not to. They did just the opposite. They simply forgave and purposely showed more love towards their ten remaining children.

Did we miss our little brother? Of course we did! After his death, our young hearts continued to ache as we drew strength from our parents until we matured and learned to rely on the promises of God.

There is no better Counselor than our heavenly Father. He knew how much it hurt my mother and dad to lose one of their precious gifts from Him. After all, God experienced the loss of a Son too. Rather than focus on hatred and vindication, they diverted their attention to teaching and training the remaining children on how wondrously blessed we were. They knew even during this period of grief that God was still holding them accountable for not only doing what was right, but for teaching it to their children as well.

As parents, we are responsible for teaching our children all of the qualities and values of love that are exhibited in the life of Jesus and to prepare them for a future with God. My parents did a laudable job in raising their ten children, and now all of us are fully responsible for establishing our own love walk in the likeness of Jesus. Romans 14:12 says, **"So then every one of us shall give account of himself to God."** It is an absolute certainty that each of us will stand before God and give an account for all of our actions or lack thereof. It makes no difference how well Mother and Daddy served the Lord. Each child needs to earn his or her own set of wings.

The best thing, and I mean the very best thing, that any parent can do for their children is to lay a strong Bible-based foundation for them to build upon. The Bible does not say that our children will not go astray or stumble. It simply states in Proverbs 22:6, **"Train up a child in the way he should go: and when he is old, he will not depart from it."** In other words, no child will permanently leave your rock solid foundation if it is built on the Word of God. Once the foundation is laid, the rest of the building is up to the child.

### "V" — Vision

The "V" in the acronym **L-O-V-E** represents *vision.* God has a plan for us that is literally out of this world! Jesus said in John 14:2-3, **"I go to prepare a place for you. And if I go and prepare a place for you, I will come again, and receive you unto myself; that where I am, there ye may be also."**

This is the ultimate vision, the one that believers in Christ are hopeful to receive during the second coming of Christ, but what about here on earth? God had a universal vision for the world and for His people on earth before He framed the worlds. God had to have a vision for us because He made provision for us in His Word. He loves us and wants us to have His very best. But as God-fearing men and women, we must step up to the plate to carry out our roles in His vision. I am not talking about a shortsighted fantasy. I am talking about long-range visions where the minds of God's people are used to change the world.

A vision is a supernatural appearance that conveys a revelation. It is a mental picture that can appear to you while you are awake or while you are asleep. Visions are how God makes His will known to us. First Samuel 3:1 says, **"And the child**

**Samuel ministered unto the Lord before Eli. And the word of the Lord was precious in those days; there was no open vision."** During the period of the judges, it was a rarity to hear from God in the form of a vision. So it is a good thing whenever God gives us an open vision.

God wants us not to just receive His vision or to have a vision, but He wants us to carry out our visions. If you are going to dream, dream big! Make a plan for the Kingdom of God with God, and watch Him do it through your belief in Jesus.

In Genesis, chapters 40 and 41, Joseph became known as an interpreter of dreams for the Pharaoh. God spoke to Joseph in his dreams. In Acts 16:9-10, the Apostle Paul's missionary journey into Europe began with his vision of a man from Macedonia appealing for help. In Genesis 15:1, God appeared to Abraham in a vision concerning his seed. He said, **"Fear not, Abram: I am thy shield, and thy exceeding great reward."** Notice, the first thing God does in His vision to Abraham is He gives Abraham courage. He says, **"Fear not."** It might be normal for you to be temporarily frightened, but your fear should last momentarily at best. Fear is a tactic of Satan.

First John 4:18 NIV says, **"There is no fear in love. But perfect love drives out fear, because fear has to do with punishment. The one who fears is not made perfect in love."** If you remain afraid or in fear, perhaps you have experienced an illusion rather than a vision. God does not give us a vision that is designed to instill fear in us. Second Timothy 1:7 says, **"For God hath not given us the spirit of fear. . . ."** God wants us to have courage, and He will give us courage when we exercise our faith and carry out any Kingdom-building vision that includes:

1. **God as the Head.**
2. **All the right motives.**

Our motives should simply be about Jesus, nothing else.

## LIFE IS SO SIMPLE WHEN
## WE CHOOSE TO LOVE GOD'S WAY

The next thing God does is He guarantees us protection. He says, **"I am thy shield"** (Genesis 15:1). So what is there for you to fear when the Creator Himself has promised to be your shield? Remember, Isaiah 54:17 says, **"No weapon that is formed against thee shall prosper. . . ."**

Once you get your assignment from God, there is no need to tarry. Get started! The least bit of procrastination opens up a bank account for excuses. And before you know it, there goes another shattered vision. Or was it really a vision? Only you can answer that. How many times in your life have you started a project and before long you decided to quit? The problem was you did not have a made-up mind, your motive was wrong, or God was not in it. God is a God of order and integrity. You cannot expect God to endorse any vision if you have the wrong motive.

Last, He promises to reward us. God tells Abraham, **"I am . . . thy exceeding great reward"** (Genesis 15:1). Not just reward, but *exceeding great reward!* "To exceed" means to go beyond, to excel, or to outdo. Whenever you step out with a Kingdom-building vision for God, He not only shows up, He shows out! God's promises are absolute when you are obedient to His Word.

Hebrews 11:6 says, **"He is a rewarder of them that diligently seek him."** God knows the exact manner in which to reward His people. Think about how the Word of God is presently spreading across the globe on TBN by a vision launched by Paul and Jan Crouch.

God has a special part for all of His children in His overall vision, but it is incumbent upon us to find our scripts and carry them out. God will use anyone who is willing to step out on the track and take the baton. It starts by studying His Word and meditating in it daily, and seeking Him to find out the will and destiny that He has planned for your life. All of us have a role in spreading the good news of Jesus Christ.

# Know God's Love
## (Simply Love)

My pastor, Dr. Michael D. Moore, of Faith Chapel Christian Center in Birmingham, Alabama, has a powerful vision for our church, the community, and the city. Part of that vision has already been executed in the form of a $15 million dome sanctuary that comfortably seats three thousand people, built without a mortgage. All of the members and contributors must continue to be active participants for all phases of his vision to come to fruition.

It makes no difference how eager we are about the vision or how much hope we have, if we do not do the work that is necessary to make it happen, it will forever remain just a vision. Habakkuk 2:3 says, **"For the vision is yet for an appointed time, but at the end it shall speak, and not lie. . . ."** A vision requires long-term standing and trusting in the Word of God. Success does not take place overnight. It's a process. However, it starts with having a made-up mind! We must be patient and know that if God has endorsed the vision, it simply will not fail.

Jeremiah 1:5 says, **"Before I formed thee in the belly I knew thee. . . ."** God predestined your life and He knew how you could be best utilized for Him long before you ever took your first steps as a child. Everything you need to fulfill your vision is in the earth. John 1:3 says, **"All things were made by him; and without him was not any thing made that was made."** Everything in this world that man has invented was already here. The inventor simply believed and made it happen through a combination of faith and works.

To this end, do you think that God would predestine your life with greatness in mind for His Kingdom, and not give you the resources necessary to make it happen? We must not build in our own effort, but meticulously carry out our orders that we receive from God. His Word is true all the time, right on time! God cannot lie. Romans 3:4 says, **"God forbid: yea, let God be true, but every man a liar. . . ."**

You must envision what the world would be like if we would love the way Jesus exemplified, exercise our faith, and proclaim the Word of God by capaciously enhancing His Kingdom. There would be fewer wars, suicide bomb attacks would cease, police departments around the world would downsize, jails would be imploded, pharmaceutical sales would take a nosedive, and it would be commonplace around the globe for people to walk the streets daily and nocturnally, fearlessly spreading and celebrating the Good News of Jesus Christ.

We have to think long range, but we must begin to do the little things in life that will eventually add up. For instance, extending our acquaintances or our circle of life to people everywhere all across the globe who do not know Jesus. How do you extend your circle of life? You extend it by incrementally reaching out to greet people whom you see for the first time, or by simply introducing yourself to someone whom you have seen before but never formally met. Most people are eager to extend their hand to you, especially if they see that you are interested in them and are not simply trying to sell them a bill of goods.

Recently, I was sitting in my vehicle with two of my children, waiting for their school bus to arrive. Suddenly, it was apparent to me that I should get out of my car whenever the bus arrived and extend my acquaintance to the gentleman and his daughter who were parked next to me. He and I parked side by side practically every school morning, but neither of us ever spoke to the other. Here were two people that I see at least five days a week. I could easily encompass them into my circle of life and the life of my children as well.

One day someone's soul might be saved because of this simple step of extending the courtesy of introduction. Maybe one day this gentleman will introduce me to other members of his family or some of his friends, or vice versa. What about our children after they were introduced? With three children, each having their own circle in life, there is an even greater propensity for their circles to increase.

Now, look at this on a much larger scale. What could happen if every God-fearing believer stepped outside of his or her comfort zone and made this a practice once or twice a week? It is simply the right thing to do. We should get to know people on purpose. God is pleased with every kind act that we perform, regardless of the splendor of the performance.

After our introduction, we experienced warmth that would have never occurred if I had continued in selfishness. We must possess a genuine spirit of love and include everyone if our vision is to be successful. Proverbs 29:18 says, **"Where there is no vision, the people perish. . . ."** If we are going to successfully get to the next spiritual level, we must not only have a vision for ourselves, but we must also have one for our children. One of the reasons some of our children fail in life is because they are not dreamers. Their dreams and imaginations have been replaced with videos, drugs, and violent gang activity. As parents we must assume some of this responsibility by helping them plot their future.

God has already given us everything that we need to fulfill the vision of love for now and for the future. It is up to us to utilize all of the resources that are at our disposal. People are God's most important resource to fulfill His vision. That is why it is so important that no one is overlooked. Once we have gained a person's friendship, we should be about winning their soul to Jesus. No God-fearing Christian should ever pass up an opportunity to spread the Good News of Jesus Christ. Remember, the optimum goal for every Christian year in and year out should be to win countless souls for the Kingdom of God through our Savior and Lord, Jesus Christ.

## "E" — Emotion

The "E" of the acronym **L-O-V-E** represents *emotion.*

We love to get our emotions involved in almost everything that we say and do. However, contrary to popular belief, love is not simply an emotion, and it should never be predicated on emotions. It is good for us to have and to occasionally show our emotions. Emotions have a purpose. Even Jesus showed emotions. Emotions can reveal the philanthropic side of people who were thought to be stoic or insensitive. There is nothing harmful about a good cry regardless of whether it represents happiness or sadness.

John 11:35 says of our Savior and Lord, **"Jesus wept"** after the death of Lazarus whom He loved dearly. This, being the shortest verse in the Bible, reinforces my belief that it's okay for us to show our emotions. However, they should only last for a short period and we should not dwell on them. According to John 11:4, the sickness and death of Lazarus, who was eventually raised from the dead by Jesus, was just an opportunity for Jesus to bring glory and honor to God. Jesus did not arbitrarily make an emotional decision to raise Lazarus.

Emotions should be removed completely from the decision-making process and the critical thinking arena. They should also be removed from any part of the yardstick for falling in love. Emotions are here today and gone tomorrow. Emotions can cause us to come to conclusions before getting any or all of the facts. This is something that almost every human has been guilty of at some point in their life. When we were children, emotions never stopped our parents from spanking us, and no matter how loud we hollered, our emotions never eased the pain! Emotions are like a roller coaster. They are up and down, and within a moment they come to an abrupt end.

When I was injured in October of 2003, bleeding profusely while lying helplessly in the cul-de-sac near my home, emotions and its best friend doubt were about to creep into my spirit when my wife arrived and whispered in my ear, "Baby, listen, let's pray in the Spirit." Afterwards, serenity that I had never experienced filled my soul.

In Matthew 14:29-30 Peter was on his way to a new level of faith, walking on water just as Jesus did, until he allowed his emotions to turn his faith to fear, causing him to sink. Our emotions can cause us to hit the panic button and sink!

What if Jesus had decided to act quickly based on the emotions of the scribes and the Pharisees who brought a woman to Him who had been caught in an adulterous affair (John 8)?

They wanted a quick response from Jesus as to how He thought she should be punished. They tried to trap Jesus so they could concoct a charge against Him. But rather than respond to their emotions or even give them an emotional response, He simply stooped down and calmly wrote on the ground, ignoring them. Obviously, this did not set well with them.

Jesus then raised Himself up and answered them with a question. **"He that is without sin among you, let him first cast a stone at her"** (v. 7). In other words, go ahead and start throwing stones if you have never sinned. Again, He stooped down and continued to write on the ground (v. 8). Before long, they had all been convicted in their own conscience and went out one by one.

Afterwards, Jesus was left alone with the woman standing before Him (v. 9). Jesus Christ is the greatest Teacher this world has ever known. He did not condemn, condone, or judge this woman. He simply won her trust, her belief, and He forgave her. Jesus, impervious to the emotions of those around, concluded by charging the woman in John 8:11, **"Go, and sin no more."**

If Jesus had responded immediately, based primarily on the surrounding host of emotions, there would perhaps be other verses interpolated in this story. Instead, He gave us the performance that He expects from all of us. Regardless of how our intellect is driven by our emotions or the emotions of others, we should not be moved, enticed, or intimidated by them. We should certainly never judge anyone based on any kind of emotion. In addition, we should not give anyone the satisfaction of knowing that something that has been said or done, or a mean, tricky plot that someone has planned, emotionally challenges us.

Isaiah 54:17 says, **"No weapon that is formed against thee shall prosper; and every tongue that shall rise against thee in judgment thou shalt condemn. . . ."** If you heed the voice of the Spirit, which is always available, then it should become part of your nature to remain cerebral and make godly decisions based on your wisdom from God. The best way to learn to make godly decisions through love is to remove your emotions. I cannot think of any situation where our emotions will bring lasting help to any one of our brothers or sisters if we are called upon to assist them. Jesus never displayed situational confidence. He showed confidence all the time. He was never rattled by emotions and neither should we be affected by emotions.

In First Samuel 16:6-7, Samuel was impressed with the sight of Jesse's son, Eliab. God is not moved emotionally by our countenance or by our stature. God told Samuel, **"For the Lord seeth not as man seeth; for man looketh on the outward appearance, but the Lord looketh on the heart"** (v. 7).

God looks past all of our emotions, facades, and features that appear to get attention from others and sees the real picture of truth for what it's worth. When we come to conclusions based on emotions, they almost always come back to haunt us. How many times have you disciplined your children only to realize an hour later that the punishment did not fit the incident, or it was simply too severe?

Our emotions can cause us to be mean to people and to use harsh words that we can never take back. Our emotions can also trick us into formulating an opinion about people that we have never met or do not know. Often, these kinds of preconceptions are based on what we heard, what we thought we saw, or what some so-called friend told us. We need to further investigate some of these situations. Many times what we have been told by our friends or what we heard during a sidebar really has no value. It is just as wrong to be governed by someone else's emotions as it is to use first impressions to guide us.

The Bible says in James 1:19, **"Let every man be swift to hear, slow to speak, slow to wrath."** It is best not to respond when we are not in control or don't have all the facts. Some people seem to think that there is something special about idle gossip, getting the last word, or having the last say. But the reality is, we will always end up saying the wrong words, and we can never fully recall them. In most cases, neither party is eager to make amends.

Look at the emotional wreck of the disciples when they were at sea during a storm, yet Jesus was on board. He was asleep on His pillow during the storm. Mark 4:38 says, **"They** [the disciples] **awake him, and say unto him, Master, carest thou not that we perish?"** After rebuking the storm, Jesus said to them, **"Why are ye so fearful? how is it that ye have no faith?"** (v. 40).

We will never know how our motor is going to perform if it has never been tested. That is why it is so important that we start out early in our Christian experience, putting our faith on the line for small matters, and then gradually increasing to greater things. Bear in mind that Jesus' disciples were men chosen by Jesus. They had been with Him as He performed breathtaking miracles throughout His earthly mission. More than anyone else, Jesus' disciples should have known that Jesus was not rattled by emotions and emotions never solved anyone's problems.

At times emotions can even complicate matters. It is only after you settle down that the problem can be understood and properly diagnosed. Possessing a calm demeanor is the only way anyone can understand what you are saying. It makes no difference how much you scream or holler, God is not moved or enticed by your repertoire of emotions. So you might as well settle down and speak the Word in faith. Your emotions will never convey to God how well you know Him or how much you love Him. If anything, your emotions will show the true measure of faith you have in God and just how much you know about His love and His Word.

Jesus said, **"He that hath my commandments, and keepeth them, he it is that loveth me . . ."** (John 14:21). We are charged to be obedient to all of God's Word and to keep His commandments. If you say that you love God and you have not been studying His Word to show yourself approved, then that simply means that you do not love God as you say.

Proverbs, one of the most familiar books of the Bible, is a collection of moral sayings and counsel that should be read by every person seeking God's wisdom. Proverbs 4:7 says, **"Wisdom is the principal thing: therefore get wisdom: and with all thy getting get understanding."**

We need to walk in the fullness of the love of God every day through Jesus. Then get firmly rooted in His Word and simply trust it. This world has no challenges that Jesus did not meet head on and overcome. He says in John 16:33, **"Be of good cheer; I have overcome the world."** God is the Source of all of our blessings. We own nothing but our souls and our sins. We do not even own ourselves. We were bought with a price and are merely instruments that God is willing to use to do His work in the earth. As His stewards, we are to reach out and help people, whoever they are and wherever they may be.

John 3:16 says, **"For God so loved the world, that he gave his only begotten Son. . . ."** "So loved" means unconditional love. He loves everyone, and His love should be continued throughout the earth as it was illustrated through His teaching. He was never rude, even at the point of death, and always placed others ahead of Himself. No love that we can muster will ever equate to the love that He gave to us.

I am so thankful that the price was paid in full to redeem us into new life in Christ. The benefits of His love are matchless. All He taught His disciples was to love and to continue in His love. Spreading the love of God and walking in His love is an ongoing process. We must not hate anyone but love them. Jesus not only showed us how to love, but He also showed us whom to love — everyone. Every person has the gift of love in them that must simply be stirred up.

Love is an action word and it must be acted out by us in all parts of the world. This is the purpose of our discipleship. Our great Savior and Lord knew that this was the only way that His love could reach all corners of the globe. His cross pointed in all four directions and so does His love. We must be loyal disciples for Jesus by sharing and showing His love to others.

It is incomprehensible and mind-boggling to me as to why so many people continue to hate for the sake of hating and kill for the sake of killing, when all of us can have God's grace, His love, joy, peace, longsuffering, gentleness, goodness, and eternal life at no cost. John 13:1 says, **"Having loved his own which were in the world, he loved them unto the end."** Jesus showed us true love until the end of His life on earth. John 17:4 says, **"I have finished the work which thou gavest me to do."** Then He ascended to His Father. According to Ephesians 1:20-21, Jesus is now seated at the Father's **"right hand in the heavenly places, far above all principality, and power, and might, and dominion, and every name that is named, not only in this world, but also in that which is to come."**

Jesus finished His course and He passed the baton to us. Now we must continue in His love. Who could have shown us a better way to love than the Son of love Himself, Jesus Christ? We must exhibit this same love for each other, lasting to the end, by *choosing to love God's way*. We are all about His love. Jesus paid the price in full, allowing God's grace and mercy to exist for everyone. Why not take full advantage of His gift of love and spread the Good News to others while there is still time, daylight, and plenty of work for all?

Now that we are conversant with God's love, let's move on and talk about some choices that will shape our future.

# Chapter 2

# Choose God Today Above All Else (Simply Choose)

Contrary to popular belief, the world in which we live is not predicated on black or white, male or female, rich or poor, or even Democrat or Republican. This world simply declares good versus evil.

According to Genesis, chapter 3, Adam and Eve disobeyed a stern command and warning from God when they ate the forbidden fruit from the tree of the knowledge of good and evil, thereby exposing mankind to this detestable form of knowledge known as evil, something that God in His goodness never intended for us to experience. Because of this flagrantly disobedient act that dealt a blow to God's original plan for mankind, you and I must make a conscious choice to live our life and serve either as a child of God or as a servant of the devil.

God, the Creator of the universe and the Father of love, dons the spirit of excellence and represents every fiber of good and very good. Satan, the diabolical one who waves and sails with the banner of sin, is unambiguously the father and the very heart and soul of evil, whose mission statement according to John 10:10 is **"to steal, and to kill, and to destroy. . . ."**

We must not only be able to recognize that there is a distinct difference between right and wrong, but we must choose to do one or the other. No one is perfect. However, a mature saint, rooted in the Word of God, has no business lacking moral restraint or vacillating in any form of sinful behavior. Doing right is a world that we should have formally met during the youthful years of our natural life, and now, because of who we serve and what we know, it should be second nature to us as we strive to an upper level of faith through the living and life-changing Word of God.

It is with your decision to choose good over evil and to choose to live for God over Satan that you cement your future with Jesus. The importance of this choice can never be overemphasized, and regardless of your current arena, you alone must make your choice. There is no middle ground. God does not remotely desire that any one of His precious creations perish. However, it is left solely up to each of us, of our own free will, as to whether or not we will make the unequivocal decision to follow the works of Jesus while we yet live.

Remember, Jesus is the One who represents good in every facet that can remotely be measured. Eternal life is a choice, and according to Romans 10:9, it is available to any person who confesses with their mouth the Lord Jesus and believes in their heart that God has raised Him from the dead. This is the only way that any of us, regardless of our status symbol, can possibly be saved.

The Apostle Paul reminds us in Romans 2:11, **"For there is no respect of persons with God."** In no way does He remotely differentiate between any of His special creations, irrespective of any biases that you may experience on earth. God is without a doubt the epitome of equal opportunity.

First Timothy 2:4 says, **"Who will have all men to be saved, and to come unto the knowledge of the truth."** Again, note the word "all," which is used throughout God's holy Word, clearly delineating that God takes a special interest in each of His precious creations. Heaven is glad for each soul that is won to Jesus. As a matter of fact, God wants all the lost children of the world to be saved. But they too must confess their sins and believe in His Son, Jesus.

# Choose God Today Above All Else
## (Simply Choose)

A personal relationship with God will only engender when you consistently study His Word and diligently seek His face. As you continue to seek His face, His will for your life will become as plain as the sun in the sky. Once you are validated as His child, you must be about His business, boldly and confidently leading others to the pathway of His Kingdom. After openly choosing God's way of life, the assignment of expanding His Kingdom becomes a part of your task too. God is depending on all of His saints to do their part in supporting and spreading the gospel throughout the world in an effort to win souls to Jesus.

Jesus knew that many of us would be doubters about truth, as were some of His own disciples, most notably Thomas, who went so far as to doubt Jesus' resurrection. In the 20th chapter of the book of John, Thomas had not seen Jesus after He had risen. In John 20:25, Thomas stated to the other disciples who had seen Jesus after His resurrection, **"Except I shall see in his hands the print of the nails, and put my finger into the print of the nails, and thrust my hand into his side, I will not believe."**

Here is a fellow, one of the twelve handpicked disciples chosen by Jesus, who witnessed as Jesus gave sight to the blind, made the lame to walk, cleansed the lepers, made the deaf to hear, raised the dead, fed the poor, and preached the gospel to the poor. That's not all. John 20:30 NIV says, **"Jesus did many other miraculous signs in the presence of his disciples, which are not recorded in this book."** This man, who spent a great deal of quality time with Jesus as he performed miracles on a daily basis, has the arrogance to make his own demands as to what it will take for him to simply believe what Jesus had told them would come to pass.

Most of us have had encounters with people like this. They would much rather believe a lie than to believe the living truth. Thomas not only doubted the truth from his fellow disciples, but he sounded a little pompous. Eight days later Jesus and His disciples met again. This time Thomas was with the disciples, and

## Life Is So Simple When
## WE CHOOSE TO LOVE GOD'S WAY

Jesus afforded him the opportunity to take his hand and touch His hands and His body where He had been pierced during the crucifixion. Having finally been convinced, Thomas said to Jesus, **"My Lord and my God"** (John 20:28). Wow! What a backstroking event this must have been! I can just imagine how small Thomas must have felt after all the dust settled and he witnessed firsthand this overwhelming evidence that he originally repudiated.

I am quite sure that a few of us, including me, have had to recant on certain issues or traditional beliefs, or have been the victim of an embarrassing incident at some time in our life. Afterwards, Jesus said to Thomas, **"Thomas, because thou hast seen me, thou hast believed: blessed are they that have not seen, and yet have believed"** (v. 29). Thomas believed simply because he was convinced through his natural senses by touching and seeing the overpowering evidence on Jesus' body.

In our Christian love walk, the things that we trust in but do not see are the very things that should keep us motivated. Even though there are still some doubters among us today, none of us have at our disposal the luxury that Thomas was afforded. Jesus is not readily available to entertain a long line of "doubting Thomases" so they can feel and view His bodily scars just to be able to categorically convince themselves that He is indeed the Christ, the Son of the living God, who was supernaturally resurrected by the power of God for the propitiation of our sins.

Even if Jesus were readily available today, there would still be doubters and unbelievers. So our overwhelming evidence today is that we are blessed with God's holy Word, which, according to Hebrews 4:12 **"is quick, and powerful, and sharper than any two-edged sword . . ."** as well as the Comforter, the Holy Spirit, who is indeed our present help.

Jesus said in Luke 12:12, **"The Holy Ghost shall teach you in the same hour what ye ought to say."** He is readily available to guide, intercede, and steer us onto the on-ramp so we might enter our personal pathways that God has designed exclusively for each of us.

God gives the unwarranted gift of salvation to anyone who believes in His work through His Son, Jesus. Hebrews 11:6 says, **"But without faith it is impossible to please him. . . ."** However, the bonus is, **"He is a rewarder of them that diligently seek him."** So don't just seek God, seek Him diligently! Seek Him steadily and energetically with every ounce and fiber of your being!

If someone from your family called you on your job and informed you that you had a reward in today's mail, you would be ecstatic. Even if you had been somewhat expecting this boon and you believe the source that informed you to be credible, there is still that drive in you that insists on you leaving your job early so you can go home and see for yourself whether or not this news is really true.

Now, on a higher scale, believe in the Word of God, but in addition, continue to intensify and build on your belief by studying and meditating in His Word so you will eventually come to the knowledge of truth for yourself, deepening your personal relationship with God. This is what God wants you to do, simply choose Him and get to know for yourself that He exists.

I pray you are receiving this information with an open mind and that you are studying God's unimpeachable Word on a daily basis. My sincere hope, however, is that you have already made Jesus Christ the Lord of your life and you are not waiting until you get "all your little ducks in a row"! Or when all of the conditions in your life are perfect, or perhaps when you feel that the playing field is finally level. If these factors must come to fruition before you study the Word, then you will never do it.

Remember in the previous chapter where we expatiated on how the scribes and Pharisees brought a woman to Jesus who was caught in an adulterous affair so He might condemn her? When it was all said and done, her accusers had vacated and there was no one present except she and Jesus. She was triumphant in the midst of her trial. Actually, her accusers concocted a subterfuge designed to trap Jesus and to condemn the woman, but in reality they wound up helping the woman by bringing her to God's court of mercy *just as she was!*

This is just another simple illustration of how the righteousness of God uses the enemy as our "footstool." Maybe she had planned to come to Jesus after one or two more rendezvous or after partaking in a few more private acts, or one or two more nights on the town. You know how we sometimes like to go at least one more round with our favorite sin? But just maybe she had no plans or intentions to ever change her life. If not for her enemies, tomorrow may have been too late.

How long do you have to live in an area that has proven to be indigenous to certain health issues to know that it would be wise to have your goods insured and your premiums paid up long before a catastrophe arises? If you stay in the world long enough and continue to live by "rolling the dice," the storms of life eventually will catch you. That is a mathematical certainty! You may be fortunate enough to make it through the first time with only negligible damage, but there is that prodigious chance you take each day that you are out of God's ark of safety.

Jesus said in Matthew 11:28, **"Come unto me, all ye that labour and are heavy laden, and I will give you rest."** Often, we get beat down in life, especially from doing things that we know are contrary to the will of God. In some instances we will never be able to muster enough strength or maintain our focus to successfully give them up on our own. You need the Word of God and the strength of Jesus sown into your life. God knew from the outset that it would indeed be an arduous task as we try gallantly to come under His wings of protection, wounded and subjugated, feeling as though the weight of the world is on our shoulders. Without God, this is an impossible task, in spite of status symbols or the amount of prestige that we continue to collect each day.

## Choose God Today Above All Else
### (Simply Choose)

Regardless of who you are or what you represent, the longer you are in the storm, removed from God's umbrella of protection, the greater the likelihood of you getting challenged by the seen as well as the unforeseen. Without the Word of God, which gives you full coverage when you choose to abide in it, your journey in life, although deceivingly pleasant at times, is doomed to derail!

We are reminded in Second Corinthians 12:9, **"My strength is made perfect in weakness. . . ."** The weakness He makes reference to is ours, of course. God has no weakness. He has already remedied all of our hindrances that have the tendency to burden us in the development of our Christian life by giving us the required strength, inner peace, and protection found only in His Word.

You must, of your own volition, take the first step. God wants you to check out what He has to offer free of charge. God will not force you into taking this coverage. It is imperative that you understand that He really wants you to come just as you are with all of your cares and concerns.

I am grateful that I have been saved for a few years, but even dating back to a couple of years ago, there were some things that I needed to do to get my life in the order that God prescribed for me. Although none of us are where we need to be, we should take solace in knowing that we are not where we used to be. It's all about making the decision to follow Jesus.

The Apostle Paul gives a scintillating account in Philippians 3:13, saying, **"Brethren, I count not myself to have apprehended: but this one thing I do, forgetting those things which are behind, and reaching forth unto those things which are before."** The race has by no means been won. However, we will never win the race, let alone finish, if we continue to peep into our past. We need to forget the past and press forward if we intend to reach the life that God has designated for us through Jesus.

There are people who view some Christians as hypocrites because they perceive them as living dual lives. Perhaps their assessment is true about some, and quite simply those Christians who fit this bill are not fully persuaded of the goodness of God. God is the evaluator and He alone will deal with each of us. In Matthew 23:3 NIV Jesus spoke to the multitude and to His disciples regarding the Pharisees: **"So you must obey them and do everything they tell you. But do not do what they do, for they do not practice what they preach."**

The Word of God will always be true, regardless who proclaims it. So be watchful and know what the Word says and do not necessarily put stock into the lifestyle of the messenger. First Corinthians 1:27 says, **"But God hath chosen the foolish things of the world to confound the wise; and God hath chosen the weak things of the world to confound the things which are mighty."** God will use any one of us to do a work for Him in this earth. The Word of God and the total lifestyle of the messenger may not always mesh. Just ensure that you know the Truth for yourself and adhere to every part of His Word.

Solomon advises us in Ecclesiastes 1:13, **"Search out by wisdom concerning all things that are done under heaven. . . ."** Anything that you want information about in this world, use the wisdom of God to "check it out" and point you in the right direction. God will grant you wisdom if you ask for it, and it starts by searching His written Word. As you search throughout the Word of God, use your faith to apply His truth in any region of your life. Acts 17:11 NIV says, **"The Bereans were of more noble character than the Thessalonians, for they received the message with great eagerness and examined the Scriptures every day to see if what Paul said was true."**

There is no reason for any child of God to be blindsided by any activity or function when we can study the Word and simply abide in it under the auspices of the Holy Spirit. You also need to be under the spiritual jurisdiction of an earthly shepherd or pastor. However, you must choose to know the Word of God for yourself regardless of what your pastor or media ministry may teach. As human beings, anyone can misconstrue or make a mistake when delivering a message. Hebrews 12:2 says, **"Looking unto Jesus the author and finisher of our faith. . . ."** Always look to God who knows the hearts of men, and if you want to know the heart of any person, God will show you if you ask Him.

All Christians, having made the choice to serve God, should at all times strive to do their best in representing Him, living out His Word as an example to others and winning souls for His Kingdom. Each of us will give an account of our actions or lack thereof.

Second Corinthians 5:11 says, **"Knowing therefore the terror of the Lord, we persuade men. . . ."** One of the reasons Christians should work so hard to win souls for Jesus is out of reverence and an awesome and inspiring fear for God. I am talking about fear as in respect, fear as in wanting to go the extra mile for our heavenly Father.

Most of us know what it's like to be a child and wanting to please our parents or guardians with everything we do. That's a microcosm of the fear I am referring to. Once we really get a revelation of God's magnificence in both power and truth, we will begin to be more concerned about not only our salvation, but the salvation of others as well, especially those who are dear and near to us in our circle of life. But it should not stop there. We should minister to people all around us. When we do, we are going to be absolutely perplexed by the number of disconsolate people who will appear to have been waiting just for us, that are in dire need of a word of encouragement, and even more so, the Good News of Jesus. Some will adhere and some will not.

Our responsibility, however, is to "let down our nets" and pray for a catch! Jesus said in Luke 9:5, **"And whosoever will not receive you, when ye go out of that city, shake off the**

**very dust from your feet for a testimony against them."** As saints of God, we are not in the business of violating the rights of people. God does not sanction any form of coercion. Our responsibility is to advise them of "thus saith the Lord." The individual who knowingly refuses to adhere to the Word of God has in essence set sail for death.

It is vitally important that you get to know God and learn His Word for yourself. You do not have enough mind, muscle, or money to make it in this world on your own. Romans 14:11-12 says, **"For it is written, As I live, saith the Lord, every knee shall bow to me, and every tongue shall confess to God. So then every one of us shall give account of himself to God."** You are responsible for your own soul. Why let one act, one person, or any group of people be responsible for writing your ticket to hell? Hell is a real place for unbelievers. In Revelation 19:20, John describes eternity as **"a lake of fire burning with brimstone."** On the other hand, heaven is the place where God dwells. John describes the future home of all believers in Revelation, chapter 21, as **"the holy city, new Jerusalem . . ."** (v. 2).

Picture yourself driving to the airport with both these descriptions of eternity in mind. Having the opportunity to take an eternal vacation to either location, free of charge, which destination would you choose? Remember, you will have to make this call on your own. To defer your choice could prove costly. God will by no means force you to accept His Son. Don't be too busy making a living that you forget to plan your future. We should be on a personal crusade actively recruiting souls for Jesus, as all believers are called to do.

Jesus said in John 8:31, **"If ye continue in my word, then are ye my disciples indeed."** It is not just your pastor's job on Sundays or after other church functions to extend invitations to accept Jesus to people whose connection to God is broken or who have genuine concerns that need to be addressed. It is the job of *every born-again believer, seven days* *a week, to use every opportunity that avails itself to tell the world about Jesus and His wondrous works and that salvation is free and readily available to all.* There is absolutely no reason for anyone to suffer unnecessarily when *a very present help* is available.

Luke 13:11 states, **"There was a woman which had a spirit of infirmity eighteen years, and was bowed together, and could in no wise lift up herself."** The NIV says she **"had been crippled by a spirit for eighteen years. She was bent over and could not straighten up at all."** Jesus healed her instantly. Similarly, we are charged to reach out with compassion and help straighten out the lives of those who are "bent over" physically and mentally and who need our help in their painful situations. Then, they are more apt to follow our directions to help them find Jesus.

God wants all sinners to come now, even if they have sunk to the hog pen of life and are saturated with filth. In this world there are inextricable situations in all of our lives that we will have to face, and no matter how hard we try to untangle them, without the Word of God burned in our spirits or without being around someone who has been there and knows what God can do, we simply will not manage. It makes no difference what your status may be, how much education you have, your level of opulence, or how much worldly experience you may have accrued over the years, one day you will meet with God.

God does not want you to run the risk of waiting too late to check in with Jesus. He wants you to come right now, while you are still circling, heading for the runway, preparing to land in what could be your final destination. If you do not soon have a complete change of mind and choose God above all else, it will be just a matter of time before your world crashes, costing you your right to claim the gift of eternal life.

You may even think that your best years are still ahead of you. Just remember, life is as beautiful as a rose, but both their beauties are evanescent at best. They are temporal and short-lived. They are here today and gone today as their memories fade into the sunset.

While your name and memories will soon become but a blur to those who are left behind, what will you tell God during the judgment prior to your sentencing when He inquires about the eternal choice that you made and about the time, talent, and finances that He entrusted to you? Jesus said in Matthew 7:22-23:

**Many will say to me in that day, Lord, Lord, have we not prophesied in thy name? and in thy name have cast out devils? and in thy name done many wonderful works?**
**And then will I profess unto them, I never knew you: depart from me, ye that work iniquity.**

If we were to reflect on years gone by, we could collectively note countless people who never reached the pinnacle of their lives. Most of them thought they had tomorrow. Wherever you go or whatever you do, always remember: Yesterday is gone, tomorrow will always be the next day or a day later, and without God's protection plan the only time that is important to you is right now, this very moment. The lives of some of our relatives and friends may have ended with shadowed visions and dreams. If so, we can only hope that they gave their life to Jesus before they left us so abruptly.

But more importantly, we should, more than anything else, use their life-span experience as a barometer to see if we need to make some immediate changes in our lives to ensure our future with God. We know that Jesus loves us unconditionally and that His undeniable love was demonstrated for us on the cross. Isaiah 53:5 says, **"But he was wounded for our transgressions, he was bruised for our iniquities: the chastisement of our peace was upon him; and with his stripes we are healed."** He has removed all of our sins, sicknesses, shortcomings, and other foibles with His precious blood. God assured us that the finished work of His Son left no stone unturned. His death covered every imaginable region of the globe and every sub-compartment of our delicate life. There is no reason for any of us to come up short and remain there, or to lack in any area of life.

To become a member of Jesus' team does not require a cumbersome application to complete, no drug or alcohol test, and no extensive background checks. There are no grueling mini camps or wind sprints. Everyone who confesses and believes in Jesus makes the team. There are no second or third stringers in His love. Together all of us make up the "first string." And I am sure you will be glad to know that there are no politics, favoritism, or vendettas involved, and no one is arbitrarily cut from His roster, unless of course they initiate the action. No writing is necessary to join since the name of Jesus is already written across your heart. Simply confess, believe, and accept Jesus as your Savior, acknowledging that He died for your sins. Then continue to meditate upon His Word each day, obey it, and enjoy the full benefits of walking in His love.

*To simply love God's way* cannot be made any easier. Romans 10:9 says, **"Thou shalt be saved."** Often, in our quest to do well, even as we listen to some of the mature pastors and ministers in the Body of Christ, they tend to make things too complicated. To walk in the fullness of everything that God has to offer takes time and involves a process. Just remember, if your train has been off the tracks for a while, even though you are finally back on course and rolling again, it will still take some time and some persistent application in the Word of God to establish your personal relationship with Him. But you can still get what He has for you if you consistently study His Word and work at building your relationship with Him. Just make Jesus a permanent choice. You will not be able to catch up overnight, but make up your mind to stay focused and stay in the race. Your success rate and your altitude will be left exclusively up to you. Your lasting success will depend on your commitment in serving Jesus through others and your eventual level of faith in God.

Some people do not relish promotions and there are various reasons for their complacency. Being on my job for over twenty-one years, I've noticed that there are some members who simply like their positions and they prefer to continue in their existing rank for the duration of their careers. Their performance is not perfunctory, and they not only love what they do, but the quality of their work is not second-guessed nor has it fallen off. Having quality experience at the entry level has its advantages because you never want to have all of your experience at the top of the pyramid and no experience at the base level. Besides, there are people at both ends of any spectrum who know very little about the love of God.

God simply desires ambassadors for His Kingdom who can relate to people in a godly manner. Whatever level you desire to attain in any area of your life is your choice exclusively. Your level of success will never preclude you from being a member of God's elite team, and it should never be used as a barometer to measure the height of your effectiveness.

Whatever your role is in the expansion of God's Kingdom, give it your best effort and always give the glory to God. Promotions come from God. Everyone who has a willing heart has a role to fill to assist in the furtherance of His Kingdom. But you must first make the choice that will save your own soul.

As children of God, our heavenly Father wants His children to know that if we want more, we can have more. Once you are saved, your footing has been established. You can now build a strong foundation, allowing the Word of God to be used as bricks to frame you as the beautiful tabernacle that God predestined long before you were conceived. The only relationship with God that you can be absolutely certain about is your own, and the only person who can establish your relationship with God is *you*. God has given you a free will.

Remember, at present you may be able to see the rising and setting of the sun, the soaring fowls of the air, the high and low tides of the ocean, and all of the adorned beauty that God chose to embellish the universe with during the creation. We will not always see these amazing expressions that we take for granted on a daily basis, but you can have a future to behold with Jesus. Most of us have gone to extraordinary lengths to ensure that whenever we do transition, our families will have sufficient funds to give us a proper burial and to move forward with their life without us. This should be a priority. But have you ever thought about what is going to happen to you when you are gone? I mean, have you really given this question serious thought?

John 5:28-30 says:

> **Marvel not at this: for the hour is coming, in the which all that are in the graves shall hear his voice,**
> **And shall come forth; they that have done good, unto the resurrection of life; and they that have done evil, unto the resurrection of damnation.**
> **I can of mine own self do nothing: as I hear, I judge and my judgment is just; because I seek not mine own will, but the will of the Father which hath sent me.**

Jesus makes it incontestably clear. If you do not meet God's specifications or His simple qualifications for obtaining eternal life before you die, you will receive neither inspiration nor consideration at the judgment. There is nothing that even Jesus Christ, our Savior, the Resurrected One, can do to bail you out then. Jesus came to earth to carry out the will of God the Father, and believe me, the Father, the Son, and the Holy Spirit are all on the same page. Once you die and you have not made Jesus your Savior and Lord, there will be no "hocus pocus" or "abracadabra" that will allow you entrance into the realm of eternal life. No sidebar will exist among God, Jesus, and the Holy Spirit to make a last-ditch effort to grant a special concession on your behalf. Jesus Christ is the only way to the Father.

You must clearly and boldly make the choice to accept Jesus while the blood runs warm in your veins, just as Joshua did when he forthrightly declared in Joshua 24:15, **"And if it** seem evil unto you to serve the Lord, choose you this day whom ye will serve; whether the gods which your fathers served that were on the other side of the flood, or the gods of the Amorites, in whose land ye dwell: but as for me and my house, we will serve the Lord."

We have to make the best decisions not only for us, but for our families as well. We pray that in making godly decisions with our families each member will be visionary enough to see the benefits in choosing God's way. But even if the family decides that they do not want to partake, or if they later decide to opt out or abandon their loyalty for any reason, you must gather yourself and go it alone. Your first-line item on life's agenda should be about your choice for eternal life encompassed with your personal relationship with God through your love for Jesus. Then it should be extended to your family, friends, and others.

Proverbs 13:22 says, **"A good man leaveth an inheritance to his children's children: and the wealth of the sinner is laid up for the just."** We should take pride in leaving possessions, property, and other procurements for our loved ones so they can have a wholesome start in life; a lifestyle that surpasses the one we lived. However, included at the very top of this package should be a strong foundation built with a godly value system for our children to follow.

This world is saturated with untapped resources as well as possessions that are intended for expanding the Kingdom of God. The Christians who diligently seek God and His righteousness have a right to the fruit of good labor, including supernatural blessings that he or she could never work enough hours to gain. Deciding to forever make Jesus the Lord of your life and working to extend the Kingdom of God will add more blessings to your life than you could ever fathom.

Deuteronomy 6:10-11 says:

**And it shall be, when the Lord thy God shall have brought thee into the land which he sware**

**unto thy fathers, to Abraham, to Isaac, and to Jacob, to give thee great and godly cities, which thou buildedst not,**

**And houses full of all good things, which thou fillest not, and wells digged, which thou diggedest not, vineyards and olive trees, which thou plantedst not; when thou shalt have eaten and be full.**

Continue to seek God first, and work His Word in your life, believing through your ever-increasing faith that He is going to bless you in such a way that you can't help but be a blessing to others. Couple this scripture passage with James 2:20: **"Faith without works is dead."** Remember, there has to be some action on your part. Like love, faith is an action word that requires belief, trust, and loyalty to God.

Have you ever had an occasion where you knew that you needed to act out on something, but for some unacceptable reason you simply refused to acknowledge it? As a result of this procrastination, laziness, or just plain indecisiveness, it only got worse.

When I started driving, my brother and I purchased an old car. One day as I was driving along I heard a knocking sound coming from the front end of the car. We concluded early on that it was probably nothing. The next day I felt relieved as I drove the car for most of the day and I did not hear that sound. During the day, I was so nonchalant about the noise that I did not give it a second thought. However, about two days later, the impeding sound returned. This time it was even louder and I was terribly embarrassed as I clacked on down the road!

When I got home, I decided to take the front wheel off. Even though I had no idea what to look for, I could not see anything that appeared to be out of place or outworn. So in amazement, I put the wheel back on and continued to drive.

During the following days, the noise would come and go. *It's nothing,* I thought. But I was only trying to convince myself, when in reality I knew that something was terribly wrong. This went on for about three more days.

On about the fourth day, the noise became unbearable. I finally decided that enough was enough, so I drove over to my friend's mechanic shop to let a professional mechanic diagnose the problem. Much to my chagrin, not only was the ball bearing completely worn, I had also done irreparable damage to the front right axle. I knew deep inside, even before the diagnosis, that something had to be awfully wrong and whatever the problem was, I could not lessen the intensity of the noise on my own. After all, I was not a mechanic.

And so it is with our lives. We were born with a void, and no matter how hard we try to ignore it, fill it with people or things, or try to fix it on our own, we simply cannot do it. It will only exacerbate. We cannot make it in this world alone. We need the love, clairvoyance, and wisdom of God, and it can only be found in His Word.

In John 14:26 Jesus says, **"But the Comforter, which is the Holy Ghost, whom the Father will send in my name, he shall teach you all things, and bring all things to your remembrance...."** The Comforter tutors us, guides us, and inspires us through edification to go forward. He consoles us in times of troubles or worries and He encourages us. Why would God send us a Comforter in the name of Jesus if He did not feel that we would need a present help every day — a personal confidant who is always available and never takes a day off? A Helper who never vacations or calls in sick? The sooner we begin to realize His purpose and take advantage of His presence, the sooner this life will begin to take on a whole new level in meaning. The more of the Holy Spirit that we involve in our decisions, the better choices we are destined to make.

Matthew 26:41 says, **"Watch and pray, that ye enter not into temptation: the spirit indeed is willing, but the flesh is weak."** Remember, Jesus walked this same earthly realm as we do. Therefore, He knows all about the temptations that we face and the variety of choices we must make each day.

## Choose God Today Above All Else
### (Simply Choose)

Our spirit has this insatiable desire to want to do right, because we are a spirit being. However, our bodies or flesh is frail and it desires to have its way as well. Whichever one you feed and let be the vanguard of your life will invariably take charge in guiding you during the course of your life's journey.

We should continue to study God's Word and activate His Spirit within us by learning His voice and adhering to it. Then we should simply remain focused and determined to stay the course, utilizing all of the routes in His Word that He has made available for us to escape the temptations of this world. God has already provided a safety net and hedge of protection all around us if we would only read and meditate on His Word daily.

Satan is on the job 24/7. First Peter 5:8 says, **"Your adversary the devil, as a roaring lion, walketh about, seeking whom he may devour."** Peter tells us that the devil is *seeking* us. Jesus tells us, **"*Seek* ye first the kingdom of God, and his righteousness . . ."** (Matthew 6:33). There is indeed a tug-of-war that is going on inside of us as we prepare to make decisions and even after our decisions have been made. Satan is on the hunt, seeking people and opportunities with the same tenacity as we are instructed to "seek God."

Satan is making every effort to locate and destroy whoever gives him permission. Ephesians 4:27 says, **"Neither give place to the devil."** We are the ones who provide Satan with employment. He can do nothing if we resist him. If we do not present him with opportunities, he is null and void. Although Satan may leave for a spell, he is bound to return. But how many times must we fall prey to the same old tricks of greed, money, sex, and drugs?

In Ecclesiastes 1:9 Solomon says, **"The thing that hath been, it is that which shall be; and that which is done is that which shall be done: and there is no new thing under the sun."** The *New International Version* says, **"What has been will be again, what has been done will be done again; there is nothing new under the sun."** We can see that Satan uses the same sleight of hand year in and year out, yet when he comes our way, we still allow him to be just as effective in manipulating us as he has done to others.

In Matthew 4:10 Jesus said to Satan, **"Get thee hence, Satan: for it is written, Thou shalt worship the Lord thy God, and him only shalt thou serve."** When we mimic what Jesus did when He was tempted by Satan, according to Matthew 4:11 two things will happen: 1) Satan will leave you, and 2) The angels will minister to you.

You will never be content in this life until you have made the unquestionable choice to make and keep Jesus Christ the Lord of your life and to make practical use of His Word every day for the rest of your life. We are subject to make negligible errors and mistakes. No one is perfect. However, no one continues to wallow in sin unless they choose to do so.

You can choose to give your life to Jesus right now and join the team of believers who has chosen to win in life and to win more souls for Jesus. It is time to get real! Simply repeat: *Heavenly Father, I repent of my sins right now. Please come into my life. I now receive Jesus as my personal Savior and Lord.*

1. Repent.
2. Receive and believe in Jesus Christ.
3. Be obedient to the Word of God.
4. Choose to love God's way.

Now that you have wisely chosen to make Jesus the Lord of your life, let's talk about the benefits of God's love.

# Chapter 3

# Know the Benefits of God's Love (Simply Benefit)

There are a myriad of benefits that a Christian inherits by virtue of being a child of God. One of the primary benefits is not only knowing that we have God's Word, but knowing that His Word is true and that He will not and cannot change His Word.

Psalm 119:160 says, **"Thy word is true from the beginning: and every one of thy righteous judgments endureth for ever."** All of His judgments are righteous and foundational words of truth which endure forever.

First Peter 1:24-25 NIV says, **"For 'all men are like grass, and all their glory is like the flowers of the field; the grass withers and the flowers fall, *but the word of the Lord stands forever.*'"** It is always good for us to give and receive due recognition from each other for the exceptional deeds we do on earth. However, the people and the accomplishments in our everyday works that we lionize and give accolades to, laudable as they may seem, are short-lived at best and will soon fade away.

Now, counter this with knowing that all of God's Word will not only last forever, but it is equally righteous, written under the inspiration of the Spirit of God, and designed exclusively to lead us and to keep us on the right course. The Word of God is tailored and geared specifically in our best interest, and we are

*LIFE IS SO SIMPLE WHEN*
*WE CHOOSE TO LOVE GOD'S WAY*

kept under the watchful eyes of God when we mimic His love and walk in His righteousness.

It is incomprehensible as to the number of relationships, whether they are marital, kindred, co-workers, or just plain friendships, that have been set apart as a result of deception, shattered vows, halfhearted commitments, or from a simple breakdown in communication. In a larger percentage of these faltered relationships unforgiveness still looms large. So it is indeed a life-changing benefit to know that the Word of God, unlike anyone else's word, will always have our best interest at heart while remaining constant and lasting forever.

Regardless of the depth of these benefits, you will only experience the magnitude and full effect of God's unimpeachable love when you spend quality time in His Word and you get to know Him on a personal level.

Here is an important **training key:** Imagine for a moment being laid off from work. Your employer gives you a severance package that includes major medical insurance along with other perks that are good for only thirty days. Four weeks (or twenty-eight days) later, you go to the hospital for an emergency. When asked for your place of employment and the name of your insurance company, you inform admissions that you are unemployed and that you do not have insurance coverage. Out of dejection, you never took the time to open and read the information contained in your severance package nor did you check with management about your benefits before your last day. Therefore, you never really learned the details or scope of your insurance policy.

The only thing you could tell the hospital staff with any amount of surety is that you were laid off about a month ago because of a reduction in the workforce. You were unaware that you still had a couple of days' coverage left on your benefit package to cover your hospitalization. The hospital staff had no knowledge of your severance package and they did not refute the information that you gave them. Thus, you end up with an astronomical bill and out-of-pocket expense simply because of a

# Know the Benefits of God's Love
## (Simply Benefit)

lack of knowledge. Through ignorance you did not become conversant with the host of benefits that were provided for you by your employer that were good for thirty days.

One year later, you find out that at the time of your emergency surgery you still had two days' coverage remaining on your insurance that would have covered the entire cost of your hospitalization if you had filed it within the thirty-day period. You were also given a fifteen-day grace period after the thirty days, but it too had lapsed. You are now bound by litigation.

After a lengthy battle in court, the justice system, the appeals process, and an arbitrator all side with your former employer, citing that at the end of the thirty-day period your policy expired and your insurance company was no longer tasked with the responsibility of paying for your hospitalization. All of this was the result of a careless oversight on your part because you refused to read to find out what benefits were included in your severance package.

In the past we have seen where all it takes is one major surgery or a lengthy illness without the benefit of insurance coverage to devastate one financially and deplete his or her assets. People are not lining up to inform you of the contents in your benefit package that you yourself should already know, if you would only take the time to read it.

This is what happens when we become buried by the cares and worries of this world and simply refuse to read the Word of God to know what it says about whatever concerns we may have. We need to read the Word for ourselves to become more adept about the knowledge of the benefits and promises that are rightfully ours as adopted children in the family of God. Your benefits in His Word will remain valid as long as you are obedient, regardless of how much reduction in force is happening around you. There is knowledge untold and information and wisdom galore in the Word of God and in other vehicles of communication that will only unravel and be revealed to you when you decide to read the contents between the lines and explore the context for yourself.

## Life Is So Simple When
### WE CHOOSE TO LOVE GOD'S WAY

Hosea 4:6 says, **"My people are destroyed for lack of knowledge. . . ."** To know God's Word and His ways are benefits that all of His children are entitled to, but we will only receive the fullness of His plan for our life when we learn not only to read, but also to study, meditate, and delight ourselves in being occupied with His Word.

Hebrews 13:8 says, **"Jesus Christ the same yesterday, and to day, and for ever."** No one in this world other than God Himself can make this incontrovertible claim and back it up! As people, we are capricious and will change from moment to moment without serving notice. I am sure that you can attest to some of the people in your everyday circle, including a colleague or two whom you may see and work with every day who at some point or another changed their mood unexpectedly.

You and I and even some of our immediate family members have also had our moments when we just plain did not want to be bothered and we never took the time to explain why. We all have our peculiarities or idiosyncrasies that seem to show up at inopportune times. But isn't it great to know that in Malachi 3:6 God says, **"For I am the Lord, I change not . . ."**?

When you confer with God during prayer or just small talk about whatever trouble you may be experiencing, you can rest assured that He is concerned. He will never snap on you nor will your business be out in the parking lot whenever you arrive at work the next day! And though you may not always get the answer from Him that you want when you want it, one thing is for certain: His love and His Word will remain genuine, and He always gives us the answer from the big picture as He has already looked all the way down to the end of the road before He responds.

Throughout the Bible there is confirmation from God that is designed to give us the confidence and the encouragement that we need to succeed in *every* area of life. Here are seven such promises:

*Psalm 23:4* — "Yea, though I walk through the valley of the shadow of death, I will fear no evil: for thou art with me. . . ."

*John 14:1* — "Let not your heart be troubled: ye believe in God, believe also in me."

*John 14:13* — "And whatsoever ye shall ask in my name, that will I do, that the Father may be glorified in the Son."

*Psalm 46:1* — "God is our refuge and strength, a very present help in trouble."

*Psalm 34:19* — "Many are the afflictions of the righteous: but the Lord delivereth him out of them all."

*Psalm 27:14* — "Wait on the Lord: be of good courage, and he shall strengthen thine heart: wait, I say, on the Lord."

*Psalm 37:25* — "I have been young, and now am old; yet have I not seen the righteous forsaken, nor his seed begging bread."

These are just a few confidence-building passages of Scripture that you can use as a starting point to give you a general idea of how specific God is in His promises. There are a myriad of other promising words that you will find as you search the Scriptures daily for words of encouragement either for yourself or for someone else who may be in need of them. So starting today, open your Bible and search for other promises.

Once we develop an unshakable faith life and become deep-seated and deep-rooted in the Word of God, we will also become astute at knowing how to stand alone on the promises of God, using His Word and our faith.

Jesus said in Matthew 24:35, **"Heaven and earth shall pass away, but my words shall not pass away."** We can bank on His Word. All of His Word is true, whether we bank on it or not. Nevertheless, we should develop our trust in His Word more and more every day.

I am convinced beyond the shadow of a doubt that choosing to give my life totally to God and trusting in His holy Word are the two best choices that I have ever made. They are two of the best decisions that you will make too. His Word has never failed.

In the book of Exodus, after the death of Moses, God promised Joshua in chapter 1, verses 5 and 6: **"As I was with Moses, so I will be with thee: I will not fail thee, nor forsake thee. Be strong and of a good courage. . . ."** God knew before He framed the worlds that we would experience moments of fear, uncertainty, and a plethora of challenges throughout our mission. However, these are but small obstacles that should never become permanent fixtures and block the path of our Christian love walk. The same guarantees and safeguards that God provided for Moses, Joshua, and others are available to us as well. Often, we lose our focus and the first thing that we surmise is, "God has abandoned me." But in actuality, we are the ones who have abandoned God. All we need to do is to believe and receive Him through His Son Jesus and continue to seek Him diligently in His Word.

Romans 2:11 says, **"For there is no respect of persons with God."** It simply makes no difference who you are, how many titles you may have, or how many abbreviations you may or may not have behind your name. You cannot merit enough attaboys or accolades to earn God's unmerited favor. Salvation is the unmerited favor of God that no one has earned or can earn. Every person is privileged to receive this benefit. There are no prejudices with God.

John 4:24 says, **"God is a Spirit: and they that worship him must worship him in spirit and in truth."** To worship Him in the Spirit is pure worship, the type of worship that God desires from all of the saints. He is a supernatural being who only knows truth. It is vitally important that we become more spirit-conscious and learn to worship Him in this manner

# Know the Benefits of God's Love
## (Simply Benefit)

because, after all, we are spirits with a body made in His own image.

The world in which we live will always take various factors into account such as your status symbol, skin and hair color, sex, height, weight, age, and of course, your personal background and use it to their advantage or to your detriment when making worldly decisions about your career or your future. But God is love and He only sees and knows truth. When we decide to live our life for Jesus and connect with God, a mind-changing process must take place. To tune your spiritual mind in and bring your life in line with Christ requires a submissive will on your behalf.

The Apostle Paul tells us in Second Corinthians 5:17, **"Therefore if any man be in Christ, he is a new creature: old things are passed away; behold, all things are become new."** Neither you nor I have enough cleansing power nor might to meet this specification and become a new creature all by ourself. But once we are *in Christ,* committed to the Word of God, and our mind-set and lifestyles are commensurate to His Word, we are indeed renewed individuals who can now fulfill God's purpose for our life. But it can only be done through Christ. It makes no difference how others view you or have viewed you in the past. Once you make the commitment to serve God through Jesus, you are a new creation and God is the One with your new scorecard. His score is the only one that matters.

Philippians 4:13 says, **"I can do all things through Christ which strengtheneth me."** That sounds like another benefit to me. There will be intricate situations that we will meet as long as there is movement on the face of the earth, some through acts of disobedience and some through no fault of our own. Some people will manage to move on with their lives while others may continue to experience repercussions. Without a doubt your love walk will be challenged. No one is exempt.

*LIFE IS SO SIMPLE WHEN*
*WE CHOOSE TO LOVE GOD'S WAY*

Proverbs 11:8 says, **"The righteous is delivered out of trouble, and the wicked cometh in his stead."** The *New International Version* says, **"The righteous man is rescued from trouble, and it comes on the wicked instead."** The Word of God tells us that the righteous will always prevail regardless of what it looks like at halftime. Through Jesus, you have the strength to overcome any imaginable deficit, seen or unforeseen. Your Father is King of the universe and His Word operates with the same effectiveness towards all of His precious creations. His love and benefit package are available to all who abide in Him through His Son Jesus. That's good news. But this opportunity won't always last.

According to Hebrews 9:27, **"It is appointed unto men once to die, but after this the judgment."** Each of us has an appointment with death, followed by judgment. Jesus will return again, but according to Hebrews 9:28, He will **"appear the second time without sin unto salvation."** In other words, He will not be returning for another sin issue. Instead, the order of business will be our salvation. So for us to die in the natural is a reality, and then the judgment will be followed by our eternal destination, which will be predicated on the choice that we made during our time here on earth. As mentioned earlier, heaven and hell are real places. So the primary message for us is that *we need to get our house in order*.

## No One Has to Spend Eternity In The Lake of Fire!

No one has to remotely flirt with the thought of dying and going to hell because Jesus has already paid our fare. All we have to do is make the connection. John 3:17 says, **"For God sent not his Son into the world to condemn the world; but that the world through him might be saved."** The price has been paid in full. Just believe it, receive it, and share the Good News with family, friends, and strangers too. You have nothing to fear if you know that you have received Jesus and your lifestyle is commensurate to what God requires of His people.

# Know the Benefits of God's Love
## (Simply Benefit)

Our God is King of kings and Lord of lords, which makes us royalty with Jesus. Jesus said in John 14:2, **"In my Father's house are many mansions: if it were not so, I would have told you."** Our heavenly Father has given us everything that we need to have success in this world and in the world to come.

Did you honor your earthly parents who raised you as a child and respect their authority while growing up? As a result, didn't they see to it that you got their best? And do you not look out for the best interest of your own children? Then, why is it so out of character for us to fathom that our heavenly Father wants to do the exact same thing for His children on earth, only on a much more imposing and more perfectly balanced scale?

There are several benefits that God has available for His children throughout His Word. We know that God is a sovereign God who owns it all. David conveyed in Psalm 24:1, **"The earth is the Lord's, and the fulness thereof; the world, and they that dwell therein."** Simply put, He owns everything! However, God delegated the interworkings of this earth to man when He gave us dominion in Genesis 1:26, which says, **"Over the fish of the sea, and over the fowl of the air, and over the cattle, and over every creeping thing that creepeth upon the earth."** So man has been permitted to rule the earth, even though God holds the deeds.

Everything in this world, whether tapped or untapped, including all of the silver and gold, the oil, the water, and the land, invariably belong to God, who has by design given us the authority, stewardship, and responsibility to govern this realm in a manner that is on par with heaven. This entails the entire earth, including all of the things in this world that have not been invented or discovered that are waiting for us to act out through our faith and seek His guidance through the Spirit to bring them full circle to glorify Him and expand His Kingdom.

Everything in this earthly realm was already here whenever we arrived. John 1:3 says, **"All things were made by him; and without him was not any thing made that was made."** Even though He is our Father through the redemptive

## Life Is So Simple When
### WE CHOOSE TO LOVE GOD'S WAY

blood of Jesus, we still must develop our own personal relationship with Him. His Word says, **"God shall supply all *your* need . . ."** (Philippians 4:19). Whatever your needs are, God will supply them. However, it is only after you become part of His family through Jesus that you become eligible to receive. Afterwards we must be about His business in our quest to expand His Kingdom through our lives, to receive the benefits that He promised us in His Word.

Hebrews 11:6 says, **"He is a rewarder of them that diligently seek him."** Christians should want to be rewarded, and God certainly wants to reward us, or He would not have given us this promise in His Word! We do not seek God to be rewarded out of an avaricious nature or for the sake of hoarding, but rather to be a blessing in assisting others who may have fallen or those who are confused and struggling and need some temporary relief. They must seek God for themselves to find their prescribed pathway to living a prosperous and abundant life.

We all know of someone through our circle of acquaintances who perhaps came from a well-to-do family, but wound up falling short in life, never quite reaching the optimum level of prominence that was mapped out for their future by their parents or loved ones. In most cases, it was clearly because they made a conscious choice to take an off route that differed from what their parents envisioned for them — a route that was noticeably out of sync with God's specific itinerary for their life.

Remember, at some point in your life you need to realize the importance of making quality decisions based on biblical principles reflecting what is best for your life and the life of your entrusted family. God has a divine plan, full of magnificent benefits that all of us can have, for a simple exchange of obedience.

In the Old Testament book of First Samuel, chapter 15, verse 22, King Saul discovered that **"To obey [God] is better than sacrifice. . . ."** Obedience to God's Word is far superior and more pleasing to Him than any sacrifice or offering that you or I could ever make. God truly wants us to know and understand the unparalleled value of obedience to His Word.

In Romans 4:21, the Apostle Paul, referring to Abraham, said, **"And being fully persuaded, that what he had promised, he was able also to perform."** God has always done and will always do exactly what He says in His Word. What He has done for others, He is willing to do for you and me regardless of how dramatic it may seem. But we must follow His way and work His living Word in our life.

In Proverbs 3:4 Solomon instructs us that God's virtue will induce favor for us **"in the sight of God and man."** He wants us to have His favor in every area of our life. Proverbs 8:35 says, **"For whoso findeth me findeth life, and shall obtain favour of the Lord."** Whatever trials you may face can readily change into triumph, but you must be discerning enough to get in His Word and trust it, as you not only read but also meditate on it daily. God hears you even when you meditate.

Some things in life will only come through God's wisdom, and wisdom also is a benefit from God. He will give you wisdom and favor to see things and find solutions through your spiritual eyes that others can't humanly see.

A prime example of favor, sometimes referred to as grace, is revealed in the life of Joseph. Genesis 39:21 says, **"But the Lord was with Joseph, and shewed him mercy, and gave him favour in the sight of the keeper of the prison."** If you are not familiar with the story of Joseph, read the book of Genesis starting with chapter 37. Joseph, who was one of the sons of Jacob, was gifted with prophetic dreams. Not only was he blessed with the favor of God, he also had paternal favor as well. The paternal favoritism may have caused some of the jealousy that his brothers had toward him. He was sold into slavery by his brothers and taken to Egypt. He was later sent to jail after his master's wife accused him of rape. After he was tossed in prison, God's favor showed up, causing him to be released from prison and rise to second in command in Egypt after interpreting Pharaoh's dream.

Psalm 84:11 says, **"No good thing will he withhold from them that walk uprightly."** God's favor will allow whatever seed He has planted in you to grow in any type of soil or terrain. It makes no difference where you are on this earth or what kind of wildlife surrounds you — as long as you know that you are in the path that God has chosen for your life and you continue to stay the course. Every weapon that the enemy presented to destroy Joseph, God removed the effectiveness of it. God protected Joseph, as only our God can do for His children, while using those very same enemy traps to give him wisdom and strength. All the while God was preparing Joseph for his promotion. God knew that Joseph was not quite ready for the real challenge.

If we are in the Body of Christ, we must always be prepared to wait for God's perfect timing in all situations. Sometimes after we have applied for a job and have met all of man's prerequisites for a desired position, we are passed over. There are times when a person may have inferior qualifications compared to yours, but they end up getting the nod instead of you. You then become despondent, feeling as though an employer, a superior, or perhaps company management snubbed you by promoting or hiring a lesser-qualified candidate. But once you have developed an inextricable relationship with God, you know that He sees everything from His view. And if you remain steadfast, faith in His Word will let you know that He has something better for you down the road.

So continue to pray for maturity in the fruit of the Spirit, and never become dismayed to the point of allowing others to see that your love walk is on the downswing. After all, we are ambassadors for the Kingdom of God. Instead, we must reflect the prudence of God and be circumspect to know that His love is still at the helm, His Word will always rise to the surface, and His justice will always prevail.

# KNOW THE BENEFITS OF GOD'S LOVE
## (SIMPLY BENEFIT)

Matthew 22:44 says, **"The Lord said unto my Lord. Sit thou on my right hand, till I make thine enemies thy footstool."** He will steer us and shield us from our enemies while at the same time use the enemies and their training facilities to take us to another level. However, patience is a virtue. Those same villainous brothers of Joseph had to journey to Egypt to purchase grain for their family. Unknown to them, they were at the mercy of the same brother whom they despised and sold as a slave.

God's wisdom and favor will give you victory over your enemies every trip of the train and will allow your enemies the opportunity to witness just how good God is to those who claim victory in the name of Jesus.

You might say, "I would love to have a certain position, but I do not know if I can handle the training." If you are not willing to study God's Word and to trust in Him enough to prepare yourself for victory, you won't ever have to worry about that because you won't qualify. You have to be willing to spend time in God's Word and establish an intimate relationship with Him to know what His will and course of direction are for your life, as well as the long-range benefits that come with it.

There is no need to fear Satan. Jesus has already defeated him. Jesus said in John 16:33, **"These things I have spoken unto you, that in me ye might have peace. In the world ye shall have tribulation: but be of good cheer; I have overcome the world."** Satan is being used every day, and he is too ignorant to see it. Whenever the average person gets in a quandary, regardless of their level of relationship with God, the first name that they unquestionably yell out is not, "Oh, dear Satan." Usually it's "Oh, my God." So you see, even in Satan's quest to separate you from God, he actually draws you nearer to Him. But instead of us using the tribulation time to get reacquainted or to improve our relationship with God, we often become embedded in our grief. Just remember:

## LIFE IS SO SIMPLE WHEN
## WE CHOOSE TO LOVE GOD'S WAY

**Without the Word of God**
**You don't want to face tomorrow.**
**And without the love of Jesus,**
**You will drown in your sorrow.**

We must learn to set aside ample time each day to soak our souls in the Word of God. Failure to do this will ultimately drive a wedge between us and the redemptive blood of Jesus. God has already provided all that we need to circumnavigate any situation that we are confronted with. God does not rejoice whenever we stumble or get overwhelmed by the concerns of this world. I do not believe that any caring, loving parent would enjoy seeing his or her children flounder or be disappointed for any reason. Neither would God.

When we do not choose Jesus as Lord of our life, we have a much greater proclivity to become hard-headed and disobedient, and it becomes increasingly easier for our hearts to harden, and for us to say and think the wrong things. Then we are forced by way of our own choosing to return to Satan's gym to allow more training. When we finally get it right and get our new promotion, we can tell the story and give God the glory.

Sometime back I was passed over for a promotion on my job. My ego was crushed. I knew I was qualified and certainly just as capable as any of the other candidates who ended up getting the nod. However, through it all, I was never contemptuous nor was I rebellious toward my superiors or subordinates because of this rather difficult situation. God knew all about my qualifications and I trusted that He would promote me in His time. So what I purposely did was wish the newly promoted officers well and continued to do my job in a professional manner. I decided to look for ways to improve my present position.

You will be absolutely startled at what you will find when you begin to diligently seek God's wisdom instead of drowning in your sorrow. Maintaining the practice of doing the opposite of what others expect simply works wonders.

# Know the Benefits of God's Love
## (Simply Benefit)

As believers, according to Deuteronomy 14:2, we are charged to be different, **"For thou art an holy people unto the Lord thy God, and the Lord hath chosen thee to be a peculiar people unto himself, above all the nations that are upon the earth."** We are called to be different in all matters of importance throughout the world. Someone is always taking notice, and we should seize every opportunity to take a winning attitude for Jesus. We are required to react differently from what would be normal in most situations. This is part of our separation from the world. We are God's most special creation in all of the earth.

At any rate, eight months later I got my promotion. It was right on time. When my superior called me up to give me the good news, he informed me of two qualities that he admired in me more than anything else: my ability to remain professional during an understandably disappointing period, and the intensity of my focus after I was passed over. He added that he could not say the same about some of the others who were in the same predicament.

It's not important whenever your ego gets crushed. That's just a pride thing. The true test of character is what you do after you pick up the pieces. Be mindful that someone is always watching you, whether you see him or her or not. Besides, God is watching and as ambassadors to the Kingdom of heaven, you don't want to ever let God down.

Matthew 5:16 says, **"Let your light so shine before men, that they may see your good works, and glorify your Father which is in heaven."** God wants us to come out of the darkness simply because there are no benefits in the dark. The only reason we should be in the dark is to use our light to lead other sisters or brothers out of it. John 3:19 says, **"Men loved darkness rather than light, because their deeds were evil."** As Christians, we are on duty at all times. We need to shine for Jesus at every turn, never squandering an opportunity.

## LIFE IS SO SIMPLE WHEN
## WE CHOOSE TO LOVE GOD'S WAY

I wound up getting an opportunity to command one of the most prestigious units in the police department, and of course, God gets all of the glory. I had absolutely no experience in the unit, but that was remedied too. Psalm 75:6-7 says, **"For promotion cometh neither from the east, nor from the west, nor from the south. But God is the judge: he putteth down one, and setteth up another."**

Promotions come from God. We have to wait for God's perfect timing for promotion. It does not make any difference how well qualified you think you are to do a job. Every job that you feel you are qualified to do may not serve God in the capacity that He wants to be served by you. This is another key benefit of being in God's family. God will not lead you down the wrong path. When we find ourselves traveling down a path that is incongruous to the one that God has chosen for us, we have no one to blame but ourselves.

David said in Psalm 23:3, **"He leadeth me in the paths of righteousness for *his name's sake*."** God wants us to know that He maintains His words of excellence. He does whatever He says in His Word. He knows that His reputation is always at stake, and He relishes the opportunity for us to trust Him. He does everything using simplicity. He does not complicate matters for our life. We are the ones responsible for that.

Jesus said in John 14:6, **"I am the way, the truth, and the life...."** Is there anything mysterious or indistinct about this passage of scripture? Jesus says He is the way. The love of God is not a mystery. Jesus is simply the truth. His way is the absolute best and only way that's tailor-made for our life, irrespective to any other ways you may know or have tried. His way is **above and beyond all others.** Quite simply, any other way is the wrong way.

To know the way of the Lord is another helpful benefit designed to keep us on course. There is nothing nebulous about the truth and the life. All of us could use and should certainly want more of both. Just think of a world saturated with "truth and life" instead of lies and untimely deaths, the latter being

## Know the Benefits of God's Love
### (Simply Benefit)

traits of evil and destruction, initiated by the debacle of Adam and Eve. God thrives on the fact that His reputation is always on the line. We worry unnecessarily about our image and reputation. But with God on our side, there is no need to worry about the fate of our reputation. Isaiah 54:17 says, **"No weapon that is formed against thee shall prosper...."**

The benefits of God's love are infinite. God has nothing to gain in leading us astray. All we need to do is to take the first step and just believe. Simply take Him at His Word and do what it says, stay on course, and wait for your breakthrough as you hone your relationship with Him a little bit more each day.

Sometimes in having to make a decision, you will be confronted with what might appear to be a good resolution. Remember, in all matters of importance, seek God first. To seek Him first also means that before you make an impetuous decision, seek His guidance. The Holy Spirit will aid you in deciding between what appears to be good and what is better. Your conscience is a dependable guide when the Holy Spirit infuses it.

I am not advocating that you reject every potentially good thing that comes your way. What I am saying, however, is that once you become familiar with God's Word and His voice and your spirit man has your ear, you will then get a better gauge of exactly what He wants you to do, what He wants you to have, and what He wants you to say.

Speaking the words of the Spirit is another invaluable benefit that is available to every Christian. First Corinthians 2:14 says, **"But the natural man receiveth not the things of the Spirit of God: for they are foolishness unto him: neither can he know them, because they are spiritually discerned."** People in the world do not have the Spirit of God; therefore, they cannot speak the language nor understand its significance until they have been born again, accepting Jesus as Lord. Every born-again Christian has this benefit within, but it is of no avail if we do not activate it.

## LIFE IS SO SIMPLE WHEN
## WE CHOOSE TO LOVE GOD'S WAY

God is all about fulfilling His Word and He will use anyone in this world who is willing to do His work in the earth. The number one method that God uses to get His message across as well as His blessings through to us is by way of people. This is why we are never to overlook any person who crosses our path.

The Word of God says in Jeremiah 1:12, **"For I will hasten my word to perform it."** The word "hasten" means to accelerate or to move or act quickly. So now we know that the Word of God can and will cause "it" to happen quickly. "It" is or "it" can be whatever desires we may have in our lives that are consistent with His Word. The things in life that we pray for, including our desires, do not have to take a lifetime to come full circle. Our heavenly Father certainly wants us to have all of what we need, but you need to know that He also wants us to have the things that we desire.

Psalm 34:10 says, **"The young lions do lack, and suffer hunger: but they that seek the Lord shall not want any good thing."** The young lion is thunderous, mighty, and ferocious, and in most instances, he is always able to get or take whatever he wants. "The young lion" symbolizes mighty men who depend on their strength alone. However, notwithstanding their might, invariably if they are fortunate, they will grow old and their strength will eventually deplete, fading into the sunset as their ability to dominate dissipates. This constitutes a severe lack that introduces suffering, which ultimately leads to their death.

In comparison, we who diligently seek the Lord may lack the physical prowess of mighty men. However, we shall never want for any good thing because we know that our heavenly Father openly rewards us by supplying our needs as well as the desires of our heart. The young lions lack, but with God there is no lack. Therefore, any saint who professes to be a child of God should have no lack in their life and should certainly never claim it, even if it appears to be present in the natural realm.

Whatever we need, God has already provided. All we need to do is put our faith in action. God wants us to have what we

# Know the Benefits of God's Love
## (Simply Benefit)

want just because He is our Father and we are His children who depend upon Him as the Source of all of our blessings.

Jesus says in Mark 9:23, **"If thou canst believe, all things are possible to him that believeth."** Just believe in God and continue to confess that He has already done it! Without God, your strength and your riches might get you close to the finish line, but you will not cross the finish line or win the race. It is all about willingness to be obedient to the Word of God and to stay focused on Him regardless of the odds. If you seek Jesus, you will find Him. Once you have truly found Him, it would behoove you never to take your eyes off of the prize.

In this world today, all of us feel a need to be protected. More importantly, we need to know the protection that is promised to us in the Word of God. Not just for our sake, but for the sake of our mates, families, and friends. Follow His lead and expect His protection, His favor, and His supernatural blessings.

In Psalm 23:1 David said, **"The Lord is my shepherd; I shall not want."** Why should you want or how can you want when there is no scarcity in God? It's simply awesome to be a child of God and to know the benefits that we have in Him. It is by no means arrogance. It is just having a feeling of unrivaled security while exuding confidence as we should. There is no fictitious character or make-believe supernatural hero who will lead us and guide us through this life's journey. That is, no one other than the guidance of the One who made us and left us with written instructions to follow for a fulfilled life according to His purpose. No one but God, the Creator of the universe, can do that. He is THE SHEPHERD.

Jesus says in John 10:11, **"I am the *good* shepherd. . . ."** Jesus is forthright, always concise and to the point. He lets us know from the outset that we need to be on guard, as there are other so-called shepherds in this world with a self-centered agenda and who are not operating in heaven's best interest. There are imposters and charlatans in all walks of life. The

Church is not immune as Satan continues to prowl, lurking all around for any sign of stray sheep longing for a shepherd.

God made us and He knows all about us, and whenever we decide to quiet down and listen carefully inwardly, we will hear Him giving us cadence. David personalized Him by saying the Lord is "my shepherd." You and I can make this claim as well once we accept Jesus as our Savior and develop a personal relationship with God through Him.

Anyone can verbalize that God is his or her shepherd, but it's only true when we seek and find Him and live our lives according to His Word and allow His Word to undeniably lead us the rest of the way. Truth breeds success, and if we are living examples that God is our shepherd, our lives should somehow promulgate that not only are our needs met, but that we are just as concerned about the salvation and needs of others. With God as our Shepherd, we should have an oversupply.

So don't let your excess bewilder you. Just continue to thank God for what He allows you to have. Your excess is provided so you can be a blessing to others. It is a blessing to be abundantly blessed. It symbolizes that you have won God's approval to the extent that He trusts you to continue to sow seeds on other good ground so that His presence can continue to flourish and be felt throughout the earth. Our godly benefits, without a doubt, just got better. In Psalm 23:5 David says, **"Thou preparest a table before me in the presence of mine enemies. . . ."**

Think about the odds that were stacked against Moses as we reflect on the book of Exodus, starting with chapter 2. When Moses was born, his people were slaves in Egypt. Pharaoh feared that the Egyptians might eventually take over his country, so he ordered all baby boys killed at birth. Moses' mother hid him in a basket at the Nile River where the daughter of Pharaoh found him and reared him as an Egyptian. Of course, Moses grew up as an Egyptian, but once he found out he was Hebrew, he never forgot. This became evident as he murdered an Egyptian and fled Egypt. Later God spoke to

Moses from a burning bush and told him he must go back and free the Hebrews from slavery.

We cannot remotely visualize the depth of God's wisdom and how He can purpose in our heart what He wants us to do and how He has the uncanny ability in His Word alone to get us to do it. God now gets Moses to go back to Egypt and free the Hebrews from slavery. You know the story. After several plagues and the eventual death of Pharaoh's son, Pharaoh finally released the Hebrew slaves.

Now, imagine being a fugitive from justice, having to go back to the very place where you committed a murder and you had to flee from that place. Then, you have the audacity to tell the Pharaoh several times, while threatening him and showering his country with unimaginable pestilence and plagues, **"Thus saith the Lord God of Israel, Let my people go . . ."** (Exodus 5:1). If you serve Almighty God, Creator of the universe, and if you know that He has sanctioned your mission, then you better believe it's okay. Furthermore, it behooves all of us to do whatever the Spirit of God instructs us to do, especially when you know that it coincides with the Word of God.

God will guide your steps whenever you decide that you are going to trust Him and take the first step. God is a God of order. With Him, it is always one step at a time. Remember, we had to crawl before we ever walked. However, that does not preclude God from doing things supernaturally in our life. But in most cases, a process is involved, which starts with accepting Jesus as your personal Savior.

Another prime benefit in God's love is that when He gives you an assignment or authorizes your vision, He has already equipped you with everything that you will need to succeed. He has also prepared every heart that you will encounter during your journey. As a matter of fact, everything that you need to begin your journey is right in front of you. It's left up to you to seek and find it. Through Jesus, it is already done and so are eternal life and an abundant life with God's enduring grace and mercy.

## Life Is So Simple When
## WE CHOOSE TO LOVE GOD'S WAY

God's love and benefit package are available to all of His special creations who will abide in Jesus. However, you cannot live a sin-infested life and expect to abide under God's umbrella of protection and receive your benefits. God hates sin. Proverbs 16:25 says, **"There is a way that seemeth right unto a man, but the end thereof are the ways of death."** Death is the pinnacle of our unforgiven sins and we can only be redeemed through acceptance of the death, burial, and resurrection of our Savior and Lord, Jesus Christ.

Salvation is always the **benefit de jour** (benefit of the day), and without a doubt the most important benefit that we will ever receive. What is especially great about this benefit is that it is available to all of us, whether we are currently employed or seeking employment. So why not take full advantage of this priceless gift from God?

# Chapter 4

# What Does the Bible Say About Love? (Simply Study)

*G*od's living Word, the Bible, is our universal road map, designed specifically to lead, guide, and protect us as we travel through the pathways of this abundant life en route to our hope of eternal life. God is love and His love is the all-embracing language that was expressed exclusively for all of mankind through the sacrificial death of Jesus, His only begotten Son.

It matters not if you are in the United States or Iraq, South America, or Southeast Asia. It makes no difference if you are wealthy, miserly, impoverished, or unskilled, and your resources are limited. Whether you are red, yellow, black, or white, the effective power of the Word of God and His compassionate Spirit are present-day helps available to everyone. If you allow His Word to be the helm of your life, it will successfully navigate you and anyone else on board safely throughout this world, taking only the pathway of least resistance.

John 3:16 says, **"For God so loved the world, that he gave his only begotten Son, that whosoever believeth in him should not perish, but have everlasting life."** This is one of the most renowned, beloved, and memorable Bible verses in the entire world. Yet how many of us have really taken the time to study and meditate on this passage of Scripture and understand the very essence of what it means?

## LIFE IS SO SIMPLE WHEN
## WE CHOOSE TO LOVE GOD'S WAY

God's love for us is more than simply unique. While unique is still considered a quality word, over the years it has become somewhat vogue and has lost some of its luster and effectiveness because of its overblown usage. So it would be a terrible injustice for us to conclude that God's proven love for us is simply unique. Instead, His love is inimitable, unprecedented, and unparalleled. It can never be duplicated, emulated, or compared to any other love that we know.

Think about **"God so loved the world."** He loved us to an unspecified extent, to an extremity, if you will, with a wide open love, better known as *"agape"* love, a Greek word for selfless or unconditional love. God knew that without Jesus at the forefront of His repurchasing plan, all of us would eventually self-destruct and never reach Him to experience the beauty of living in His holiness. He knew that if we were left without His grace that we would continue to sink and eventually drown in our shortcomings.

Furthermore, the only way these discrepancies could ever be rectified would be through the redemptive blood of His Son Jesus. So now through Jesus, we too can have and openly give His love once we confess and continue in His completed work.

*Agape* love characterizes the altruism of God and the love that He showed for us when He sacrificed the life of His only Son. The mere thought of having someone love us this much is matchless. Jesus Himself accentuated the magnanimity of this love in John 15:13 when He said, **"Greater love hath no man than this, that a man lay down his life for his friends."** This epitomizes the love of Jesus, who lived a short life here on earth, but was and still is our model. His life was a paragon that will never be forgotten.

Jesus' life was not taken. He simply laid it down, gave it up of His own volition because of the mandated will of God the Father. Not only did He lay down His life for you and me, but for all of us, even for the strangers in the world who have yet to find the time, inclination, or common courtesy to simply pause from their busy schedules and get to know Him! There is nothing in this world that is remotely comparable to His ineffable display of love that was freely given to all. Quite simply, God sacrificed the best that He had.

For the most part, the cursory "I love you's" that we express to each other on a daily basis are based on some sort of emotion, a tit-for-tat natural reciprocity that we enjoy receiving and we feel obligated to respond to. That's why occasionally people do not reach out and receive our love with sincerity when we offer or attempt to express to them what we view as the God-kind of love. To them this love is strange or fallacious and it does not appear to be natural or authentic. For a number of people this is simply not what they have grown accustomed to receiving, as they have never expressed or received love of any kind from anyone.

Not everyone was fortunate to have experienced a childhood with a prototypical love-filled family background. So we must be compassionate and continue to learn and embrace the ways of Jesus through the Word of God to develop and administer the patience of His Spirit through the fruit of our spirit towards everyone we meet.

Some people do not comprehend rejection, so when someone tends to balk at receiving our love or our invitation to get to know Jesus, sometimes our emotions get involved and our feelings become hurt. A few may consequently discontinue their commitment to spreading the Good News about Jesus.

Galatians 6:9 says, **"And let us not be weary in well doing: for in due season we shall reap, if we faint not."** Whenever you strive to do good, especially specific things for the Kingdom of God, learn to be impervious to what others think. Don't ever quit! Your harvest for doing well is right around the corner. Think process! Getting you to quit is one of the top ten line items on Satan's "to do" list, specifically designed and geared towards the destruction of good deeds. All of us know of someone, or perhaps we have been a quitter at one time or another. Quitting a good work does nothing to enhance the Kingdom of God.

## Life Is So Simple When
## WE CHOOSE TO LOVE GOD'S WAY

Ephesians 6:8 says, **"Knowing that whatsoever good thing any man doeth, the same shall he receive of the Lord, whether he be bond or free."** There are a myriad of people in this world who would be more than happy to sit a spell with you and tell you all about the consequences that you will experience in quitting, and how their minds have since looked back and wondered, *If I had only toughed it out,* or *I wish I had the opportunity to relive that moment.* These are all good intentions and afterthoughts, but that's about all they are. They are all for nought. There are no celebrations, appreciations, or trophies for quitters.

Have you ever thought about why some people succeed in their endeavors while others fail, whether in their careers, in their personal life, or in their quest to further the Kingdom of God? It's because those who fail become feeble or weary in their well doing and they succumb and simply throw in the towel. They are fully aware of what they need to do to succeed, and there is no doubt about their motives or their qualifications. They simply become weak, jaded, frustrated, and impatient, eventually leading them to abandon the ship.

It may come as a surprise to you, but from time to time even the best of people get a little tired and frustrated. However, if we are going to be top-notch soldiers in the army of God, we simply cannot afford to drop the towel, raise our hands, and subjugate to Satan whenever the first sign of rejection or disappointment comes our way.

Imagine if the adversary could force all of us to become weary and implode. We need to start out on our journey by thinking success. Think positive by looking at the end result of how the finished product is going to look before you ever get started.

In First Samuel, chapter 17, David spoke with gloating faith and he was so confident that he was going to defeat Goliath that he asked the men of Israel, **"What shall be done to the man that killeth this Philistine?"** (1 Samuel 17:26). In other words, speak like David and know that through your faith in

God you already have the victory! Think back to what Jesus sacrificed at the cross. What if God had given up on us, or if Jesus had decided to succumb to the temptations of Satan and opt out of His Father's plan?

Now, visualize what your finished product will look like when you begin to think from within and use your intestinal fortitude to act tough and finish what you start. Just because we see a good opportunity does not mean that we will not have to be a little aggressive. With Jesus no obstacle can possibly stop your progress. Isaiah 54:17 says, **"No weapon that is formed against thee shall prosper...."** Complete the process! And always remember,

### The benefits in completion
### Will outlive the satisfaction in quitting.

Learn to *go the distance and* finish what you start. God needs Christians with winning attitudes for His Kingdom, Christians who are willing to stay the course and ride the wave until the very end. If by chance you stumble, simply straighten up, compose yourself, and keep right on going. Jesus said, **"I will never leave thee, nor forsake thee"** (Hebrews 13:5). That's all the love and guarantee that you will ever need to successfully complete any good work in Jesus' name.

Try and understand the significance of honing all of your skills in a godly fashion. The work that Jesus started must continue in the earth, and everyday people like you and me will play a vital role in getting it done. Remember, **"In due season we shall reap, if we faint not"** (Galatians 6:9). Fainting is simply a sign of giving up. Hang in there and finish the job that you started.

First John 2:17 says, **"And the world passeth away, and the lust thereof: but he that doeth the will of God abideth for ever."** It's all about our consistent obedience to doing what is right. The sinful pleasures, desires, and cares of this world, regardless of how fascinating they may seem at the time, will always pass quickly out of existence. Regardless of how long they keep you in the game, you will always fall short of the end zone.

Everyone and everything in this world that is not representative of the Father will eventually find their way to eternal damnation. That's why we must pray without ceasing for the will of God to be done in our life in earth as it is in heaven. We must thank God for His grace and mercy as we permeate our minds with His Word and soak our hearts with His love — the love that we must have to be undaunted to rejection and to what people think about us as we gallantly spread the Good News of Jesus.

Stop wasting time trying to find something or someone else in this life to fill your void and to stir you up. Stir up yourself with the promises of God and pray that the spiritual minds of unbelievers be enlightened and receptive to the purpose of Jesus' life, death, and resurrection.

In Matthew 22:36-39, one of the Pharisees who was a lawyer, asked Jesus a question regarding the commandments and Jesus responded to him:

> **Master, which is the great commandment in the law?**
> **Jesus said unto him, Thou shalt love the Lord thy God with all thy heart, and with all thy soul, and with all thy mind.**
> **This is the first and great commandment.**
> **And the second is like unto it, Thou shalt love thy neighbour as thyself.**

Only with *agape* love are we able to love God as prescribed by Jesus and love others whether they love us or not, while continuing to reach out to save a dying world lost in sin with the same tenacity, zest, and zeal that Jesus had. Notice, Jesus spelled out three specific areas that are critically viewed when our love for God is placed under the scope. We are to love God with all of our **heart, soul, and mind.**

# What Does the Bible Say About Love?
## (Simply Study)

Think about the word "all." As mentioned previously, "all" means the whole amount. It encompasses everyone, including you and me, giving every ounce of our being to God. Quite frankly, it means giving entirely the very best of what we have to offer. If something is broken, lacking, or if something is missing, then it's not your all. Your all is not what you have compared to your best friend, your next-door neighbor, and certainly not your leftovers. Your all is based on the absolute best of what you have been blessed with, on the inside and on the outside.

When you love God with all of your heart, no one has to tell you or make you lift up the name of Jesus. It should be an honor to you to know that you can always be connected to the Creator of the universe through His Son and through His living Word.

So do you love God with your absolute best, living your life by His unimpeachable Word? It's time for a self-evaluation, not designed to berate you, but simply to point out the flaws in your love walk that may be keeping your blessings from breaking through. This is a way for you to truly know whether you love God with all of your heart. Obviously, He already knows! You simply cannot give Him your all when something in your life is missing, especially when that someone missing is Jesus. When you love God with all your heart, you deservingly and understandably place Him in a category all by Himself. You keep Him there regardless of how you feel from day to day, or what you may be going through.

The heart happens to be the center of our life, our very existence. Our emotions, feelings, and expressions come from the heart, so we are to love God with all of life, with all of our innermost affections, emotions, and feelings, holding nothing back. Keeping Him first, not only in all we do but also before anything we do, just to ensure that He approves and has sanctioned our first steps before we proceed any further in whatever our endeavors may be.

## Life Is So Simple When
## WE CHOOSE TO LOVE GOD'S WAY

Whenever we love God with all of our heart, we leave all of our effort on the field. We leave no gaps or cracks for doubt to creep in or for anything ungodly to be desired. There is never an "I'm not quite sure," "I just don't know," or "I know I am supposed to love Him but. . . ." It would serve you tremendously to etch the words **"God first loved me"** in the core of your heart.

Matthew 15:18-19 says:

> **But those things which proceed out of the mouth come forth from the heart; and they defile the man.**
> **For out of the heart proceed evil thoughts, murders, adulteries, fornications, thefts, false witness, blasphemies.**

The best barometer to use to gauge the character of any person is to monitor what comes out of their mouth. Start listening more carefully to what you are saying. We need to realize from this point forward that we frame our life just a little bit more each day with bricks that are made from the things that we say.

> **Your end results,**
> **Whether intentional or not,**
> **Are parallel to the words**
> **That flow from your mouth.**

Did you know that your end results and your behavior mirror what is in your heart? Is what you are saying consistent with what you are doing? Our actions will almost always indicate what's really going on inside of our hearts. What are your actions saying? The Bible is God's Word and His Word will never change. If you want to have good success, then adhere to His living Word. Hebrews 4:12 says, **"For the word of God is quick, and powerful, and sharper than any twoedged sword, piercing even to the dividing asunder of soul and spirit, and of the joints and marrow, and is a discerner of the thoughts and intents of the heart."**

# What Does the Bible Say About Love?
## (Simply Study)

The true and living Word of God not only predicts our future, but it calls us out as well. The lasting results that we get in life will be directly proportionate to the measure of God's Word that either we apply or do not apply in our life. His Word has already predicted the results. If you want to do an in-depth study on your results, start by checking the words that you say every day.

Jesus advises us in Matthew 24:35, **"Heaven and earth shall pass away, but my words shall not pass away."** All we need to do is trust and obey His written Word. God will always keep His Word and it would behoove us to always keep ours. It's not what goes into your mouth, but it's what comes out of your mouth that unveils you and accurately reports your truthfulness.

Choose your words carefully before speaking. If you do not plan to honor a commitment, don't make the promise. In Ecclesiastes 5:2 Solomon said, **"Be not rash with thy mouth, and let not thine heart be hasty to utter any thing before God: for God is in heaven, and thou upon earth: therefore let thy words be few."** Sometimes we say things and make promises that we know from the outset we have no intention to honor. There is no shame in saying, "I am not quite sure," because if you want to know the truth about it, there are very few things in life that we can be absolutely certain of. However, God's Word and His love are absolutes. Don't even think about making God a promise if you're not going to keep it. God already knows your heart. He predestined your life before you were conceived, and according to Matthew 10:30, **"The very hairs of your head are all numbered."**

Jesus also said that we are to love God with all of our soul. Your soul is your inward appetite or that inner part of you that has the insatiable desire to always urge for something else. It is your will to say "yes" or "no" to God. It is your guide for doing right or wrong. Jesus said, **"If ye love me, keep my commandments"** (John 14:15). Are you keeping God's commandments?

In Luke 8:21 Jesus said, **"My mother and my brethren are these which hear the word of God, and do it."** Are you in the family? Do you fit the bill? Can you manage to stay focused on the righteousness of God regardless of everything else that is going on around you? Do you have that unquenchable thirst to continue to love God and keep His sayings, or are you still wrestling with trying to stay on the right side of the fence? Which side of you is winning the battle: your will to follow God, or your will not to follow Him? These are questions that only you can answer. But you can rest assured that whatever path you choose to follow, your final score will be tallied and recorded, whether you are keeping score or not.

In Matthew 26:41 Jesus said, **"Watch and pray, that ye enter not into temptation: the spirit indeed is willing, but the flesh is weak."** Temptations of all sorts loom large in this world. Our bodies are frail and they have this insatiable desire for instant gratification. Jesus was tempted and we will also be tempted. You can count on it. So when you get down to the final analysis, the only thing that will matter is not whether or not you were tempted, but did you:

**Reject the invitation, or
Succumb to temptation?**

It is imperative that we stay prayed up and fueled up with the Word of God. Learn to listen inwardly so you can become more conversant with that soft voice that gives heavenly advice and information that is congruent with the Word of God. When you spend time in the Word of God, there should be no reluctance on your part to follow the inner voice of your spirit.

The Apostle Paul in Acts 23:1 said, **"Men and brethren, I have lived in all good conscience before God until this day."** What about you? Can you say that since giving your life to God you are still serving Him with a good conscience? You do the math. Not just on Sundays but during the week too and especially after hours. Paul makes a bold statement with surety as he speaks like a man with complete confidence in his

# What Does the Bible Say About Love?
## (Simply Study)

faithfulness and service to God, demonstrated in his love walk. There is no vacillating in his words or actions.

When you know the love of God for you, you should not be afraid to make bold statements of truth. Not that you are boasting, arrogant, or condescending. It's just exuding supreme confidence in what you do as the Word of God guides you.

James 1:8 says, **"A double minded man is unstable in all his ways."** If you are double minded, it simply means you have not completely given your life to God. There is still uncertainty in almost everything that you do because you have adopted a dual lifestyle. You want to receive God's best and be a part of His team, while still appearing in Satan's lineup. When you are unstable with your love for God, you are sure to experience unstableness in other areas of your life. There is bound to be uncertainty in your relationships with people as well as inconsistencies on your job.

A closer check will no doubt reveal that you are not consistently studying the Word of God. The only way that you can accurately assess specific areas of your life, especially your love for God, is by knowing what the Word of God says about your situation. If you are not in the Word of God, talking to Him on a daily basis, how can you know that you love God with all your soul and that God has authorized your love walk? When you love God with all of your soul, no one has to tell you to do what's right, because you will have that uncanny desire to keep the mind of Jesus, not desiring to cause any embarrassment to yourself or to the Kingdom of God during your trials and temptations, regardless of who may be doing the tempting.

Your love for God will withstand any test, and even though all of us are bound to hit bumps and potholes on the interstate of life, your love for God will simply refuse to allow you to exit off His Word.

Can you incontestably say that you love God with your entire mind? Your mind is where your real or true feelings are initiated. Everything starts with a thought. The mind is where you do your reasoning and rehearsing. This is where we contemplate, compute, or give consideration or regard to a matter. Your mind determines your conduct. The Bible often refers to the heart and mind as being the same.

Philippians 2:5 says, **"Let this mind be in you, which was also in Christ Jesus."** In other words, we should be an extension of the same will, intentions, thoughts, and feelings that are trademarks of Jesus. In Psalm 19:14 the Psalmist said, **"Let the words of my mouth, and the meditation of my heart, be acceptable in thy sight, O Lord, my strength, and my redeemer."**

Often, we say whatever we think without giving it much consideration. We should strive to please the Lord with all of our thinking as well as with all of what we say. The words that we choose to speak and the majority of the thoughts that we ruminate in our minds will reveal overwhelming evidence as to whether or not we are fully persuaded to please God. Even with the small battles that are constantly brewing inside of us, your will to do right should always win.

Whenever saints decide to place themselves in a setting that is not conducive to the Kingdom of God, it grieves the Holy Spirit. With this in mind, you should decide to make your way to the nearest exit as soon as you find it. Isaiah 26:3 says, **"Thou wilt keep him in perfect peace, whose mind is stayed on thee; because he trusteth in thee."** When you keep your mind stayed on God, He will give you perfect peace or a supernatural peace based on your faith in Him. Perfect peace would include but is not limited to wholeness, good health, prosperity, and essentially every kind of goodness possible.

Only God's children are privy to His peace. Philippians 4:7 NIV says, **"And the peace of God, which transcends all understanding, will guard your hearts and your minds in Christ Jesus."** No faculty of your natural mind has the percipience to comprehend the peace of God. This peace that God gives is a blessing and it supersedes or overrides any other state of mind regardless of your circumstances or feelings.

The believer is not ashamed to take His Spirit everywhere he or she goes, and whenever there is an uneasy feeling about where you should take Him, it simply means that you should not be there. This is your cue either to not go or to simply get up and leave immediately.

Ephesians 4:30 says, **"And grieve not the holy Spirit of God, whereby ye are sealed unto the day of redemption."** As children of God, we have been stamped and labeled with His seal and identified as His property for the day of redemption. Your part is to honor God by remembering Him in the way that you live and in all that you do.

When we *choose to love God's way,* our representation of the Kingdom of God is seen in us wherever we go, and as secondary as it may seem, it all starts with the execution of a simple thought that enters our mind. Our job is to take care of God and His work throughout the earth. When we do this, He takes care of us in a manner befitting to children of the Most High. When your mind is committed to pleasing God and spreading His wondrous works in the earth that He drafted in His will for your life, you are showing a diligence that pleases Him. Remember, Hebrews 11:6 says, **"He is a rewarder of them that diligently seek him."**

## Paul's Description of Love

When we take another look at what the Bible says about love, First Corinthians 13 gives a beautiful rendition as recorded by the Apostle Paul. This text helps some of us realize just how much our love walk needs to be overhauled.

First Corinthians 13:1-2 says:

> **Though I speak with the tongues of men and of angels, and have not charity, I am become as sounding brass, or a tinkling cymbal.**

## Life Is So Simple When
## WE CHOOSE TO LOVE GOD'S WAY

**And though I have the gift of prophecy, and understand all mysteries, and all knowledge; and though I have all faith, so that I could remove mountains, and have not charity, I am nothing.**

What a heart-piercing message that cuts right to the core. We can instantly see that charity [love] has nothing to do with words. It makes no difference as to the loftiness of your vocabulary or your native or angelic language. It matters not whether you prophesy, teach, or preach. God can and will use anyone of us to deliver His messages, the point being, God is love. And without the love of God in your heart, whose love is in His Word, your gifts amount to the fleeting sound of clashing cymbals. God is not interested in our self-importance.

I believe that love is the greatest and most enduring of all Christian virtues, and without it, all that you have done and all that you can and will do is the equivalent of a tinkling cymbal. And as you may well know, the sound of a tinkling cymbal or sounding brass disappears in a nanosecond. In other words, it loses its value before it can ever be appreciated. That's quicker than you can blink your eyes, bow your head, or snap your finger. That is what your talent and contributions are worth if they are not interwoven with the love of God in your heart. This is so vitally important, because we need to know that even though a person may never speak a word or possess breathtaking talents, their love, beauty, and truth can still be found in everything that they are as well as in everything they do.

As an afterthought, did you know that people who are incapable of expressing themselves with words can still convey to you that they love you? Maybe they can't speak the language or tell you verbally, but you know that they love you. For example, what if you are married or have been living with a relative for any period of time. Suddenly, you or your relative or perhaps someone else that you know becomes unable to express or communicate their love to you in the traditional way because of some unfortunate incident. Does this mean that their love or their need for love has stopped? Of course not! Remember, we said earlier that love is an action word. Love is not what it says, *it is what it does.*

A young child of six months may not be able to speak fluently, but he or she knows their mother's love strictly by action alone. Most people are capable of taking words or expressions in any language and using them to their advantage. In an effort to keep us divided, Satan does this every day. But when we chose to follow God's itinerary for our life, we tend to please Him in a way that no one else can.

I simply refuse to forfeit another opportunity to please my heavenly Father. And if I were you, I would get to know Him and never forego another chance to express the truth to a lost brother or sister about the love and knowledge of the Word of God. We must be willing to promulgate His plan by supplying this world with His love that's found throughout His Word. He has provided a specific role for each of us. He is not hung up on your past or your present status. There are people in and around our circles of life who long to hear, and more importantly, need to hear and know the truth about the awesome power of the living Word of God.

First Corinthians 13:3 says, **"And though I bestow all my goods to feed the poor, and though I give my body to be burned, and have not charity, it profiteth me nothing."** It's not about you or me or us. It's about Jesus and the love of God. The Kingdom of God must encompass all of the teachings of Jesus whose hallmark was and is love. This same love emphasized by Jesus must be our primary motive.

Several early Christians sacrificed their lives. You too can sacrifice your time, money, or anything else of value that you like for His cause. God is pleased when we are great humanitarians or philanthropists. But regardless of what sacrifices we make in this life, it does not give us an edge if the love of God is not at the forefront.

We have motives for doing whatever we do. Every day people make sacrifices for different reasons. Nevertheless, if you are not living and exemplifying the life of Jesus, who emphasized loving God and loving one another with the love of God embedded in your heart, then all of your giving, including your personal sacrifices, will lose some of its effectiveness.

Jesus said in Matthew 23:26, **"Cleanse first that which is within the cup and the platter, that the outside of them may be clean also."** Listen very carefully. The Word of God does not advocate that you should simply stop your giving and cease from helping people. Quite the contrary. Jesus was all about giving Himself. He has also shown us how we are to be about God's business by following His philanthropic footsteps of love and compassion for people.

We should by all means continue to give and give even more of our time, talent, and increase towards reaching other people for the Kingdom of God. Be very careful of your ostensible motives and ensure that your heart is in the right place. That is to say, the love of God must be out front, followed by genuine love for one another.

If you read the Word of God with an open mind, His Word will convict you and point out the flaws in your love walk. In other words, He will show you "your hitch in your get up"! This is one of many reasons why we need the Word of God as our guide. Whenever the Word of God convicts us, we should simply make adjustments and get back at once to serve the needs of others.

It is easy for us to know where we stand with our heavenly Father. All we need to do is simply get in His Word and He will show us. His Word will also give us a bird's-eye view of the significance of what Jesus did for us on the cross. Each day of our life, all of us need to inspect, assess, and correct our priorities, using God's Word alone as our barometer so we can know what we need to do to grow closer to becoming more like Him and more valuable to Him.

It is best that we help one another to grow in love and not ever give up on anyone. We are God's greatest creation. He wants the very best for us, and we should want the very best for each other. That's what the love of God is all about. He knows that the best way to win people for His Kingdom is through His loving saints who have decided to live out the love of Jesus and not through their gifts alone. Our love is to be like His love.

Ephesians 2:4 says, **"But God, who is rich in mercy, for his great love wherewith he loved us."** God does not simply love us. He loves us with great love. Every day He affords the lost another opportunity to get right with Him and receive the gift of salvation through His Son, as He provides us with His grace and mercy that endureth forever.

It is only befitting that His love is titled "great love." He instructs us to love our neighbors with the same veracity as we love ourselves. Everything that God does starts with His love. Remember, He first loved us and He is love.

First Corinthians 13:4 says, **"Charity suffereth long, and is kind; charity envieth not; charity vaunteth not itself, is not puffed up."** Are you impatient, unkind, jealous, or braggadocios? Do you acknowledge people from all walks of life? Do you separate yourself from people, looking down on them, based solely on your position in life? What about your temperament? Are you a mean person? Everyone has their quirks, and from time to time, we don't mind showing flashes of them. But I'm talking about something much larger like the real you or your total personality. Because of the very nature of Jesus, we should always strive to be kind and patient. There is simply no place in the Kingdom of God for a condescending disposition and especially envy, when our Father is King to all of His children.

There is more than enough for all of us. All we need to do is ask Him. James 4:2-3 NIV says, **"You do not have, because you do not ask God. When you ask, you do not receive, because you ask with wrong motives. . . ."**

God already knows your pretext before you approach Him, so don't waste your time going to Him for anything when your motives are wrong. That time and energy can be better spent reading His Word and asking Him for deliverance. You have no idea what level of faith, painstaking measures, or nocturnal labor other people may have sacrificed before they obtained their level of success or any other personal achievements.

It should take you all of the twenty-four hours in your day to encourage yourself and to acknowledge what you need to do to address your shortcomings. Proverbs 16:25 says, **"There is a way that seemeth right to a man, but the end thereof are the ways of death."** Doing right will always win. Mark 4:24 says, **"With what measure ye mete, it shall be measured to you. . . ."** You are responsible for your dividends, and you control your returns with everything that you do in life.

Giving and receiving is a universal law. You give love and you will receive love. It works the same for everyone and with everything that you give in life. All you need to do is check your record of giving. You do not need to make any phone calls for this one. Just ask yourself, what have I been dishing out lately? Go ahead and ask yourself right now. And if you still have not asked yourself this question, then I know that you are not serious about your self-assessment. This is a tool to help you in becoming the best example possible for Jesus.

As long as we can control what we give, we will always be responsible for what we receive. So what kind of goods have you been handing out lately? Life is somewhat like a boomerang in that whatever you throw out, sooner or later it will return. It's only a matter of time. I have never seen it fail. And of course whenever it returns, you will be able to recall the precise time that you planted it. Your returns will follow you wherever you go in this world. Why don't you follow the prudent advice of David in Psalm 37:4 and shift your focus to: **"Delight thyself also in the Lord; and he shall give thee the desires of thine heart."**

# What Does the Bible Say About Love?
## (Simply Study)

Notice, He did not say, "Keep up with the Joneses," nor did he say, "Find a second job." Instead, he charges us with finding satisfaction in learning more about the ways of God. Only the truth found in His Word can equip us with the things we will need to make us complete. So learn to be happy in the Lord and obedient to His instructions. He is our heavenly Father and He has left us His Fatherly advice in His Word. The more we seek His face, the more likely He is to reward us by granting our desires.

**"Charity vaunteth not itself, is not puffed up"** (1 Corinthians 13:4). There is no need to brag about our achievements, especially around people who are less faithful or whose blessings have not arrived yet. We should never pompously look down on others or think that we are a little bit more or that we are far superior to others in any form or fashion. That simply does not bring glory and honor to God. In fact, the only time we are to look down on another brother or sister is when we are lending a helping hand to pick them up or when we are bending over to see and hear what we can do to render assistance. As believers, we should never be lifted up in pride. If you really want to know the truth, some of us are exactly one incident away from being in another person's shoes.

First Corinthians 13:8 says, **"Charity never faileth...."** God's love has never failed us and our love for each other should never fail. His love functions consistently with the same effectiveness. Hebrews 13:8 says, **"Jesus Christ the same yesterday, and to day, and for ever."** He is a model of consistency and His love and His Word will always mesh. We are sometimes capricious in nature, suddenly changing our mood and countenance, all in one breath, for no valid reason.

God's love is constant. If we are His children, mimicking His kind of love, we should not disappoint Him or purposely let one another down. We should pull for each other to succeed and always hope for the best and hope for truth. We need to constantly evaluate our thinking and change our mind-set, if needed. We should be proud of people when they are promoted or elevated, and we should love to see others receive accolades and good news for jobs well done. Be happy whenever the truth is unveiled.

Likewise, your heart should go out to people when they experience a misfortune, but rejoice with them if and whenever their misfortunes have been rectified through the justice of God and the criminal justice system.

Not long ago I saw where DNA evidence exculpated a young man who had been wrongfully imprisoned for several years. Stop and think for a minute. Can you imagine this happening to you or to someone close to you? To lose your liberty through no fault of your own is certainly regrettable. It was unfortunate that this happened, but justice did prevail and it always will. My heart leaped for him as he got back his long-awaited freedom.

We should always hope for the best for people during their unfortunate trials and tests. Love is a vehicle that calls for action. Though unfortunate events may cause our vehicles to momentarily stall, our love should always seek ways to rejoice. Always be ready to forgive and to help others get to their next level of success and happiness.

First Corinthians 13:13 says, **"And now abideth faith, hope, charity, these three; but the greatest of these is charity."** The Apostle Paul says that of these three, love is the greatest or the most important. We know that nothing outranks or supersedes the living Word of God. But when you think about the greatest of these three, how can you not say the greatest is love? First John 4:8 says, **"He that loveth not knoweth not God; for God is love."** Love is indeed the greatest, simply because nothing precedes the love of God. *Choosing to love God's way* is the highest-ranking quality that any human can ever embody. Having and sharing the love of God is the only role in life, bar none, that covers all bases!

The Christian love walk is a lifestyle. I pray that you have made your choice to walk in love for life. It's really not difficult, because Jesus showed us how.

# Chapter 5

# How Do I Improve My Love Walk? (Simply Improve)

*In* order to improve your love walk, you must make an earnest effort to remove the debris that is blocking your entrance to the pathway that God has ordained specifically for your life. Some of this debris may indicate a flaw in your mental attitude that consequently affects the way you view your life, yourself, and your perspective of others. It could also have a bearing on other major matters of concern that we are faced with in today's society.

The Apostle Paul emphatically reminds us in Romans 12:2, **"But be ye transformed by the renewing of your mind, that ye may prove what is that good, and acceptable, and perfect, will of God."** Notwithstanding any changes that may instantaneously affect your appearance, long-term changes must first take place within the mind. With this renewing of the mind you begin the process of renovating your inner man, bringing to a halt any degree of corruptible thinking that might lead to undesirable behavior and a depraved mind. We must learn to do what is right simply because it is right.

When we become saints of God, our thinking must mirror a lifestyle that depicts a disciple of Jesus, aspiring to spend eternity with God. And if by chance your new attitude does not consistently reflect His compassionate Spirit, then your mental transformation has not taken place.

Maybe you are challenged with a conglomerate of other shortcomings and biases that are by no means conducive to a God-quality of life. It is by instituting positive changes, embraced with godly wisdom, that the faculties of your spirit can begin to fully grasp God's way and His perfect plan for your life.

So as a preamble for improving your love walk, reflect back on the years of your life that you have allowed this debris to accumulate or to stack up and block the specially designed path that God has made exclusively for your life. I know that this sounds a little like work, but according to James 2:20, **"Faith without works is dead."** Faith, like love, is an action word. There must be a reasonable correlation between what we believe and what we do.

So quickly picture in your mind water flowing smoothly down the drain once a pipe has finally been unclogged after a long period of blockage. At first, this task may seem arduous, tedious, and quite challenging. But there is one thing for certain. This completed process will have a more wholesome effect on your spiritual growth and your personal development than you could ever possibly imagine. As a matter of fact, I can tell you from personal experience that it will aid you tremendously, provided you are now willing to consistently study the Word of God and heed the voice of His Spirit as you allow Him to guide you every step of the way.

In Second Corinthians 4:16, the Apostle Paul said, **"For which cause we faint not; but though our outward man perish, yet the inward man is renewed day by day."** The term "day by day" makes it unquestionably clear that renewing the mind entails a process. The *New International Version* of this verse states, **"Therefore we do not lose heart. Though outwardly we are wasting away, yet inwardly we are being renewed day by day."** A change can begin to take place immediately, just by executing a simple thought in your mind. However, in order to succeed in your Christian endeavor, it will require habitual service over a period of time.

# How Do I Improve My Love Walk?
## (Simply Improve)

The benefits of this change are immeasurable as God's way is burned into your spirit. If you are really serious about being God's best and having an impact in renovating the world in which you live, then you must be absolutely truthful, starting with yourself and starting right now as you begin to evaluate, challenge, and then rectify your love walk.

Your love walk is the total you. It is your present-day results based on allowing or not allowing the living Word of God to be an example in every area of your life that can possibly be measured. In other words, it is the sum of your complete lifestyle relative to the Word of God.

In Ephesians 4:1, the Apostle Paul, who was imprisoned in Rome, makes a humble plea to Christians to **"walk worthy of the vocation wherewith ye are called."** The *New International Version* says, **"Live a life worthy of the calling you have received."** As Christians our vocation is our divine calling to the life of Jesus and it should be extended to the strangers that we meet and even modeled for the companies that employ us.

And get this: No Christian is exempt! We are commissioned to be representatives of heaven, extensions of everything that Jesus is a proponent of, and willing to stand with Him in unity against anything He opposes in His Word. To walk worthy means:

*To walk with consistency*
*With your integrity.*

As ambassadors of the Kingdom of God, our life should mirror the very image of Christ. So we should make it a point to evaluate our love walk on an ongoing basis. In Isaiah 55:8 God says, **"For my thoughts are not your thoughts, neither are your ways my ways. . . ."** In our continuous effort to be more like Jesus, we must be mindful during each day that a tremendous amount of work, including daily assessments, geared specifically towards tweaking our love walk, are essential. God is on high and we are down low. Our efforts to improve our love walk should be loaded with teeth, claws, and spikes as we become lifetime climbers striving to be more like the Lord. His thoughts and ways are far superior to ours; therefore, we should never become complacent with our accomplishments in life or with our existing conditions.

Look at it from this perspective. Regardless of how great your keyboard skills are, if you are idle for any length of time, you are subject to fall short of the home row. Seeking God and meditating in His Word will improve your love walk. It should be done with such regularity that it becomes a constant among all Christians.

During the fall of 2003, as I shared earlier, I experienced a severe injury, and for over five months I was idle with very limited mobility. It was during the lateral period of my downtime that I came to myself and began to utilize this time to evaluate my love walk and to put my life in perspective. God does not plan special events in the life of His children to experience any semblance of pain. However, if we do experience a misfortune, He has already figured out all of our "what if's."

Paul stated in Romans 5:20, **"But where sin abounded, grace did much more abound."** The *New International Version* reads, **"But where sin increased, grace increased all the more."** The soot of sin, personal failures, or any shortcomings that we face are never too much for the mighty grace of God. Your conviction, through the Word of God, actually challenges you to take control of whatever you may be experiencing. Even after you have put yourself in a position for God to apply more of His grace and mercy on more than one occasion, you must be willing to submit to His will for your life.

God loves us so much that long before we experienced any turbulence in this life, He had the clairvoyance to make the provision that would allow us to get back on track if we would simply shift our focus from our circumstances and ourselves to Him and His Kingdom.

## How Do I Improve My Love Walk?
### (Simply Improve)

As Christians, it is mandated that we be held to a much higher standard than unbelievers and the world in which they live — not because of who we are, but simply because of the God we serve.

Second Corinthians 3:18 says, **"But we all, with open face beholding as in a glass the glory of the Lord, are changed into the same image from glory to glory, even as by the Spirit of the Lord."** The *New International Version* says, **"And we, who with unveiled faces all reflect the Lord's glory, are being transformed into his likeness with ever-increasing glory, which comes from the Lord, who is the Spirit."**

As followers of Jesus, with each passing day it should become more evident that our love walk is developing more and more in the likeness of Him. Some of the more notable increments that are highlighted on the barometer used for measuring the Christian's love walk include:

1. Lowliness and meekness (humility).
2. Longsuffering and patience.
3. Our unity in Christ.
4. A complete makeover (our newness in Christ).
5. Our love for each other.

When I think about the meekness and humility, submissiveness and self-denial immediately come to mind. In Matthew 16:24 Jesus said to His disciples, **"If any man will come after me, let him deny himself, and take up his cross, and follow me."** When you deny yourself, your selfishness and self-importance go out the window. You should consider the needs and feelings of others ahead of your own. It does not matter whom we meet or where we meet them. It makes no difference whether they are leaders with authority or rank and file. As born-again believers, we are sisters and brothers in Christ, not to be proud, overbearing, or haughty in appearance, but showing kindliness and respect towards everyone.

Kindness does not mean weakness or gullible. Instead, kindness is strength, having a gentle and sympathetic spirit, always eager to listen to the concerns of others, assisting them with their headaches while putting yours on hold. Kindness can be worn and easily recognized on your face. Kindness can be warmth that is felt during a routine telephone conversation from miles away as you render assistance to some stranger in need.

Kindness can also be recognized in a smile — not a fake smile or a factitious one, but a genuine smile, the kind that has value and will last for a while. Not the kind of smile that we wear simply because we are vying to get your business or that quick, snapshot smile that we sometimes give to people in passing. You know the kind of smile I am alluding to.

When we are kind to people, we can easily tell them the truth without sugarcoating it and not be overly occupied with who will get hurt. Not that we are unconcerned about the troubles of our sisters and brothers, because as saints of God, we are charged with giving everyone the truth in kindliness and in love. And if by chance some feelings get hurt, we simply continue in kindliness, for through our faith, we know that truth will always prevail.

Ephesians 4:32 says, **"And be ye kind one to another, tenderhearted, forgiving one another, even as God for Christ's sake hath forgiven you."** Kindness also plays a huge role in forgiveness. A kind smile can give assurance that you have been genuinely forgiven. And if by chance you are still wrestling with forgiveness, simply reflect on what Jesus did at the cross. Where would any of us be if God had not provided a forgiveness plan for us?

There is so much energy in kindliness. Did you know that an unkind spirit will deprive you of your blessings and even drain you of your own energy? Kindness helps to win people over to Christ. God wants His children to be winners! It is certainly a blessing anytime you are able to help another sister or brother. However, it is also a plus to be gracious when you render assistance. During His time here on earth, Jesus exuded kindness to the highest degree and so should we.

Even when you successfully help people to fulfill their needs and desires, if you are not kind when you assist them, they will tend to lend more credence to your unkind behavior than to the remembrance of what you did to assist them. It costs you absolutely nothing to be kind to everyone you meet and greet. Kindness is an absolute must if you are sincere about improving your love walk. Be kind on purpose!

God is love and He is also the author of patience and longsuffering. Thank God for His patience, which is intended to bring people to repentance. Second Peter 3:9 says, **"The Lord is not slack concerning his promise, as some men count slackness, but is longsuffering to usward, not willing that any should perish, but that all should come to repentance."** The *New International Version* says, **"The Lord is not slow in keeping his promise, as some understand slowness. He is patient with you, not wanting anyone to perish, but everyone to come to repentance."**

It is certainly not God's desire that any one of His marvelous creations spend eternity in the lake of fire. If that were the case, the plug would have been pulled on a large number of us a long time ago. I thank God every day for His mercy, that the Lord does not return in another day for those among us who are lost and haven't found our way back to the fold. None of us is qualified to be a poster child for patience, and we certainly were not qualified before we became saved by His grace.

Even today your own cement is still not quite as dry as you may think. One might conclude that it should be relatively easy for us to be patient with each other, simply because we are God's greatest creation, God is love, and God has been and is still very patient with us. Patience, however, is one of those highly contested areas in our love walk that needs continual prayer for improvement. So concerning your spouse, your lost child, or maybe one of your siblings or friends who is still circling the world and out of God's ark of safety, don't give up on them.

The same can be said for a brother or sister in Christ who is not where we are in our faith. Don't give up on them either. Continue to pray for all of them and be patient. You might give them a call, offer to take them out to lunch, or send them a card to let them know that you are thinking about them. You can't imagine how great this might make them feel or how much closer it might bring them towards giving their life to Christ. If they say they aren't ready to receive Him, don't get all religious on them. Instead, take one step at a time and continue to pray and be kind. Yes, it is important to be persistent and not give up, but the key is to be patient. If the truth were known, someone was probably patient with you!

All of us at one time or another will no doubt face a battle or two in life. Our optimum level of success will ultimately depend on our level of faith and a surrounding cast of God-fearing people. Of course, all of us are not on the same faith level.

I am on another level from where I was one year ago, even a few months ago. During my life, I have had to weather some storms too, and someone had to be patient with me. I certainly did not make it to this point in my life without some struggles. Paul says in First Thessalonians 5:14, **"Now we exhort you, brethren, warn them that are unruly, comfort the feebleminded, support the weak, be patient toward all men."** Wow! That sounds like there is some work that needs to be done both inside and outside the church.

More importantly, as children of God and leaders in the Body of Christ, it all starts with us. There is a role for each of us to play. It's about everyone doing his or her part as members in the Body of Christ. God is concerned even about the small stuff, so learn to be patient with everyone.

A Christian with an unruly disposition who does not don a kind and gentle spirit should pray earnestly for guidance to

# How Do I Improve My Love Walk?
## (Simply Improve)

activate the fruit of their spirit. An unruly Christian is simply out of order. Being out of order can consist of a multiplicity of negative features involving behavior that is not conducive to the Body of Christ. Paul strongly advises us to warn them of their conduct.

As children of God, we should be docile, self-governing, and always eager to serve. We should never need to be reminded of every little thing to do. We should be eager to explain to people who cannot understand and eager to understand people who cannot explain. As saints of God we are not on the same level as the people in the world. We are called to be different. One bad attitude in any organization can severely hamper the attainment of any objective, especially when that attitude is in a position of leadership. Followers will always mimic their leaders. So we should be mindful of the negative vibes that we can easily give to others, even though they are sometimes unintentional.

Remember, we must honestly evaluate our love walk daily, making improvements where needed. If you are not going to contribute to the increase of the Kingdom, just be sure that you do nothing to hamper it. We are to be patient toward all men. This simply means with everyone. Not short, hasty, or impetuous, thinking only of yourself and a few select others.

Make it a point each time you attend church or any civic gathering to extend your hand to someone you don't know. Don't just stop at giving a cursory greeting at the advice of your pastor. I'm talking about after your meeting when you really have a chance to look an unfamiliar brother or sister eyeball to eyeball so they will know that you are congenial and your motive is crystal clear. God wants us to extend our circle of life by including additional people into our cadre.

It is simply amazing how easily our opinions can be skewed and how we are more apt to be dictated by someone who in our eyes is cute, exhibits an elegant lifestyle, or perhaps is extravagantly colorful with words. People with these features usually get more attention from us than we give to others, given the exact set of circumstances. But God is no respecter of persons.

## LIFE IS SO SIMPLE WHEN
## WE CHOOSE TO LOVE GOD'S WAY

Only God knows how many blessings and blown opportunities have fallen through the cracks or have been missed, simply because we decided to make life-changing decisions based solely on what we viewed and speculated with our human intellect. Once we abandon these kinds of bias practices and get our spiritual faculties more involved in our decisions, our love walk will begin to make precipitous strides as we move ahead to another level.

When unity comes to mind, think commitment. Having one wife, one husband, one job, one church home, and of course, serving the one and only true and living God! No organization or plan will succeed without unity. If you are chasing two separate dreams you could very well lose sight of both. Unity is a pledge to oneness.

Galatians 3:28 says, **"There is neither Jew nor Greek, there is neither bond nor free, there is neither male nor female: for ye are all one in Christ Jesus."** All of us are entitled to the same godly benefits through our belief in Jesus. It makes no difference what your talent level is or what gift you have been blessed with, they all belong to God. All of us have the same rights and privileges in Christ. As parents, do you not afford your children the same benefits, given they respect you and adhere to your rules, regulations, and principles?

The Church is the Body of Christ and is a single unit in one accord. Ephesians 4:4-5 spells out the Christian unification:

1. One body (together we are one body, the Body of Christ).
2. One Spirit (the Holy Spirit).
3. One hope (the Christian's inspiration and motivation to serve).
4. One Lord (our Lord is Jesus Christ).
5. One faith (our trust in the Person of Jesus).
6. One baptism (the unity of Christ's death, burial, and resurrection).

Ephesians 4:6 says there is **"one God and Father of all, who is above all, and through all, and in you all."** As

## How Do I Improve My Love Walk?
### (Simply Improve)

Christians we are a meticulously ordained unit known as the Body of Christ, representing the Kingdom of God. We serve the one and only true and living God. We have been given unmerited favor through our faith in Jesus. He is supreme above everything else, and as He lives in us we fill every place in the earth with His presence. Our corporate love walk benefits tremendously when we strive to maintain this unity and peace that are produced and given to all of us whenever we adhere to the Spirit of God. What a gracious and mighty God we serve!

Did you know that in Christ you have been made over? How do you view your makeover? Second Corinthians 5:17 says, **"Therefore if any man be in Christ, he is a new creature: old things are passed away; behold, all things are become new."** The *New International Version* says, **"The old has gone, the new has come!"**

It makes no difference about your past history or your past credit report. As Christians, we become new creations through our relationship with Christ. We are no longer permitted to indulge in the sin-filled life of yesterday. The old things are passed away, meaning the former behavior and frame of mind has been buried. You are new, completely made over, and not defective as some man-made products are, even as they are catapulted off the assembly line! You are made whole through the redemptive blood of Jesus.

Evaluate your love walk, and if you are continuously doing the same old things that you know do not magnify the life of Jesus, you are simply not living in Christ. Instead, you are an imposture! Remember, **"the new has come."** If your new-found relationship with Christ is genuine, it will be indicated by the way that you do the things that you do. Your new and improved love walk will speak for you without you ever having to open your mouth. The people whom you associate with, the places where you go, and the words that come out of your mouth are fruit of your testimony. Becoming a new creature in Christ is more than a title change. **It's a life change.** As I once heard my mother say, "I would rather see a sermon walked than to hear one preached."

There will always be a need for us to improve our love walk, because *choosing to love God's way* simply has no end. It's a lifestyle change that involves work every day. Are you walking **"in love,"** as Paul expresses in Ephesians 5:2, **"as Christ also hath loved us?"** The love, faith, and obedience in your love walk are three of the most important concomitants to the success of your relationship with God. Hebrews 11:6 says, **"But without faith it is impossible to please him: for he that cometh to God must believe that he is. . . ."** "Impossible" means incapable of being done. So before you go to God in prayer with a faithless request, vacillating in doubt, know that your request is already denied! You simply cannot satisfy God without faith. You need to begin by asking God to help your unbelief. It is not possible to please Him when you waver.

Are you mirroring the walk of obedience set out by Jesus? What will it take for your love walk to reach the apex? Why do we sometimes choose to take the scenic route like Jonah instead of the one prescribed to us by God?

In the Old Testament book of Jonah, chapters 1 and 2, Jonah decided to purposely circumnavigate the presence of the Lord and sail in the opposite direction of Nineveh, the place where the Lord had instructed him to go. In doing so, Jonah removed himself from God's ark of safety as some of us have done today. The Lord, being who He is, allowed a great wind to rattle the seas, causing the sailors aboard the ship with Jonah to be frightened as the ship was now in total disarray.

When the sailors realized that the cause of the high winds and raging seas was Jonah, who was being chastened by the Lord for his disobedience, they tossed Jonah overboard. Shortly thereafter, the sea ceased its raging.

This is the way life usually goes when we arbitrarily decide to do our own thing and elude the exclusive path that God has chosen for us. During the course of our disobedience, when we

## How Do I Improve My Love Walk?
(Simply Improve)

decide to walk in someone else's path instead of the path that God has purposed for us, people whom we may or may not be acquainted with will toss us to and fro and trample us. Or, we just might get tossed overboard too. Satan has a plethora of facilities that you could wind up working out in during the course of your disobedience.

After Jonah was thrown into the raging sea, according to Jonah 1:17, **"The Lord had prepared a great fish to swallow up Jonah. And Jonah was in the belly of the fish three days and three nights."** We can reasonably conclude that while in the fish's belly, Jonah was no doubt trying to strike a deal with the Lord while doing some serious praying. Jonah 2:10 says, **"And the Lord spake unto the fish, and it vomited out Jonah upon the dry land."** Jonah then got his act together, and I would imagine he had somewhat of a swagger in his walk as he made his way to Nineveh to do the will of God.

We ought to know by now that God is going to get His work done and get His glory too, one way or the other. We *can* pay Him now or we *will* pay later! Whether we decide to be like the prodigal son who, in Luke, chapter 15, verse 17, **"came to himself"** only after he had squandered his inheritance and was reduced to the hog pen of life. Or like Jonah, who left his ordained path and decided to take the scenic route, but wound up touring the whale's belly for three days and three nights because of his flagrant disobedience.

Whoever said experience is the best teacher? I beg to differ. I cannot think of anyone right off hand who would relish the opportunity to eat with hogs or who would love to stand in line to get swallowed by a whale and lodge there for three days on an involuntary fast, just to see if obedience is better than sacrifice.

These are two examples of people who were given another chance to make it right. We should do our best to learn from their past, from our past, and from mistakes made by others. God is indeed a God of many chances, but remember, when you are out of His ark of safety, you are rolling the dice of life while running strictly on fumes. You could run completely out of grace before safely landing, as your final chapter of life begins to close in on you. God cannot and will not change His Word just for it to benefit us, or to work exclusively in our situation.

Let me digress for a moment. In your quest to seek God first and as a token of your love and appreciation to Him, how much of your time, talent, and finances do you contribute to the furtherance of His Kingdom in the earth? The New Testament stresses the commandments of loving God, loving each other, and voluntarily giving from the heart. Second Corinthians 9:7 says, **"As he purposeth in his heart, so let him give; not grudgingly, or of necessity: for God loveth a cheerful giver."** In other words, we should give voluntarily from the heart, with eagerness, without feeling compelled to do so. God wants us to want to give cheerfully.

As you give from your heart, much is revealed about your character. God already knows the heart of every person. In Proverbs 4:23, we are instructed, **"Keep thy heart with all diligence; for out of it are the issues of life."** The heart is the center of all our thoughts. From the heart we act and speak truthfully what we really feel about everything. Our hearts will bring forth the good or evil deeds that we fulfill in the earth.

In Luke 11:41, the giving of alms, inward giving, or giving from the heart, is emphasized. Again, the focus is placed upon free will giving and not giving as a result of any form of coercion. The scribes and Pharisees placed their intensity on outward giving and other matters of outward concern like hand washing before meals, healing forbidden on the Sabbath day, and building and rebuilding memorials, while they completely overlooked the qualities of their spirit. These outward traditions continued to clog their hearts and minds while at the same time placed more debris in the minds of the people who respected their views and opted not to think for themselves.

Jesus said in Matthew 23:23, as He admonished the scribes and Pharisees, **"Woe unto you, scribes and Pharisees, hyp-**

ocrites! for ye pay tithe of mint and anise and cummin, and have omitted the weightier matters of the law, judgment, mercy, and faith: these ought ye to have done, and not to leave the other undone."** The *New International Version* says, **"Woe to you, teachers of the law and Pharisees, you hypocrites! You give a tenth of your spices — mint, dill and cummin. But [or except that] you have neglected the more important matters of the law — justice, mercy and faithfulness...."**

Jesus did not proclaim that tithing or giving a tenth was antiquated or thought to be irrelevant. However, He proceeds with the conjunction "but," indicating that there is a connection between the two sentences. Jesus concludes by saying, **"You should have practiced the latter, without neglecting the former"** (v. 23 NIV). In His response, Jesus did *not* remotely reprehend the principle of tithing or giving a tenth. He simply admonished the hypocrisy of the scribes and Pharisees as they emphasized eternal laws but lacked scruples regarding the things of the spirit, such as mercy, judgment, and faith. Essentially what the Pharisees did was they emphasized their works of the flesh and totally disregarded the more important works of edifying and developing their spirit. This clearly delineates that Jesus did not condemn the practice of tithes and offerings.

I believe tithing is not stressed as much in the New Testament because in the Old Testament people were apt to endorse this external principle in an effort to gain favor, without lending any credence to the Spirit. As mature saints of God, adhering to this principle does not automatically punch our ticket to heaven! We are convinced beyond a shadow of a doubt, however, that giving and receiving is a natural law that will work for anyone, including sinners.

Ephesians 6:8 says, **"Knowing that whatsoever good thing any man doeth, the same shall he receive of the Lord, whether he be bond or free."** Following the principle of tithes and offerings affords us a very special opportunity to show that God and His Kingdom are truly first in our life. It's easy for us to say that we love God and that His work is primary or first in our life. But what are we doing to show it besides talking? Jesus exemplified the perfect life of liberality in giving as He gave His precious life for us.

As for my family and me, tithing from our finances as well as from our time and talents will forever remain our free and voluntary giving of 10 percent or more from every applicable increase that we receive, which in our experience always yields prolific results. We should all want full coverage from God.

Proverbs 3:9-10 says:

**Honour the Lord with thy substance, and with the firstfruits of all thine increase:**
**So shall thy barns be filled with plenty, and thy presses shall burst out with new wine.**

Notice, he says, **"Honour the Lord with the firstfruits of *all thine increase*."** The word "increase" means to grow or enlarge and is used here as a general term to represent a gain. This includes any applicable resources with which God blesses you. Your firstfruits would include giving the first of your best, or in laymen's terms, "giving off the top of your increase." So again, we see from the scriptures the benefits and the rewards that come when we are faithful in giving our best to God.

Second Corinthians 9:8 says, **"And God is able to make all grace abound toward you; that ye, always having all sufficiency in all things, may abound to every good work."** Through your obedience and cheerful readiness in giving, God can cause you to have a supernatural abundance in everything you need in every area of your life. In other words, through your obedience to the works of God on earth, He will reward you with much too much!

Spreading the Word of God and assisting our sisters and brothers in need can only be done through people and resources. God loves a cheerful and hilarious giver, and He will

## How Do I Improve My Love Walk?
### (Simply Improve)

enlarge our harvest simply because of our willingness of heart to give Him our best. I am certainly not opposed to God blessing me because of my cheerful giving, nor am I opposed to receiving an increase because of my obedience to scripture. Does this automatically make me a better Christian than one who doesn't tithe and give? Of course not! This is not a salvation issue.

Tithing your time and talent is just as important as tithing from your financial increase. However, the added coverage and blessings that come from this simple act of obediently and consistently giving the best of what you have to God's Kingdom are matchless. I advocate giving God your absolute best at all times, both internally and externally.

As far as I am concerned this is not a debate. It's a choice. So if you are struggling with giving and are not conversant with the benefits in heartily giving to the Kingdom of God and you desire additional wisdom and knowledge on the subject, I advise you to seek and search out the Scriptures and other related reading materials for yourself.

Pastor Michael D. Moore of Faith Chapel Christian Center, Birmingham, Alabama, has an informing book that I recommend called *Tithing, What a Difference a Dime Makes*. More importantly, be obedient to the Word. Pray and ask God for His wisdom and understanding. Philippians 2:13 says, **"For it is God which worketh in you both to will and to do of his good pleasure."** If you really desire the will to do what is right, even when it comes to giving, God will energize you to do His will according to His purpose in your life, without you questioning it. Again, I emphasize that you have to "want to."

We should always pray and do what the Spirit of God tells us to do in all matters. Jesus says in Matthew 22:21, **"Render therefore unto Caesar the things which are Caesar's; and unto God the things that are God's."** Remember what I said earlier? *God is not going to change His Word to fit our needs*. He can, however, put a willingness in your heart. Just continue to seek God first! When we seek Him first on a daily basis, His will indeed becomes the center of our life.

Isaiah 55:11 says, **"So shall my word be that goeth forth out of my mouth: it shall not return unto me void, but it shall accomplish that which I please, and it shall prosper in the thing whereto I sent it."** The Word of God is going to do exactly what it says, period. I simply believe it because God said it! His Word is not ambiguous and it is not designed to leave you hanging.

Besides our giving, there are other areas in our life that also must improve to upgrade or overhaul our love walk. But first, who would need to improve their love walk? Everyone from the church house to the jailhouse! All of us have some area in our love walk that needs to be tweaked or improved, so let's hear your response to the following questions:

1. Do you fear God?
2. Do you love God with all your heart, with all your soul, and with your entire mind?
3. Do you keep His commandments and statutes?
4. Do you walk in His ways and love everyone?
5. Is Jesus Lord of your life?
6. Are you a compassionate person, concerned about the welfare of others?

Take time out and attempt to answer each question honestly and make changes wherever you feel they are needed. Proverbs 1:7 says, **"The fear of the Lord is the beginning of knowledge: but fools despise wisdom and instruction."**

When I think about the perfect example of fearing the Lord and fools despising wisdom all in the same breath, my mind drifts back to the crucifixion of Jesus. It simply mystifies me as to how many practical examples Jesus illustrated for us, not just in living but also just before He laid down His life while nailed to the cross on Calvary. In Luke 23:39, one of the two thieves crucified with Jesus stated, **"If thou be Christ, save**

# How Do I Improve My Love Walk?
## (Simply Improve)

thyself and us." But the other thief said, **"Dost not thou fear God, seeing thou art in the same condemnation?"** (v. 40). One of the thieves proceeded to take full advantage of being in the presence of God through Jesus and being under the same sentence by intelligently requesting in Luke 23:42, **"Lord, remember me when thou comest into thy kingdom."** As a reward for his reverence of the Lord, Jesus said to him, **"To day shalt thou be with me in paradise"** (v. 43).

So immediately we can see that to have a relationship with God, reverence and respect must be established. The beginning of knowledge is where it all starts. Even at the point of dying, both of these thieves had the same opportunity to improve their condition.

As long as you have the breath of life in you, you are afforded an opportunity to make Jesus Lord of your life. To take advantage of this opportunity will most assuredly make any situation that you face seem rather negligible, no matter who you are and regardless of the odds, even at the point of dying. But it begins with fearing the Lord, not fear as in fright or flight. This type of fear is a tactic of Satan. According to Second Timothy 1:7, **"God hath not given us the spirit of fear; but of power, and of love, and of a sound mind."** God sent us the Holy Ghost, a companion for us in all situations, ready and willing to guide us in our love walk.

John 14:16 says, **"And I will pray the Father, and he shall give you another Comforter, that he may abide with you for ever."** The Holy Ghost is our main highway that God uses to give us the wisdom and instructions we need every day to make quality decisions in every facet of life. Think about it! All of us are privileged to have God, the love of Jesus, and the Holy Ghost. God's salvation packet is free to all.

Peter said in Acts 10:34, **"Of a truth I perceive that God is no respecter of persons."** Whatever He does or has done for others, regardless of rank or position, He is more than willing to do for us. God in no way relates to discrimination or partiality. However, unless we first respect and reverence God and truly know who He is, all of our godly benefits will fall on stony ground. God knew that fear (reverence) for authority would be essential towards our goal in receiving abundant life as well as eternal life.

This is why He instructs us to teach our children at an early age not only to respect His authority, but to respect parental authority. How can we expect our children to respect others if they do not respect our authority? And if they do not respect our authority, they simply cannot jump the chain of command and receive the promise of God. Exodus 20:12 says, **"Honour thy father and thy mother: that thy days may be long upon the land which the Lord thy God giveth thee."** This is the first commandment with promise.

Life is all about steps. If a child does not honor authority in the family structure, then he or she will not fear or reverence Almighty God and the promises of His Word. Fear or reverence of the Lord commands obedience. All of us must remain in compliance with divine order if we intend to receive the goodness, mercy, and blessings of God.

To reverence God is to have a feeling of deep respect and awe, devoted to worshiping Him and obeying His Word. Jesus says in John 14:15, **"If ye love me, keep my commandments."** In other words, if you love Me, show Me by doing as I have commanded you. It should be reflected in our everyday love walk, especially in how we treat people.

Jesus is the universal Commander in Chief of customer service, and we are His ambassadors. Jesus loves people. This is evident in how He showed compassion and met the needs of people everywhere He went. It's like the old adage, "People don't care how much you know until they know how much you care."

Some of us struggle with the little things in life, like saying, "Please," "Good morning," "Thank you," "I'm sorry," "Will you forgive me?" or "I made a mistake." I am aware that these are small bites, but I am thoroughly convinced that we must begin

# How Do I Improve My Love Walk?
## (Simply Improve)

taking small steps every day to improve our love walk, starting with the small talk. Small bites catch large fish, but this will not happen on its own. Again, it is a process and you will need God's help to sustain.

Remember, as Christians we must be about God's business of spreading the Good News of Jesus, not just by telling people what He did for us, but by being examples and demonstrating His love through our love. Examples should never be limited to just words. They should be reflected in our actions. Our love for Jesus can never take a day off. It would be a tragedy to come in contact with anyone who is on their final chapter in this earthly realm and be afforded an opportunity to impart some soul-saving wisdom into their life, but because of a technicality in our own love walk, we allow the door to slam shut. We squander a golden opportunity to win another soul for Jesus.

As saints of God, we are responsible for making others aware that the salvation of God is free. This is why every morning before we prepare for our day, we need to fuel our spiritual tank with the Word of God and with a will to win. Romans 3:23 says, **"For all have sinned, and come short of the glory of God."** No one is perfect. All of us need to examine and reexamine our love walk.

Most people are familiar with that small pest called the termite. Regardless of how strong you think your wooden frame house or structure might be, all it takes is for one termite to penetrate a small crack in your framework and the process of tearing down your house begins.

On a much larger plane, all Satan needs to tear down a life is just a small opening in the mind to implant a negative thought. That one small negative thought that Satan places in your mind that you decide to execute has the capability of destroying your life and possibly the life of someone else. This is why it is so important that we guard our thought life by maintaining habitual fellowship with God.

### Life Is So Simple When
### WE CHOOSE TO LOVE GOD'S WAY

Proverbs 21:5 says, **"The thoughts of the diligent tend only to plenteousness; but of every one that is hasty only to want."** The *New International Version* says, **"The plans of the diligent lead to profit as surely as haste leads to poverty."** We live in a microwave society where we want what we want when we want it and how we want it. But when we steadily seek God and consistently give Him our best efforts, we will be rewarded with a spirit of affluence and abundance in every area of our life. Our efforts, however, must continue to be steady and persistent.

For us to expect God to give us microwave solutions after we arbitrarily exclude His wisdom at every turn, using only our intellect and might, is nothing short of an ill-fated illusion. We cannot create a pathway of bad decisions and expect God to exterminate the results overnight. There are some things that must be baked in the oven, and no matter how many times you try to microwave them, they will never reach perfection. Perfection is the best friend of patience.

We need to take full advantage of every safety net that God has provided for us. Diligence happens to be one of them. We must continue in steadfastness and persistency, never vacillating or wavering in our faith. Instead, we must develop an attitude of faith much like the centurion in Matthew 8:8 whose undaunted faith permitted him to request Jesus to just **"speak the word only, and my servant shall be healed."**

Without utilizing our safety net of standing on the Word, our love walk will never successfully enter the gate to the pathway that God has chosen for our life. Like most paths, our path in life is narrow and by nature we have the tendency to want to shift in a counterclockwise direction. However, we can ill afford to lose our focus.

Our love walk must consistently be about doing the right things at all times, even when we do not feel like it. The only way any instrument is given logical consideration for improvement is that the value of that instrument be fully warranted and understood. Jesus constantly showed us the value of a

# How Do I Improve My Love Walk?
## (Simply Improve)

godly love walk. In the four Gospels, Jesus demonstrated His love walk daily by healing the sick, feeding the poor and preaching the gospel to them, and restoring the sight of the blind, just to name a few deeds. He was saturated with compassion for people, always sensitive to their needs as He consistently denied Himself. Inasmuch as we desire to be like Jesus, we simply cannot do it on our own. We need to summon the help of the Spirit on a daily basis, staying focused in His Word with every fiber of our mind.

None of us is an authoritarian on any subject, so as long as we are alive, our minds should always be positioned somewhere in the learning mode. If a person has a reasonable stance on an issue, afford him or her the courtesy to be heard. If you listen, you just might learn something. But remember, I said, "If they have a reasonable stance on an issue." There are some beliefs and stances in life that people portray that from the outset may appear to be plausible, but they are simply not scriptural, neither can they be justified.

Like placing people in categories or putting tags on people and saying things like, "That group is responsible for this," or "That group is responsible for that," we should simply not attempt to entertain these kinds of suppositions.

In Matthew 12:36 Jesus says, **"But I say unto you, That every idle word that men shall speak, they shall give account thereof in the day of judgment."** It has been my experience that meekness and calmness will overcome dogmatic ignorance in such an unexpected and wonderful way that it will simply confuse the aggressor and anyone else who might be listening. People will be absolutely astonished at how you manage, in most cases, to diffuse caustic situations, threats, and a barrage of other incidents by simply using biblical principles and by listening carefully to all parties involved.

Kindness has the propensity to penetrate the heart like only God can. Jesus was kindhearted and never discourteous, even to the irreligious characters or the so-called experts in religion that He constantly came in contact with. He was never involved in idle conversation, wordiness, or wasting words.

In Romans 12:2, the Apostle Paul makes a heart-piercing supplication to us to **"be not conformed to this world...."** Paul, who wrote two thirds of the New Testament, is certainly qualified to tell us what is required to improve our love walk, especially with all of the life experiences that he encountered. He reminds us not to be so quick to fashion our life or choices on the external things that we see during our everyday walk of life. Instead, we are to develop the mind of Jesus by changing our present mind-set and see for ourselves that God's way is not only the best way, but it is simply the only way.

You will be incredibly delighted at how you can change your destiny by simply retooling the way that you think. You will experience more of God's favor whenever you choose to find and then remain on the path that He has chosen for your life. However, you will never know what that path is if you do not study His Word and seek Him for yourself on a consistent basis.

Once you decide to live for Jesus, you are formally recognized as a threat to Satan. He now looks at you as a possible termite, armed with the Word of God and fully capable of inflicting damage to his framework and to his employment. So you will need to fully understand that the battle for you is just beginning. However, First Samuel 17:47 says, **"For the battle is the Lord's...."**

With the Lord, you are never alone. But as a babe in Christ, you really need to stay in the Word and etch it deep down in your soul to get rooted and to know what it guarantees in whatever situation you may be facing, as you rely on the Holy Spirit to guide your steps. Satan would have you believe that being saved is a one- or perhaps a two-day emotional high, and that you will be right back at first base, hanging out with your old buddies as your emotional roller-coaster crests the hill, speeds up momentarily, and eventually comes to a screeching stop.

# How Do I Improve My Love Walk?
## (Simply Improve)

Have you ever noticed or wondered why after some people get saved, their intentions at the time are genuine, but after a few brief Sunday appearances, they suddenly disappear like a puff of smoke, and you don't see them in church anymore? In this same vein, some Christians who have been saved a little longer than babes leave the church and return to Satan's world for another tour of duty. Neither one quite understands that Satan has pulled out all stops and has engendered an all-out war. He is ready to do battle with anyone whom he feels might infringe upon what he has been afforded, by some of us, to think in his turf. Especially the new babes in Christ who recently switched to God's team and now pose a threat to his livelihood and his little kingdom.

Bear in mind that according to Luke 4:13 Satan also tempted Jesus. **"And when the devil had ended all the temptation, he departed from him for a season."** Satan's departure is always temporary. He will use any means necessary to trip you up and steal the Word of God out of your life. Remember, part of his M.O. (Modus Operandi) is to steal. The Bible says after his failed attempt on Jesus, Satan departed for a season. We must burn deep down in our mind that he is never going to quit.

When you are born again, you become a new creature with a brand-new life and a brand-new beginning. Just believe it, and know that there is supremacy in the Word of God. God knows all about the opposition. His Word and the presence of His Spirit will see you through any situation if you are disciplined enough to dress in all of His armor and continue to put all of your trust in Him no matter what.

Psalm 91:2 says, **"I will say of the Lord, He is my refuge and my fortress: my God; in him will I trust."** With a guarantee like this, Satan does not stand a chance. We will never know how far we can go in the Lord if we choose to remain as babes and do not take the initiative to advance our knowledge in the Word of God. We must get grounded in the Word and cultivate our minds for continual growth.

## LIFE IS SO SIMPLE WHEN
## WE CHOOSE TO LOVE GOD'S WAY

Proverbs 3:5-6 says, **"Trust in the Lord with all thine heart; and lean not unto thine own understanding. In all thy ways acknowledge him, and he shall direct thy paths."** God does not want you to even think about doing something on your own when you can rely on the guidance of the Holy Spirit. So why would anyone want to jump the fence, when God has a nearby gate that is wide open and readily available with a pathway made exclusively for you?

You are one of God's many diamonds, even though you may still be in the rough! Stay with your commitment to be honed and shaped every day by the Word of God. Don't give up. Even as you build yourself up in the Spirit and begin to feel confident, you will still meet challenges and opposition and need God's constant protection. He wants us to always depend on His Word and the comforting guidance of His Holy Spirit.

As long as you live, improving your love walk will never be complete. You know how easy it is for us to become vain and to get all wrapped up in self-gratification, as though we did everything by ourselves. We must continue to stay humbly focused on Jesus as we search for continual improvement in our love walk, always maintaining a spirit of submissiveness as we meditate daily in His Word.

To meditate requires not only quiet time and deep thinking, but it also calls for asking God questions and waiting for His answer. However, you may never really feel comfortable asking God questions if you have not developed a personal relationship with Him. You will never be limited to the types of questions that you can ask God. You should feel free to talk to your heavenly Father about anything.

James 4:2 NIV says, **"You do not have, because you do not ask God."** Feel free to ask your heavenly Father whatever you desire or the things that you have need of. A sincere daily and honest evaluation of yourself is designed to reveal to you any areas of your love walk that need improving. If you genuinely do not know what foibles exist in your love walk, simply ask God to search your heart and reveal them to you. There is

# How Do I Improve My Love Walk?
## (Simply Improve)

one thing that is absolutely certain, and that is, God already knows our hearts and our every thought. So it would behoove us to come clean with God. We cannot bamboozle (hoodwink) Him, for He made us.

This is why David charged his son Solomon in First Chronicles 28:9 to **"know thou the God of thy father, and serve him with a perfect heart and with a willing mind: for the Lord searcheth all hearts, and understandeth the imaginations of the thoughts. . . ."**

Most people enjoy revealing or talking about their strong suits and their good qualities, but they often refuse to acknowledge their weaknesses or areas in their life that warrant a change or improvement. To depend on any system where the success is not predicated on even a smidgen of the Word of God is a time bomb waiting to happen. God's Word is the truth, and if you are not walking in it, it will eventually call you out! It is vitally important that we:

1. Find a good Bible-based church home.
2. Search the Scriptures daily.
3. Learn to *totally* trust in God.

This will aid you tremendously in improving your love walk. It is critical that we get good biblical teaching and training from an established, true shepherd of God. In Acts, chapter 11, Barnabas went to Tarsus looking for Saul (Paul). After he found him, he brought him to Antioch. Acts 11:26 NIV says, **"So for a whole year Barnabas and Saul met with the church and taught great numbers of people. . . ."**

When our great Teacher and Savior Jesus chose Peter and Andrew to be His disciples, He said to them, "I will make you fishers of men." In other words, "I will teach you what you need to do and what you need to know and say in order to win souls for Me." Jesus knew before selecting them that they were not qualified at that time to do what His Father envisioned. However, he knew their hearts, and more importantly, He knew that they were teachable and could mature through His teaching.

Are you teachable? Jesus realized early on that a good student-teacher relationship would be paramount to the success of His discipleship and for the establishment of the Church. As Christians we are charged to be "fishers of men." We must use whatever talent God has blessed us with as bait to reel sinners in with the Word of God. This is not a subterfuge nor is there any trickery involved. Your bait is your gift, which may include but is not restricted to, your employment, your personality, your talent, and your mere ability to draw one's attention to God in any manner that is pleasing to Him.

Afterwards, we should simply follow our charge to let the lost know that God loves them and what is required of them to take advantage of His salvation plan while there is still time. When we fail to do what we are commissioned to do, we not only rob God, we also rob the world. The only Jesus that some people will see is the Jesus that they see in you and me today. This is why it is so important that we find a church home.

In your church home, your pastor is there to show you the way by planting godly seeds as he teaches the unadulterated Word of God. However, it is up to the individual to receive the Word and to get rooted in it by watering and nourishing it daily to grow and mature in the knowledge of the truth. God allows us to grow in it according to our measure of faith. The cycle repeats itself, and as we are properly fed and nurtured, we can better impart to others "thus saith the Lord." The fruit from our labor will be evidence as we continue to grow and mature in our love walk.

So now we can become even more productive as believers who are delighted in winning lost souls for Jesus. If you desire to grow in the Lord and you are not advancing, even though you are studying and adhering to the Word daily and attending your church home and Bible study consistently, all while under the spiritual jurisdiction of a shepherd called by God, then something is wrong with your picture.

# How Do I Improve My Love Walk?
## (Simply Improve)

We often evaluate our careers, our neighborhoods, our children's school system, and even the car that we drive, consequently making changes as needed. But what about our church home? This is the most critical arena of your life, so you should not be satisfied with simply miring in mediocrity. God will give you the wisdom to make key decisions and changes in every corner of your life, including finding the right church home geared specifically for you and your family. He will even let you know if the problem lies within you and not in your church home, if you pray earnestly and you are willing to listen. Again, simply go to Him. According to James 1:5, God will give you wisdom if you ask.

Remember, people are the primary mechanism used by God to spread the Good News about the gift of salvation and anything else that He desires. We must all get busy. Our discrepancies will never be rectified if we stay in constant denial and if we refuse to become students of His Word. God knows that our way is not His way. This is why He wants us to submit our way of doing things to His way. His plan for our life is a much better plan than ours. It is also much easier to follow. Besides, following His plan will always yield prolific results.

Disappointments will surface in all of our lives. Without the knowledge found in the Word of God, we will not be equipped to handle them properly. But when we give them to God and trust Him to do what He says, we cannot go wrong.

Often, in our quest to improve our love walk, we go to God in prayer and tell Him all about the concerns that we are having based solely on what He has said in His Word. However, because of a low level of faith, we have the proclivity to keep dabbing in the issue as if God needs our help in finding the solution that we could not come up with before giving it to Him.

Granted, we should always do for ourselves the things in life that God has equipped us to do, but when the load is obviously more than we can handle and we summon the Spirit of God for guidance, we should simply remind Him of what He said in His Word. Then efface ourselves from that situation, and just stand, expecting the best possible answer from Him alone.

## LIFE IS SO SIMPLE WHEN
## WE CHOOSE TO LOVE GOD'S WAY

Have you ever noticed how a sore on your body actually heals itself without your assistance? Yet if we are not careful, we find ourselves rubbing and picking at it, sometimes without being cognizant that we are actually prolonging the healing process. But when we take our hands off and remove it from our minds, in due time it heals.

This is much the same manner that God works things out for us. Whenever we decide to take our hands and minds off whatever cares or concerns that we have given to Him and just trust what He says in His Word at face value, our prayers and requests that are consistent with His Word will be met. Even if He does not readily respond, remain focused. You can rest assured that He knows the perfect timing. If you are dissatisfied with His final disposition, you need to reassess your love walk because therein lies some of the problem.

Never put limits on God or on what He can do. It would be idiotic for God to have made this world and everything that is in it, yet not be knowledgeable or discerning in conveying to us how best to live in it and manage all of the intricate matters we face. Moreover, He knows what is best for His children, and He loves us so much that He left us with a road map to a successful life in this world and in the world to come — the Bible. He also left us a Personal Instructor and Tour Guide for life — the Holy Spirit. Still, His Word must be the focal point of your being. You must have an earnest desire to increase your wisdom, knowledge, and understanding of His Word.

The results of meditating in God's Word are impeccable. Psalm 1:3 says, **"And he shall be like a tree planted by the rivers of water...."** You are destined for success, like a well-developed tree that never has to concern itself with prevailing winds or the scorching sun, which may indicate trouble on the horizon. Instead, you will produce good results in a timely fashion as the hands of God Himself nurture you. But that's not all!

Have you ever noticed how all the leaves and branches on a well-nourished tree appear to be in one accord and not in contrast with one another? I believe this is God's vision for the unity of His people on earth, walking and living in His perfect peace, the peace that surpasses all understanding, as we worship Him in spirit and in truth. This is an imitation of the unison of this world when we choose to improve our love walk together and find our God-ordained paths.

As we bear good fruit from our labor, we repudiate the perception of the unbeliever, who proclaims that we do not have a changed heart. When your heart is changed, your light shines. When your light shines as prescribed by the Word of God, it will have an indelible impact on. . .

**The glorification of God,
The magnification of Jesus, and
The multiplication of the Kingdom.**

Beware that when you take on your new identity and have transitioned to the family of Jesus, people will tend to take notice and immediately place you under the scope. That's okay because we need to get their minds focused on God's way for their own sake. Be sure you understand the ideals that come with being designed in the image of God and commissioned to model the ways of Jesus.

Realistically, we cannot blame the world for putting some of us under the scope. There are many charlatans and hypocrites who have falsely represented the Kingdom of God. So consistency is another yardstick that will be used to gauge our behavior in the Christian love walk.

Satan will continue to circle like a vulture, waiting on you to take one step backwards and stumble so he can make his next move. But let me warn you. Once you have come to the knowledge of the truth, don't even think about abandonment or reversing your commitment. Second Peter 2:21 says, **"For it had been better for them not to have known the way of righteousness, than, after they have known it, to turn from the holy commandment delivered unto them."** We have been commissioned and sanctioned by God and expected to win souls for Jesus because the truth has been unveiled in our lives and our level of knowledge in Christ has been raised.

## Life Is So Simple When
## WE CHOOSE TO LOVE GOD'S WAY

Once a person is saved, if he chooses to go back into the world, it is by choice that he does so, and no excuse will be valid.

With increased knowledge comes added responsibility. So now you can no longer say, "No one told me." In other words, now you know! The more Word you are exposed to for improving your love walk, the more is required of you. You are now a full-fledged ambassador of God, expected to go out and advise people in the world that they need to be ready *before* the Judgment Day arrives.

It does not set well with heaven when we come to the knowledge of the truth, and instead of going out in the world to reel in sinners, we decide to return to our former way of life for an encore, only to find that things are just as we left them! The only thing that has changed is the face of some of the players, along with a few new plays. The rules and the object of Satan's game will remain intact — to steal, kill, and destroy.

Second Peter 2:22 says, **"The dog is turned to his own vomit again; and the sow that was washed to her wallowing in the mire."** Peter equates this unfortunate Christian reversal to a dog going back to eat his regurgitation and a hog reentering a muddy hog pen after being washed. This negative connotation is not only pathetic and dishonorable to the Kingdom of God. It also brings immeasurable disrespect to the knowledge of the truth of the Word of God.

My dear brothers and sisters, Jesus will be back at an hour and at a moment when we least expect Him! It would behoove us to leave the filth and get cleansed before His absolute certain return.

The Apostle Paul tells us in First Corinthians 13:9, **"For we know in part, and we prophesy in part."** Our knowledge and prophecy, regardless of how current, are both partial, but will someday be made full in the presence of Jesus. We are forever learning as the knowledge of God is infinite. If we knew unequivocally what the next day was going to bring, our mindset would be such that we simply could not manage to get through this day. The incompleteness of today will soon be replaced by the completeness of Jesus. It is paramount that we continue to search the scriptures every day to grow stronger in the knowledge and ways of Christ, and to continue to trust in the truth no matter what. It's a very simple recipe to follow.

## Balance

There is one other key component to improving your love. It's called "balance." God wants us to rejoice always and maintain balance in our life. He did not say, "Seek Me every minute of the hour and take responsibility for nothing." He simply wants us to seek Him first, placing Him before everything else. Seek Him for consultation before rash decisions are made. God has our best interest at heart, and like any good father, He wants us to have the very best of what He has to offer. So to ensure this, you need only confer with Him through His Word in prayer and to follow the prudent advice of the Spirit. The Holy Spirit is standing by to help guide your steps in the special path that God has designed exclusively for your life.

Keep your faith on the line, praying daily. When complex decisions are to be made and time permits, there is no need to make an impetuous decision. Simply speak the Word and follow His wisdom in faith. If confronted with an exigent situation, simply stand on your faith and on His Word.

God's system for winning souls for Jesus and for your total success in life is not designed to wear you down, burn you out, or drive a wedge between your family and you. In Exodus 18, Moses' father-in-law Jethro had the discernment to realize that Moses had taken on much more responsibility than he could handle, and that he should delegate some of his responsibilities to others so as not to get jaded. In Exodus 18:17-18 Jethro advises Moses: **"The thing that thou doest is not good. Thou wilt surely wear away, both thou, and this people that is with thee: for this thing is too heavy for thee: thou art not able to perform it thyself alone."**

Jesus showed us right from the start that we should recruit and train others and learn to delegate some of our works and responsibilities as He demonstrated with His disciples daily. You can only stretch rubber so far. God understands that our bodies are frail and they require daily replenishment. Making time for the Word and praying daily to our heavenly Father are premiums that should never be circumvented. We must still find a medium between all that we do, including but not limited to, working in the church, spending time with our families, accomplishing good success on the job, and maintaining a healthy diet.

A balanced life is one of the keys to successful living. This is why God wants us to take advantage of His Spirit who will navigate us correctly when we choose to follow Him as a guide. God gets no pleasure in seeing His children fall prey to bankruptcy, divorce courts, the justice system, or succumbing to illness. Jesus said in Matthew 11:30, **"For my yoke is easy, and my burden is light."**

Continue to seek God's face in faith and enhance your relationship with Him by meditating in His Word each day. Then watch as your pathway becomes more salient, debris free, and your love walk is the pathway that God designed specifically for you.

To improve your love walk is not designed to criticize but to purify, not to condemn but to improve, and not to impose but to evaluate. Each day is simply another opportunity for us to stay on top of prompting others in the knowledge of God. It is paramount that we evaluate our love walk daily, making adjustments when needed. And if by chance we have fallen short, we must get back in the Word of God and stay there.

*Choose to love God's way* by making Jesus your main course for the rest of your life, and always be mindful to

***Keep balance in your life!***

# Chapter 6

# Recognize the Importance of Forgiveness (Simply Forgive)

The importance of each component that we will address in *choosing to love God's way* is incalculable. However, there is none more paramount in the life of a Christian than the possession of a genuine spirit of forgiveness.

If you are in possession of an unforgiving spirit, suffice it to say, you are disconnected from God's will for your life and headed downstream on a collision course with no visible sign of either truth or life. There is absolutely no positive percentage in setting sail with an unforgiving spirit on board.

Matthew 6:14-15 NIV says:

> **For if you forgive men when they sin against you, your heavenly Father will also forgive you.**
> **But if you do not forgive men their sins, your Father will not forgive your sins.**

Simply put, we cannot expect God to do for us what we blatantly refuse to do for others. There certainly may be other shortcomings in and around our lives that we need to deal with, but for now all eyes are on *forgiveness*.

As saints of God, we must become reciprocals of forgiveness. To forgive is not an option; it is a prerequisite that is necessary for all Christians who desire to model the life of Christ.

## LIFE IS SO SIMPLE WHEN
## WE CHOOSE TO LOVE GOD'S WAY

Jesus said to forgive men "when" they sin. The word "when" means at or during that time. Forgiveness is not arbitrary, so it does not mean at our earliest convenience or when we get ready, and it certainly does not mean whenever we feel like it. We are to forgive on impact, and then quickly move on with our lives. Untold time is lost when we refuse to forgive immediately.

We were not designed to spend the rest of our life begging others for forgiveness, nor should we expect others to spend the rest of their lives begging us to forgive them. So the moment we sense or recognize that we have been wronged, our hearts should be preparing to forgive our trespassers even while they are in the embryonic stages of whatever act they propose to commit against us. It is only after you are able to grasp how important forgiveness is to life that you can fully comprehend and visualize with intensity the true measure of how Jesus demonstrated forgiveness to us, even while laying down His life at the hands of the enemy. As a nation of people, we must learn to simply forgive.

James 2:13 says, **"For he shall have judgment without mercy, that hath shewed no mercy; and mercy rejoiceth against judgment."** All of us are beneficiaries of the goodness and mercy of God whether we ever admit it or not. So God is going to deal with those of us who refuse to show mercy or who refuse to forgive people who have allegedly wronged us in the same vein that we administer forgiveness to them.

Think about the difference between winning and losing. Now that you have done that, think about the difference between mercy and judgment. Stop! Your time is up! Mercy will always win over judgment. Whenever you judge, you lose. Whether your trespasser ever asks you for forgiveness is irrelevant and of no consequence to you. The value of how others may choose to respond or react towards us in any situation has absolutely nothing to do with what God expects from us.

Hebrews 12:14 says, **"Follow peace with all men, and holiness, without which no man shall see the Lord."** The

*New International Version* of this verse says, **"Make every effort to live in peace with all men and to be holy; without holiness no one will see the Lord."** God is holy and He expects all of His children to follow the model that Jesus laid out for us during His life and revealed in His Word. If we fail to comply, we will simply have to bear the consequences. We are set apart and sanctified for service to God.

Psalm 4:3 NIV says, **"Know that the Lord has set apart the godly for himself. . . ."** For us to be holy we must simply be in compliance with the views, beliefs, and ways of God — not just the ones that depict how someone has treated us or the ones that are no longer a problem for us to keep because of our age, our level of maturity, or because father time has simply caught up with us and most of our youthful desires have dissipated. God's commandments and views must be followed.

We must be soaked with the mind of Christ, and we can only have His mind if we are in Him and He is in us. As Christians, we are encouraged to follow or pursue peace with all people. Without walking in the peace of God, we are simply not strong enough to forgive or overcome the need for forgiveness in the manner prescribed by God. His peace is designed to give us freedom from civil unrest and disturbances, freedom from oppressive and depressive thoughts, as well as freedom from our shortcomings and from our overbearing emotions.

Perfect peace has its source in God, in Jesus, and in the Holy Spirit. Philippians 4:7 says, **"The peace of God, which passeth all understanding. . . ."** In other words, the peace that is found in God, or the peace that He provides for His children by way of our personal relationship through His Son, is a supernatural peace that is inexpressible. Neither you nor I can perceive through our intellectual abilities the depth of the serenity expressed in God's peace. God graciously uses His peace to guard our hearts and our minds through our relationship with Jesus. As born-again Christians, we have the peace of God in our spirit, and we can execute it by stirring it up when we simply choose to exercise authority in our life.

## LIFE IS SO SIMPLE WHEN
## WE CHOOSE TO LOVE GOD'S WAY

Before His ascension to the Father, Jesus left us the gift of peace. In John 14:27 NIV, He says, **"Peace I leave with you; my peace I give you. I do not give to you as the world gives. . . ."** Jesus explains in this simple, yet perfect verbal expression, that there is a difference between the peace of this world and His gift of peace. There is indeed a huge difference. First of all, Jesus leaves us peace in the form of a gift and just like God's gift of salvation, you have to choose of your own volition to receive it. Jesus left His peace with us. Whenever something is left for you, it is yours only when you claim it. You have to pick it up and utilize it for yourself. It is incumbent on your part to initiate the action. The giver's responsibility is to leave the gift, but he cannot be held accountable for the lack of application or the unappreciative behavior of the recipient.

As with love and faith, peace must also be stirred up or acted out by choice. The love of Jesus does not force us. He simply lets us know that we have the gift of peace readily available in His benefit package. Once we receive Him, we have His peace. All we need to do is stir it up. And if Jesus says there is a difference between His gift of peace and the peace of the world, then that's good enough for me.

Most of us, based on our personal experience alone, can lend credence to the fact that the peace that the world gives is fragile. It can easily be damaged, destroyed, or even taken back without reason or warning. The type of peace that we experience from the world is ineffective, temporal, and is not equipped with the longsuffering or patience of God. Jesus left His peace in the form of a gift. "Gift" means it is free, without compensation, or with no strings attached. In contrast, the peace of the world is predicated on the perfect relationships, perfect settings, and with absolutely no room for human error.

In Galatians 5:22, peace is produced in all Christians through the power of the Holy Spirit, which He graciously gives to all men. The general phrase "all men" includes every man, woman, boy, and girl through their belief in Jesus Christ. If the

# Recognize the Importance of Forgiveness
## (Simply Forgive)

Holy Spirit indwells us, then we should mirror His ways and share in His peace.

If we are believers and we do not mirror the ways of the Holy Spirit, then it is by our choice alone that we lack inner peace or any other fruit of the Spirit. We can equate this to having the propensity to love but simply choosing not to. Love and peace are within the spirit of every born-again Christian. So hatred is a choice. The same is true for joy. In most cases, your peace can be detected primarily from your reactions or your behavior. Regardless of how we feel about certain people or what we feel they have unjustly done to us, we are to forgive them and love them. God is a God of order. If we are to be imitators of God in both goodness and in righteousness, and if we have been made righteous through the redemptive blood of Jesus, then it is an absolute requirement that we lay our weapons down and simply forgive as Christ did.

Romans 5:19 NIV says, **"For just as through the disobedience of the one man the many were made sinners, so also through the obedience of the one man the many will be made righteous."** Adam and Eve put the brakes on God's original plan. However, through God's plan of redemption, Jesus demonstrated to us during His life and even during His death that there are absolutely no benefits, nothing to gain, nothing righteous, and certainly nothing healthy about carrying the unnecessary weight and burden of an unforgiving heart while we live, or when we go to the grave. God made us and He knows all of the things that can have a pernicious effect on our well-being.

When you forgive, your forgiveness not only frees the trespasser, but it releases you as well. So it is imperative that we become adept at asking for forgiveness as well as forgiving others. Not because we anticipate sinning in advance or that we intend to incessantly violate someone. Quite the contrary. We simply want God's forgiveness in all situations, even in those rare instances where we may have unknowingly hurt someone. None of us are keen enough to know just how many of our words, deeds, or actions, though unintentional, may affect people every day as we venture down the highway of life, crossing others' paths.

In Matthew 18:21-22 Peter asked Jesus about the number of times we are to forgive and Jesus responded:

> **Lord, how oft shall my brother sin against me, and I forgive him? till seven times?**
> **Jesus said unto him, I say not unto thee, Until seven times: but, Until seventy times seven.**

Jesus knew exactly where Peter was going with his curiosity on forgiveness.

The grapevine is a powerful device that can be used to transport erroneous information that is capable of causing great devastation. In today's society, we know that the venom from this treacherous vehicle can come from miles away with velocity untold. And for reasons unknown to most of us, there are still some of us who are fascinated by this diabolical machination. It has been around a long time and appears to pick up speed at will. However, Jesus immediately cleared this grapevine before it was ever launched and rooted, and at the same time He dismantled the forgiveness cap of "seven times" that Peter alluded to. God does not put a limit or a cap on the number of times that we should forgive or be forgiven, and neither should we. We are to forgive each other as often as needed.

Just imagine for a moment God embracing or entertaining the thought of putting limitations or a cap on the number of times that we can be forgiven. Most of us would have used up our allotment long before our spiritual eyes were ever opened or long before we could ever grasp just how this was going to affect us in the grand scheme of life.

It absolutely bewilders me as to some of the made-up, self-imposed numbers and trite statements that we promulgate on a daily basis. And while we may be able to successfully limit ourselves with strongholds, we have absolutely no authority to even attempt to place limitations on the power of God. When we put limitations on God and promote erroneous information about what He can or cannot do, we are essentially precluding our own blessings, while perhaps blocking the blessings of others too.

Let's take a look at the following two questions that could very well determine your future:

1. Are you holding any inmates in your prison of unforgiveness?
2. Is there anyone you need to ask forgiveness of?

If the answer to either of these questions is "yes," then you need to set things right at your earliest convenience. This, of course, means right now. "Right now" is the only guaranteed time that we will ever have on earth. This time yesterday was "right now," and this time tomorrow will be "right now." That's why Jesus is specific when He instructs us to forgive people when they sin. So don't let your expiration date catch you with a heart full of unforgiveness.

Remember, forgiving does not mean forgetting. It simply means that you have chosen to free that person and yourself and move on with your life. As far as you are concerned, your relationship has been reconciled and made amiable again. If you find yourself periodically bringing up matters of the past for all the wrong reasons, then chances are you are still holding that person hostage and have not forgiven him or her.

There are no degrees of forgiveness. There is no forgiveness in the first, second, or third degree. Either you have forgiven or you have not. When God forgives us, He never washes our face with any of the particulars ever again.

Remember the woman caught in the adulterous affair who was brought to Jesus by the scribes and the Pharisees? (See John, chapter 8.) Jesus did not condone her behavior nor did He pronounce her guilty. Instead, He set her free, and according to John 8:11, He instructed her to **"go, and sin no more."**

Sin separates us from God, but forgiveness reestablishes the propensity for friendly relationships. Psalm 103:12 says, **"As far as the east is from the west, so far hath he removed our transgressions from us."** With God, through Jesus, forgiveness is a done deal. Be mindful, however, that even though your relationship with God is reconciled, there are still consequences for disobedience. Some consequences are more detrimental than others. Nevertheless, Galatians 6:7 says, **"Be not deceived; God is not mocked: for whatsoever a man soweth, that shall he also reap."** This promise from the Word of God has nothing to do with your inclination to receive the gift of salvation. This is a law of nature as well as a divine promise.

Second Corinthians 9:6 says, **"He which soweth sparingly shall reap also sparingly; and he which soweth bountifully shall reap also bountifully."** Depending on what you plant, either it will work to your advantage or to your detriment. Even if someone commits a crime such as murder, assault, or robbery, regardless whether the person asks and receives forgiveness from God, the victim, or the victim's family, that person must still pay the judicial penalty. God forgives us as we forgive others, *but we must pay the consequences for our acts of disobedience.* However, through the name of Jesus, we can always ask God for His mercy. So a reminder, if you don't want it, don't plant it, because you will see it again!

An unforgiving spirit will clog the path to our love walk and stifle our personal growth. On the other hand, forgiveness unclogs our pipes and reestablishes an affluent connection to God, allowing a proper allotment of godly benefits to resume flowing. Whenever we choose to remain obstinate and not forgive, we end up on the losing side, while the trespassers usually proceed with their life. We can never know the full effect of hurt and ill will that we extend to our families and others when we decide not to forgive. If forgiveness involves our

## RECOGNIZE THE IMPORTANCE OF FORGIVENESS
## (SIMPLY FORGIVE)

job, we tend to bring a few sparks home to our spouse and children, and as you well know, sparks are fully capable of turning into flames.

In personal relationships where we refuse to forgive or when someone refuses to forgive us, usually there is a bleed over onto the job. We tend to let some of our colleagues have an ear full of our mind if we are rubbed the wrong way. Most of this second-hand anger that we pass along will eventually lead to other problems — problems that ordinarily have nothing to do with our family or job.

Hopefully, you can see that when we refuse to forgive or ask for forgiveness, we tend to contaminate other relationships out of this pure act of selfishness. Unforgiveness cannot be permanently swept under the rug. It will never go away on its own. In most situations, it will only exacerbate.

So your choices are either you can forgive or you can continue to miserably punish yourself and hurt other important people in your life. Your love walk will take on insurmountable heights when you get rid of an unforgiving spirit, a characteristic that must be donned by all true worshipers. Remember, if the Spirit of God dwells in us, then all we need to do is simply exercise our authority and model His demeanor through the fruit of our spirit.

We should begin each day with a prayer of thanksgiving, culminated by an earnest prayer of forgiveness. Evaluate yourself at the conclusion of each day. Then ask God to forgive you for all of your deliberate acts of wrongness as well as blown opportunities that you permitted to fall through the cracks. Each day there are things that you and I should have done that we did not do.

So after you have made it right with God, complete the cycle by searching and locating anyone that you may have offended, and at your earliest convenience, go to them and personally ask them to forgive you. It is really a sad indictment when you think about the number of people walking around with the weight of an unforgiving heart that's ready to explode. It is an even sadder note when people actually die with unforgiveness lodged in their heart, but it happens.

Unforgiveness is simply wild weed that Satan uses to choke the life out of your life and the Word of God out of your life. If your spirit continues to go uncultivated, the ramifications will become fatal. At some point during your life, you may have experienced some kind of battle with forgiveness or you may presently be involved in a battle. Try to view whatever someone did to you as a trial. Not a trial caused by God, but a simple yardstick that you can use as a test to see where you are in your faith as it relates to the Word of God. Remember, you are not responsible for what others say or do to you, but you will be held accountable for your reactions.

God understands when we feel hurt, dejected, or let down. A temporary mark has been left on the inside of you. However, it should only be temporary and it should never be permitted to remain there and become a permanent fixture that's geared to navigate you for a long period of time or even for the rest of your life.

Colossians 3:13 says, **"Forbearing one another, and forgiving one another, if any man have a quarrel against any: even as Christ forgave you, so also do ye."** In other words, be patient with each other and forgive when warranted. Have compassion for people as Jesus had for us. Never take an offense personally. In this life, we cannot pick and choose who is going to hurt or disappoint us any more than we can pick or choose whom we want to forgive. To forgive is a direct order from God! Whatever differences you may have, make an unrelenting effort to work them out.

It is mandated that we forgive one another as our heavenly Father has forgiven us. So by going to God and forgiving your trespasser in advance, you will never be found guilty of holding the keys to their prison cell of forgiveness, regardless of whether they ever ask you for forgiveness or not.

# Recognize the Importance of Forgiveness
## (Simply Forgive)

I can go back to my childhood and vividly recall a painful experience that had me somewhat vexed for a long time. When I was about twelve years old, most of the boys in our community would play a game called marbles. One of the boys in the neighborhood was an excellent player, and I thought we were pretty good friends.

One day after school I saw my friend and some other boys in the neighborhood outside playing marbles, so I thought I would join them. However, when they saw me coming, they gathered their marbles off the ground and left the area, walking briskly towards the roadway.

After realizing what was happening, I finally stopped walking and watched them as they turned the corner and disappeared. For reasons unknown to me, my friend not only stopped playing with me, he also stopped speaking to me. I could not figure out what went wrong.

This is exactly how we make people feel when they so desperately need our forgiveness but we opt to give them an obstinate ear. At least we owe them the common courtesy to have a hearing to answer whether they are guilty or not guilty before we officially charge them. This would be similar to holding a cordial conversation with your friend when suddenly he or she turns away and walks off without saying why or even good-bye.

Much to my chagrin, my friend never explained to me what, if anything, I had done to offend him. I knew this was not a figment of my imagination, because for about two weeks he avoided me at every turn. Then I began to feel really bad, wondering what on earth I had done. Does this sound familiar to you?

Time has a way of healing all wounds, so I soon began to feel better as I had thoroughly searched my young heart for anything that I could have possibly done to cause this sudden aloofness. During each search, I came up with nothing to justify his unexpected change. Even though I was only twelve, I still knew that it was totally out of character for my friend of most of my young years to suddenly act this way towards me.

After about three weeks of the silent treatment, my friend had the audacity to come and knock on my backdoor to see if I wanted to come outside and play with him. I simply tied my shoes, tucked my shirt, and we began to play as though nothing had ever happened. Again, does this sound familiar? Have you ever received the silent treatment from someone who you thought was a friend and could not understand why, only to have them burst back into your life as abruptly as they left, with no explanation?

We played together for many, many years after that. He never brought up the issue and neither did I. But for a long time I wondered, *What did I do wrong? Did one of the other kids poison his mind about me, or did I inadvertently hurt his feelings?* If I saw him today, I would love to talk to him and jokingly ask, "What really caused our separation when we were kids?" But I will never get that opportunity, for he died a sudden, untimely death a few years ago.

Now I ask you on a much larger scale, is there a forgiveness issue in your life? It would behoove you to resolve it rather quickly, because the only time that you may ever have to get it right is right now!

Forgiveness relieves pressure like nothing else and it washes away sin. Jesus demonstrated how important it was to forgive, even at the point of dying. Jesus showed us that it is to our advantage to forgive and release people and to be an example of truth rather than to take unforgiveness or strife to the grave. Even though Jesus had done no wrong, He still asked the Father to "forgive them." What a classic illustration of *choosing to love God's way!*

Unforgiveness is inexcusable. Not only did Jesus show us how to live and how to forgive while He was on the cross, but listen to what He did after He had risen. In Mark, chapter 16, Mary Magdalene, Mary, and Salome went to Jesus' tomb to anoint His body. When they got to the tomb, they saw an angel who told them, **"He is risen"** (v. 6). The angel said, **"Tell his disciples *and Peter* that he goeth before you into Galilee: there shall ye see him, as he said unto you"** (v. 7).

Isn't it amazing that immediately after Jesus arose from the grave, one of the first things He did was to show compassion for Peter by sending him a personal message? Remember, this was the very same disciple who denied Him three times.

Romans 15:1 says, **"We then that are strong ought to bear the infirmities of the weak, and not to please ourselves."** As mature Christians, we are not charged to downplay sinful acts committed by anyone, even those done by babes in Christ. However, we should feel compelled to be patient with all men during their tests and trials and feel a sense of compassion towards any of our sisters and brothers who are not on the same level as we are in our faith and in our overall walk with God.

Ephesians 4:26 says, **"Be ye angry, and sin not: let not the sun go down upon your wrath."** Verses 26 and 27 NIV say, **"'In your anger do not sin': Do not let the sun go down while you are still angry, and do not give the devil a foothold."** The best way to deal with forgiveness is to:

### Just apologize and live.
### Say, "I'm sorry" and forgive!

Some might say, "Maybe it's good that I experienced rejection as a child so it won't hurt quite as much as an adult." This could not be further from the truth. There are some things in life that we never get used to and one is to be rejected by someone. But we can manage through the strength of Christ to learn to deal with rejection. Nevertheless, we should never linger in rejection. Instead, we should pick up the pieces and move on with our life.

The only thing that we should dwell on in this world is the living Word of God. Yet some of us, including some mature

## LIFE IS SO SIMPLE WHEN
## WE CHOOSE TO LOVE GOD'S WAY

Christians, walk around every day with chips on our shoulders, encased with an unforgiving spirit. Forgiveness is so essential to our everyday love walk that our heavenly Father incorporated it in our model prayer where Jesus said, **"And forgive us our debts, as we forgive our debtors"** (Matthew 6:12).

Why do you think Jesus included forgiveness in our model prayer? Simply because He wanted to remind us daily, especially at the end of each day when we have a chance to reflect back on the day, that a contrary heart and an unforgiving spirit will absolutely prevent us from experiencing God's best.

There is too much unnecessary risk involved in carrying around an unforgiving heart. All of us have heard regrettable stories told by disconsolate people who all say they wish they had another chance to say, "I'm sorry," "I forgive you," or "Will you forgive me?" So starting this moment, why not let their experiences work for you and proceed to do the right thing?

Have you ever wondered what contributing factors could possibly bear the brunt for your unanswered prayers? You may have become frustrated and begin thinking out loud: *I love everyone. I have been living right. I pay my tithes and I give offerings. I don't drink anymore. I've quit smoking. I've never cheated. What's wrong, God?*

Have you ever thought that maybe you need to ask someone to forgive you, or perhaps you are still vilifying someone who is despondent and they really need you to accept their apology? Maybe you need to reflect over your life to see what has taken place or what may presently exist in your life that could be hindering you from receiving God's best. Or getting to other levels in life that God has for those who have chosen to simply *love His way*.

I was once in that predicament myself. I decided to go to God in prayer because He made us and He knows all about our parts and why they are defective and not functioning properly at times. By the way, He does not have to hook you up to a computer and run a diagnostic test to determine what He thinks is

# Recognize the Importance of Forgiveness
## (Simply Forgive)

wrong! You can go to a medical doctor for some of your troubles, but there are other problems that will arise in this life that only the Manufacturer, the One who made you, can fix.

I don't know about you, but I expect all of my prayers that are consistent with the Word of God to be answered, especially when I feel I am making an earnest effort to line up perfectly with His Word. Are you making an earnest effort to line up with the Word of God?

At any rate, God, who is the Manufacturer, instructed me to go and pay someone in full for an outstanding debt that I incurred a long time ago. I owed someone who, I might add, is still very dear and near to me and was there when I needed them the most. This transaction took place over sixteen years ago, yet somehow the importance of my being grateful for this magnanimous feat simply fell through the cracks and never made it to the deserving recipient.

When I borrowed this money, I was in dire need of some instant relief, and God touched this person's heart to give me the assistance that I needed so badly. There was never any doubt that I still owed the money, even though it was never brought up in any of our conversations. I vividly recalled receiving this favor as though it was yesterday. How could anyone be so foolish to allow this kind act of goodness from such a courageously spirited person to fall on deaf ears?

We have very little difficulty forgetting the things that we want to forget. Usually, it's the innocuous things that we choose not to forget or forgive that seem to keep us disconnected from the love of God. However, we should be determined to never let anyone or anything keep us from doing things God's way.

The next day, I not only repaid the money with accumulated interest, I also asked for and received forgiveness. That required courage and humility. If the Spirit of God indwells you, then all you need to do is flip the switch, because whatever you need is on the inside. God wants us to be:

### Innovators, not procrastinators!

Once we learn better, we ought to do better. It makes no sense that after you have asked God for help, and He tells you exactly what you need to do, that for whatever reason you refuse to finish the process. I have made up my mind that I am going to be a finisher. I want every drop of every benefit that our heavenly Father has promised us.

After taking care of this issue, a couple of weeks passed and I still felt like something was missing, so I chose to go back to God in my prayer closet for consultation. The Spirit of God advised me a couple of days later that there was still something from my past that I needed to rectify.

You see, often we change church homes and never give a thought to acknowledging the shepherd or pastor who nourished us and had spiritual jurisdiction over our life for a period of time. We should know by now that our heavenly Father is a God of order, and He is concerned about every compartment of our life. Even if it becomes necessary for you to change your church membership to be in the place where you are to be, there is still an orderly manner in which the transition should be handled.

The next order of forgiveness for me was to contact my former pastor and ask his forgiveness. I left his church a few years ago and did not have the common courtesy to tell him that I was moving on and to thank him for nurturing me. Being a member of any organization for over forty years, let alone the same church home, deserved a befitting transition. Besides, all of us are brothers and sisters in the Body of Christ, and all Christians or followers of Christ should be able to fellowship together, regardless of denomination or tradition.

Before officially leaving my old church, I should have told my former pastor that I had been led by the Spirit to transition to another church home, but that we would always remain brothers in Christ. Then, simply wish him God's best. That would have sufficed.

# RECOGNIZE THE IMPORTANCE OF FORGIVENESS
## (SIMPLY FORGIVE)

There is no reason why any pastor should have to inquire or find out from anyone other than the source as to the membership status of any person in his congregation. So I called my former pastor as soon as the opportunity presented itself. He recognized my voice almost immediately. Without further delay, I told him just how wrong I was, not for leaving so abruptly, but for not informing him in an appropriate manner. Then, I asked him if he would forgive me and accept my apology.

He said, "My brother, it has already been done." I wish I had cameras and recorders set up to record that moment. We both were overjoyed as we continued our conversation a little longer. But more importantly, it pleased God the Father, and my prayers since that time have been answered.

You may say, "That was just a little thing." Song of Solomon 2:15 says it is **"the little foxes, that spoil the vines: for our vines have tender grapes."** I simply refuse to let any matter, big or small, block my blessings. My new church home is indeed where I am to be. I am taught that God is a God of integrity, and He wants us to exude Him in every aspect of life. Even our smallest accomplishments in integrity bring glory and honor to God.

There is simply no price to put on the happiness you experience when your heart has been relieved and you are firmly placed in God's path for your life. Whenever you forgive others, it affords them the opportunity to experience this same kind of happiness. God loves relationships. The Spirit grieves when our relationships are severed, but He loves when we manage to seek His divine wisdom without delay and carefully follow His Word as to how we should repair them.

Do not be caught with any form of unforgiveness lodged in your heart because of an egregious childhood experience, some unfortunate incident, or something that someone said that may or may not be true. One of the most important things you can do when there is unforgiveness in your life is to acknowledge it

*Life Is So Simple When*
*WE CHOOSE TO LOVE GOD'S WAY*

to God in prayer. He hears an earnest prayer and He wants us to bring our heavy hearts to Him.

Psalm 32:5 says, **"I acknowledged my sin unto thee, and mine iniquity have I not hid...."** When you get serious minded enough to take something to God through Jesus in prayer, He will forgive you and give you the inclination to make it right with anyone. Just make sure that you give it all to Him. We must show ourselves approved by God.

Mark 11:24 says, **"What things soever ye desire, when ye pray, believe that ye receive them...."** God wants us to be forgiven. If we go to Him believing that we have received forgiveness, we will be forgiven whether our neighbor is willing to forgive us or not. It is such a wonderful feeling to finally abandon an overdue load that has been unnecessarily weighing you down. People in the world today are simply carrying too much unnecessary weight on the inside that will eventually show up on the outside. There are no winners whenever there is never-ending dissension. This can also cause ineffectiveness in our desire to please God.

If you feel you need professional help, then my advice to you is to get it. However, God is still the best doctor in the world. He is concerned about all of your concerns and He has neither stopped loving you nor has He stopped making house calls.

In Mark 5:25, there was a woman who had an issue of blood for twelve years who had spent all that she had on many physicians who still could not remotely resolve this issue. It was only after she made personal contact with Jesus that her problem was rectified.

God has given us the best medical encyclopedia available in His living Word. He wants to see us succeed in this life and receive everlasting life. It all starts with contacting Jesus.

I cannot over express the importance of eliminating unforgiveness from your life. In Matthew 5:22-25, Jesus makes it unquestionably clear that the value of your forgiveness, or the

## RECOGNIZE THE IMPORTANCE OF FORGIVENESS
### (SIMPLY FORGIVE)

lack thereof, far exceeds any gift that you or anyone else in this world could ever bring to the altar as an offering. That also includes your service. He instructs us in Matthew 5:24, **"Leave there thy gift before the altar, and go thy way; first be reconciled to thy brother, and then come and offer thy gift."**

The tithe and the offering are of utmost importance for the furtherance of the Kingdom of God. You already know that. But God values relationships immensely. God would much rather see us working together in harmony, winning souls for Jesus, than to bring our gifts to the altar with unforgiveness and strife passing through the pores of our hearts. He already has more silver and gold than we could ever fathom.

In describing some of the dimensions of the New Jerusalem, John says in Revelation 21:11 NIV, **"It shone with the glory of God, and its brilliance was like that of a very precious jewel, like a jasper, clear as crystal."** Verse 18 says, **"The wall was made of jasper, and the city of pure gold, as pure as glass."** What can you and I possibly bring to the altar to match that? With that being said, God wants us to *simply love His way*.

So whether the damaged relationships in your life involve your spouse, siblings, parents, or friends, make their relationship right as soon as possible. It makes no difference how it began or whose fault it was. Sometimes we are enraged with such bitterness and strife that when we do pray, we do not think about the real purpose of our personal communication with God.

First Peter 5:7 says, **"Casting all your care upon him; for he careth for you."** God naturally wants us to do the things in life that we can do for ourselves. However, the things that surface during our journey in life that we cannot handle, regardless of how negligible they may seem to others, He simply wants us to bring them to Him. When things get too hard for us, they are just right for God. By not acknowledging and dealing with strife and unforgiveness, you can preclude your prayers from being answered.

Most of us have visions of long life and eternal life. Psalm 90:10 NIV says, **"The length of our days is seventy years — or eighty, if we have the strength; yet their span is but trouble and sorrow, for they quickly pass, and we fly away."** No one can say with absolute certainty how long he or she or anyone else will endure this earthly tabernacle. But we do know what God has promised and that the years that He promised will pass rather quickly. So we need to make amends and forgive while the blood still flows in our veins.

We discussed earlier how Jesus did the opposite of what would be the norm when He was on the cross. He showed us how to deal with adversity. He asked God the Father to "forgive them." This is precisely what is required of us when we have been wronged by our transgressors. It is a necessary requirement, according to Matthew 5:44, to **"pray for them which despitefully use you, and persecute you."** When you pray, you are petitioning God with a never-ending "to do" list, so while you are at it, why don't you simply ask Him to forgive your transgressors and help those who have despitefully used you or persecuted you?

Ask yourself this question: Would I rather be in a position to ask God to help me and someone in my life put out a little brush fire, or would I rather be on the other side of the world fighting in some foreign land, not knowing when or where the next attack will take place? When you talk to someone who has experienced both ends of the spectrum, you will be quick to agree that there is really no comparison.

As believers, we are responsible for revealing the love and awesome power of God everywhere we go and do battle in this world. It is our responsibility as children of God to fill the earth everywhere with the presence of Jesus. However, the problems we think we have in life are not nearly as intricate when compared to the hardships that others may be experiencing. We should count our blessings at every turn and give this charge to

## Recognize the Importance of Forgiveness
### (Simply Forgive)

others as well, as we continue our efforts to share the knowledge of God with them.

Most people really want to be forgiven and accepted. From my own personal experience, I know how much it hurts to be rejected by someone who was previously loyal to you. But we should put our continuous trust in God, because receiving His love through His Son Jesus is the only love that matters. Continue to do well and do what is right, simply because it is right. Don't give up or abandon ship. Even though we get weary sometimes as we face complicated matters and resistance from the opposition, choose to stay in prayer as you ask forgiveness and forgive your transgressors.

When you accept Jesus as Savior and Lord and place God above all else in your life, He will guide you and infuse you with the power of the Holy Spirit. And if you are infused with the Holy Spirit, then all you need to do is activate Him, because in Him you already have every comfort that you will ever need to succeed in this world. That would also include having the propensity to take care of some long overdue forgiveness issues.

Remember to apologize and live. Say, "I'm sorry" and "I forgive." To ask for forgiveness and to forgive are two vitally important concomitants found in the love of God. They are two life-saving addictions that no Christian should ever abandon.

# Chapter 7

# Consider the Consequences of Disobedience (Simply Obey)

*H*ave you ever wondered why some people continuously try to justify their sinful acts as well as their unscrupulous behavior? And why do they run and hide after they have knowingly committed a crime? And when they are captured and brought to justice, they show neither signs of remorse nor a twinge of compunction?

Why do people seem to show very little concern as they lie effortlessly under oath, during a trial, or while giving a deposition? Yet when most are found guilty as charged by a jury of their peers, they are torn apart with irrepressible emotions.

The answer is that, like most of us, they are well aware of the free will that God has given us to say "yes" or "no" to any situation. But once the truth has been unveiled and reality sets in, they must now pay a penalty for their acts of disobedience. They were falsely allured into believing that their behavior would support their lies which would later aid them in their quest to escape punishment and the wrath of God.

It has been permeated in the very nature of man to willfully lie and deceive each other ever since the universal sin of Adam and Eve, who through their contemptuous disobedience, exposed mankind to evil. According to Genesis, chapter 3, the serpent — the craftiest beast that God ever made — approached Eve in the Garden with an underhanded game plan that included one of the world's first lies: **"You shall *not***

**surely die"** (Genesis 3:4). The Bible does not address specifically where Adam was **at that moment.** It is conceivable that he was at her side or perhaps he wasn't.

Most of us would tend to agree that a man and his wife should always make quality decisions *together* to provide a "check and balance" for each other, especially when a decision carries significant weight and controls the pendulum of life and death. For all intent and purposes we are talking about married couples, the union between a man and a woman, joined together by God. During critical decisions, one spouse should not roll the dice or arbitrarily make an off-the-cuff decision without receiving input from their mate. If one mate were approached regarding any family matter of significance, why would they even consider making that call alone without first conferring with their mate? That is, unless of course there is imminent danger or the decision is of an exigent nature and a rapid response is needed.

In Ephesians, chapter 5, the Apostle Paul highlights love and obedience between the husband and the wife. He further expatiates on their roles in First Corinthians, chapter 7. Of course, this is another lesson all by itself. There is a plethora of useful information on marriage throughout the Word of God that you should read and study. In a marital relationship joined by God, only when warranted in certain situations does separation or domination by either spouse have merit.

According to Genesis 2:24, **"They shall be one flesh."** In other words, their function should be inextricable and not independent of each other. However, before God made Eve, He gave Adam a direct order, a precise command, if you will. Genesis 2:16-17 says:

> **And the Lord God commanded *the man*, saying, Of every tree of the garden thou mayest freely eat:**
> **But of the tree of the knowledge of good and evil, thou shalt not eat of it: for in the day that thou eatest thereof thou shalt surely die.**

## Consider the Consequences of Disobedience
### (Simply Obey)

Is there anything questionable, nebulous, or even ambiguous about the command that God gave to Adam in this passage of Scripture? This simple command or statement of order was precise as it mandated strict obedience and adherence, while including the severity of the consequences and ramifications if disobeyed. It is in direct contrast to the lie that the serpent succinctly stated to Eve.

So even today, why do we continue to allow Satan to persuade or convince us to do things that will not only be detrimental to our life, but could also be damaging or fatal to the life of our family, others, or future generations?

Adam was given a charge, and we too have been properly instructed with facts, knowledge, and wisdom from the Word of God that far exceeds any mathematical certainty, that failure to comply with the Word of God *always* produces injurious results. And if our attitudes of noncompliance are not eradicated, ultimately they will lead to untimely deaths.

Jesus said in John 15:10, **"If ye keep my commandments, ye shall abide in my love; even as I have kept my Father's commandments, and abide in his love."** Is it that we don't care to abide in the love of God, or is it that we just don't comprehend? We can easily look back and study the shortcomings in the lives of others. Whether they were hoodwinked, avaricious, or just plain gullible to know that the devious thoughts we contemplate are not tenable, and if executed, they are not going to effectually benefit our family or us.

Before all is said and done, they will no doubt bring about unfavorable consequences. Even when you think you are totally ready to execute a villainous plan, there are so many additional things that can possibly go wrong and you are not prepared for half of them!

Several hundred years after the infamous debacle of Adam and Eve, we are still a stubbornly disobedient species, looking out exclusively for number one, just for the sake of having our way. God made it distinctively clear to Adam when He declared, **"Of every tree of the garden thou mayest freely eat: but of the tree of the knowledge of good and evil, thou shalt not eat of it . . ."** (Genesis 2:16-17).

So what was Adam's problem? Were the trees in the Garden that God gave to him futile? Surely he and Eve had several discussions or sidebars pertaining to this command. After all, he was given the run of the Garden except for the tree of the knowledge of good and evil. So did they run out of fruit from their choice of trees and were just plain hungry?

We can unimpeachably say, neither of these questions ever played even a meager role in their disobedience. You and I were not in the Garden and we can only speculate on its adornment and bountifulness. However, everything that God made was not just simply good. According to Genesis 1:31, **"God saw every thing that he had made, and, behold, it was *very good*. . . ."** So whatever area of the Garden God restricted Adam to was very good and capacious enough for him and his wife.

We know that God's command to Adam was neither misconstrued nor inscrutable. Eve was also conversant with God's instructions. Even though she was not present when God commanded Adam, she was still familiar with the command and quite articulate. Eve also knew that this command was from God and not from her husband as she cited to the serpent in Genesis 3:2-3:

> **We may eat of the fruit of the trees of the garden:**
> **But of the fruit of the tree which is in the midst of the garden, God hath said, Ye shall not eat of it, neither shall ye touch it, lest ye die.**

Eve even included in her articulation to the serpent that it was prohibited for them to touch it.

It has been my experience that most women are more detail oriented than men, and their memory and sense of direction are usually better too. I am not sure that Adam could have done a better job articulating to the serpent than Eve, but according to the instructions in Genesis 2:16-17, God did not say that they were prohibited from "touching it."

So actually, the moment that Eve lied, she gave place to the serpent. Ephesians 4:27 says, **"Neither give place to the devil."** In retrospect, it is plausible that it would have been far better for them had the thought of "touching it" never entered their minds. Who in their right mind would relish flirting with this kind of disaster? Why would they want to just touch it anyway?

Most of us know from personal experience that touching anything desirous usually amounts to wanting it all the more, and touching any fruit that is appealing to the eyes will almost always lead to eventually tasting it. Why would any fair-minded adult want to go near any produce that has been guaranteed to take you out if eaten?

No one can say with absolute certainty why the serpent took a circuitous route and approached Eve instead of Adam. As we alluded to earlier, it's highly possible that Adam was not immediately present during the initial contact. We cannot categorically say. Maybe the serpent figured Eve was more capable of giving him an accurate account of exactly what God had commanded to Adam, so he waited until a precise moment to find her alone. That being the case, there would be no doubt in his mind as to the course of action that he needed to take in order to successfully complete his subterfuge.

At any rate, since Adam is now standing next to Eve as she took the fruit during this tragic event, he could have and should have interjected. Why didn't he? All of us will continue to speculate about this tragedy for a long time, and just as long as we are able to grow and mature from our discussions and different perspectives, that's good.

Hopefully this book has prompted your interest and you will begin to read the Word of God on a daily basis and know for yourself that even your own consequences from walking in disobedience are highly capable of inflicting casualties on your family for generations to come. There is one thing, however, that we can agree on without a shadow of a doubt and that is, God gave the charge to Adam. He commanded Adam, not Eve.

First John 5:3 says, **"For this is the love of God, that we keep his commandment: and his commandments are not grievous."** God's commandments are not designed to cause us pain or suffering, and when we keep them, they are not meant to be burdensome or troublesome or cause us grief. It is only when we develop this insatiable desire to disobey and not keep His commandments of love that we are guaranteed to experience troubles galore, along with complicated matters that will lead to sin and ultimately death. We must be willing to turn completely away and find our pathway prescribed by God.

Some of us are quick to point out that the serpent approached Eve because she was the weaker vessel, as it relates to her strength or her lack of physical prowess. One thing that we can be certain of is that according to Genesis 3:1, **"The serpent was more subtil than any beast of the field which the Lord God had made. . . ."** He was glib, ingratiating, a smooth operator with his words and a penchant for getting your attention in the exact manner that he does today.

After the serpent was successful in getting Eve to simply listen and partake in his game plan, according to Genesis 3:6, **"She took of the fruit thereof, and did eat, and gave also unto her husband with her; and he did eat."** So now we can clearly see that at this particular stage of the dialogue, Adam was indeed within arm's reach of his wife as she took the fruit and executed the unthinkable.

Even this late in the game, there was still a great opportunity for Adam to chime in and say, "What saith the Lord?" He simply did not have to eat the forbidden fruit, even after His wife disobeyed. We should never follow disobedience in any shape, form, or fashion, regardless of who is at the forefront or waiting at the other end. This is true even if it's your spouse or if the act of disobedience has been approved, adopted, and modeled by your family for years and years.

Adam failed the challenge, and as a result, he not only disappointed God, he bankrupted mankind. The disobedience of Adam and Eve opened their eyes to evil and caused a curse to come on all of us that separated us from God. Romans 3:10 says, **"There is none righteous, no, not one."**

There were consequences when Adam and Eve sinned, and there are consequences for our sins. Adam and Eve severely damaged the benefit package that God had provided for mankind. They had it all, but they chose to squander it for a moment of pleasure, a forbidden fruit, leaving an indelible mark of shame on God's blueprint for the universe.

God will forgive our sins. However, our disobedience can be loaded with sin that is fully capable of inflicting pain and shame even to our children's children, long after we are gone and they are grown.

In spite of their sin, God still loved Adam and Eve so much that He clothed them before He banished them from the Garden. Genesis 3:21 says, **"Unto Adam also and to his wife did the Lord God make coats of skins, and clothed them."** He clothed them from their shameful nakedness. Afterwards, according to Genesis 3:24, **"So he drove out the man. . . ."**

**God loves us so very much,
But sin will drive a wedge
Between God and us.**

Sin disconnects us from God, and as a result, it puts distance between our blessings and us. The more we sin, the more blessings we drive away. The further we are driven away from God, the longer it could take for us to get back on track. But God is so merciful that anyone whose lifespan permits, who sincerely desires to get back into God's ark of safety, regardless of his or her earthly whereabouts or what they have done, can make a complete comeback and fully recover through the redemptive blood of Jesus.

We know that God's love for Adam was special simply because he was God's first. If you have children, reflect back on your firstborn. Usually there is irrepressible exuberance that comes with the birth of the first child, unlike any other. But think about this. Adam was not just the first child, he was also the first person, the first man, the first husband, and the list of firsts goes on. Needless to say, he was God's first disappointment after He had finished an impeccable work of creating the universe.

Because of the disobedience of Adam and Eve, God now provides salvation for us through His Son Jesus so that we do not have to continue to wallow in our sins and die and go to hell. Acts 4:12 says, **"Neither is there salvation in any other: for there is none other name under heaven given among men, whereby we must be saved."**

Jesus completed the unfinished work for His Father. We are now privileged to the gift of salvation through our belief in Jesus. This gift of salvation is what keeps us from the summit of what sin is all about, and that is death.

We need not go any further than to the first offspring of Adam and Eve to get a more in-depth look at other consequences of disobedience. The story of the first two sons of Adam and Eve, Cain the oldest and Abel the younger, is found in Genesis, chapter 4. Abel was a keeper of the sheep, a shepherd, and Cain was a tiller of the ground, a farmer. When it was time to make an offering unto the Lord, Cain brought **"of the fruit of the ground"** (v. 3) and Abel brought **"of the firstlings of his flock and of the fat thereof"** (v. 4).

Genesis 4:4-5 says, **"And the Lord had respect unto Abel and to his offering. But unto Cain and to his offering he had not respect...."** In perusing this chain of events, it is ostensible that the Lord did not respect the offering of Cain because it had come from the very ground that the Lord had cursed as a direct result of the sin of Adam and Eve. Genesis 3:17 says, **"Cursed is the ground for thy sake...."**

The sin of Adam and Eve had left an indefeasible stain on the universe, and because God did not respect Cain's heartless offering, Cain had the audacity to become very angry, causing his countenance to fall. I would imagine that Cain had somewhat of a nasty disposition long before God voiced His disapproval about his offering. All of this happened because the God of the universe was simply not pleased with Cain's less than satisfactory offering.

God wants and deserves our very best. Even today, we have no reason to get upset with God or others just because He is pleased with their record of giving and blesses them for their cheerful giving. Through Jesus, all of us have the same opportunity. By the way, is God pleased with your record of tithes and offerings? Do you get offended when your conscience or your inner man convicts you and gives you a warning about the ramification of your heartless giving? Do you envy people whose record of giving pleases God and who have His favor hovering over their life? These are just a few rhetorical questions that you really need to answer and make changes if needed.

Remember, we are talking about the consequences of disobedience. By all means God wants you to be obedient so that you too can receive His favor as well as man's favor in your life.

At any rate, God, being the God He is, gave Cain an opportunity to explain or perhaps to get a dialogue going so that he could cool off and possibly avoid any ideas of committing any further acts of disobedience that would produce more severe ramifications. Cain was no doubt a disdainful man who was easily angered. God already knew his heart and He knows our hearts too. God does not want to see us fail. This is why He gives us an opportunity at every turn to come to Him through His Son just the way we are.

I thank God for His patience. If we would just take a second thought and overhaul the assailable things that we think about committing during our thought life, then our behavior, actions, and the results would cause our minds to bounce back and begin to take small steps in the right direction.

In Genesis 4:6-7 God said to Cain: **"Why art thou wroth? and why is thy countenance fallen? If thou doest well, shalt thou not be accepted? and if thou doest not well, sin lieth at the door. And unto thee shall be his desire, and thou shalt rule over him."**

These verses in the *New International Version* say, **"Then the Lord said to Cain, 'Why are you angry? Why is your face downcast? If you do what is right, will you not be accepted? But if you do not do what is right, sin is crouching at your door; it desires to have you, but you must master it.'"**

God served Cain notice, and it would behoove us to heed this advice as well. With Jesus, we are fully capable of mastering the sin game. However, Cain's retort was simply not good. The handwriting was on the wall as Cain's entire demeanor had changed. When God observed his rage, He gave Cain every conceivable chance to chill out, to change his course of direction, and to escape. He knew that Cain's mind-set was such that he was about to do something that would have a deleterious effect, not only on his life, but also on his entire family. God wanted Cain to know that this was not the end of the line, and there would indeed be other opportunities for him to make it right.

Disappointments in life are not designed to be disastrous. It is by our might that we choose to go awry. It is a sad indictment when we know what we need to do to rectify a situation, but we blatantly refuse and continue to point our fingers at others. We know that the easiest thing in this world to do is to make excuses.

In no way did God discriminate or show favoritism between the two brothers. As a matter of fact, God actually spent additional time with Cain, coaching him, trying to get him to step up his game. But Cain chose to display his real attitude — an attitude that is all too familiar to some of us today, always trying to pass the blame or the reason for failure on to someone or something other than to simply take our medicine and make it right.

This is commensurate to what Adam and Eve, his mother and dad, did when they put the blame for eating from the forbidden tree on the serpent, when all they had to do was what God had commanded.

We have the Word of God and the Holy Spirit, who is always available to us, ready to operate in our life, if we would only listen. He is always giving us quiet warnings that will keep us from the eternal fire if we would only take the time to listen and adhere. However, without studying the Word of God, we have no idea what to listen for or to know if what we hear inside is analogous to the Word of God.

Paul says in Romans 6:14, **"For sin shall not have dominion over you. . . ."** Like Cain, we have a choice. When we choose to allow sin to rule over our life, while disregarding heavenly advice, as soon as our shortcomings appear, and they will appear, we have no reason to hold others accountable. Sin is just like a magnet. It has that uncanny ability to attract any magnetic force that it comes near. However, like a magnet, we have to place ourselves in position to allow the force of sin to attract us. *We have the wherewithal of the Spirit to repel the magnetic force of sin if we choose to do so.*

God warned Cain, "Sin lies at the door." If sin is at the door, that simply means that sin is waiting on the prime opportunity to lunge. If sin is present and is knocking at your door, it is left entirely up to you as to whether or not you will succumb and let it into your life. Our door is right in front of us, and it is with us everywhere we go. Whenever your countenance or demeanor falls, you simply become vulnerable and you can easily be overtaken with a fault anywhere you turn.

This is why if you are going to heed advice from a friend, make sure that whoever you respect enough to listen to has the mind of Jesus and will tell you what is true and not simply what you want to hear. As an ambassador of God, it is a disservice and you do not represent heaven's best interest when you give a trusted friend erroneous advice, agreeing with them when they are wrong instead of giving them the godly advice that they need. Often, we don't want to listen to true friends who love us and do not mind telling us when we are wrong or when we are headed in the wrong direction. Whenever we refuse to heed sound advice, invariably we get ourselves into situations that we can never back down from.

Genesis 4:8 says, **"And Cain talked with Abel his brother: and it came to pass, when they are in the field, that Cain rose up against Abel his brother, and slew him."** Apparently Cain could not muster enough repulsion to keep from committing the first homicide in the universe. This was another first for God, and like the detestable sin of Adam and Eve, it was another first that God could not be pleased with.

This is the kind of thing that can happen to us when "sin lies at our door" and we afford it an opportunity to come in. Once it lunges and gets inside, we give life to it. Sin will never turn down your invitation to come in. Whenever you become weak and allow sin to come through your door, you can rest assured that sin will bring all of its friends in the form of trouble and complicated matters that you did not prepare for, and they will simply load you up.

The sins of life are dirty and they don't play fair. They never let you know in advance about the cliff that's at the end of your pleasurable ride. Usually at the time, you are so wrapped up in the moment's anger or the moment's pleasure that you cannot see it or fathom it until you come near the end of your ride. By then it's simply too late to jump off.

When your mind is infiltrated with wrath and anger, you will wind up taking a journey that you will one day wish was only a dream. The next time that you find yourself getting so angry that you feel like resorting to violence, just reflect on

## Consider the Consequences of Disobedience
### (Simply Obey)

what Jesus did and said at the cross. Remember, if sin is at your door, you have to be prudent enough not to grant it entrance into your life. If you wait long enough, sin will leave your door. Even though it will return after a season, it simply will not wait around crouching forever.

This was a terrible thing that Cain let happen. Murder is one of the most scandalous crimes known to man. Very few people truly know the pain that Adam and Eve must have felt after this terrible sequence of events, which invariably affected every member of the first family of the universe.

Most of us can paint a mental picture of wanting the absolute best for our children, but to have their dreams and your dreams shattered for no ostensible reason by a sibling is such a tragedy. Like Adam and Eve who went to a restricted area they should have stayed away from, Cain went to talk to his brother in the field, a location that he most certainly should have avoided, at least until his mind was more rational.

The first repercussion of Adam and Eve's sin came when they fell from God's grace and were banished from the Garden. Now comes the excruciating pain from the tragedy of the older son killing the younger. Hopefully you can see that when you walk in continual disobedience, you are stripped of your godly benefits and placed in a culpable position.

Hebrews 10:26 says, **"For if we sin willfully after that we have received the knowledge of the truth, there remaineth no more sacrifice for sins."** The *New International Version* says, **"If we deliberately keep on sinning after we have received the knowledge of the truth, no sacrifice for sins is left."** When we learn better, we must simply do better. Outside of Christ, there is no other sacrifice for sin. When you fall from the grace of God, subsequently you fly away from His wings of protection.

Everything that God has ever done or made for us was not only "very good," but it was done for our good. Of course, none of us can know the disappointment that God feels when we let

Him down and continue to circumnavigate His chosen path for our lives.

The Lord now confronts Cain who lies, denying any knowledge of his brother's whereabouts. This is precisely what some of us do when we sin. Invariably, one lie will follow another. The sin family and the lie family are first cousins! Until we finally decide to come clean, it will always be one lie, then another. There is no remedy when we tell a lie. We should have learned from our childhood experiences that one lie does not cure all. The Lord tells Cain in Genesis 4:11-12, **"And now art thou cursed from the earth, which hath openeth her mouth to receive thy brother's blood from thy hand . . . a fugitive and a vagabond shalt thou be in the earth."** We cannot fully deduce that Cain's disobedience was a direct consequence of his parents' disobedient act in the Garden of Eden. Obviously, it had some bearing, if only because of the vicarious predicament that was caused by Adam and Eve's exile from their set place in the Garden.

It is vitally important that we find our set place and remain there. Nothing positive can come from roaming. However, according to First John 3:12, Cain slew Abel **"because his own works were evil, and his brother's righteous."** It sounds like Cain was a hot-tempered man with a bad attitude, full of hatred and jealousy.

At the time we commit our selfish acts of sin, we are not clairvoyant enough to know the magnitude of how deep the impact will end up affecting not only our families but also generations of families to come. Many of us today, unlike Cain, must learn to properly manage our anger. Proverbs 15:18 says, **"A wrathful man stirreth up strife: but he that is slow to anger appeaseth strive."** The *New International Version* says, **"A hot-tempered man stirs up dissension, but a patient man calms a quarrel."** God gave Cain every opportunity to calm down. Cain lost control of himself through no one's fault but his own.

# Consider the Consequences of Disobedience
## (Simply Obey)

The Word of God leaves no doubt in Romans 6:23 as to the consequences of unforgiven sin: **"For the wages of sin is death; but the gift of God is eternal life through Jesus Christ our Lord."**

When we study the Word of God, it will guide us with invaluable and practical advice while at the same time show us the end results of just how corruptible and destructible sin really is. When God gave the commandments to Moses, He included the first commandment of promise in Exodus 20:12: **"Honour thy father and thy mother: that thy days may be long upon the land which the Lord thy God giveth thee."** God wants our children to know early on that they too are neither exempt from sin nor the consequences of disobedience. He advises us to get a handle on our children. He instructs us in Proverbs 22:6: **"Train up a child in the way he should go: and when he is old, he will not depart from it."**

Sheep have the tendency to go astray. This is why the shepherd is so important in our life. We need to be in a good Bible-based church, our set place, under the spiritual jurisdiction of a shepherd. Romans 10:14-15 says:

> **How then shall they call on him in whom they have not believed? and how shall they believe in him of whom they have not heard? and how shall they hear without a preacher?**
> **And how shall they preach, except they be sent? . . .**

Here in reverse order Paul gives us the steps of how to be saved:

- A preacher must be sent.
- The message must be preached.
- We must hear from the preacher.
- Then we must simply believe.

God is our Shepherd and in Psalm 23, David gives such a splendid rendition of His role as Shepherd in our life. God simply wants to protect us and provide His best for us as we honor Him through His Son. He has given us authority over our children, a job that we should never take lightly. God knows the sinful nature of this world and that we were born in sin. However, we do not have to remain there, as God gives us a free will to choose Him.

We have access to His wisdom, His Word, and the power of His Spirit, that came to us in the form of the Comforter, appearing after Jesus ascended to heaven.

In John 15:26, Jesus said, **"He shall testify of me."** This is evident every day as we experience the presence of the Spirit of God.

The wisdom that comes from studying and meditating in God's Word and the awesome power derived from the knowledge of knowing who God is through a personal relationship with Jesus, are awesome tools available to everyone. A good father should know that his children will be met by a diversity of challenges as they continue to grow physically, mentally, and spiritually in this realm of life. By getting rooted in the Word of God, maturing spiritually, we ought to become wiser and more knowledgeable, prompting us to gradually abandon the cares of this world and give them to God in faith.

Now God wants us to advance His Kingdom by sharing the knowledge and wisdom that He has imparted in us with our spouse, our children, and others whom we meet as we cross paths and sojourn to win souls. We often hear that experience is the best teacher. It depends on who you ask as to what response you will get. While experience is quite helpful in sports, it is not necessarily the best teacher in life.

Why would anyone want to wander in the wilderness for forty years when they can study and benefit from the mistakes and experiences of others who have already traveled that same route? We should not want our children to fall in the same pits and run into the same dead ends that we met as we were searching to find ourselves before finally setting our sights and finding our set place in Christ. And by the same token, we

## Consider the Consequences of Disobedience
## (Simply Obey)

should not want them to experience or inherit any consequences from acts of disobedience caused by us. As parents, we need to understand that we are responsible for raising our children in a wholesome setting. Our children are God's precious jewels whom He has entrusted to our care.

A cursory look at Abraham and Sarah depicts the yardstick used to measure the lengths that some people will go just to possess God's precious jewelry (children) to share in their blessings from God. In Genesis 12:3-4, God made Abram a promise when he was seventy-five years old:

> **And I will bless them that bless thee, and curse them that curseth thee: and in thee shall all families of the earth be blessed. . . .**
> **Abraham was seventy and five years old when he departed out of Haran.**

Abram and his wife Sarai became impatient with God in waiting for His promise of a child, so Sarai came up with this magnificent plan to help God speed up the process. Sarai gave her maid, Hagar, to Abram. Hagar becomes pregnant by Abram and the problems that engendered from Sarai's conception of this idea started to unfold.

At times we get these insatiable urges to want to help God put our life on the fast track, even after He gives us a vision or has promised to never leave us or forsake us. We need to be mindful that whenever we do take our cares to God in prayer, we should patiently abide in His Word and continue to do exactly what it says. Then, on a daily basis simply remind God of the promises that He made to us in His Word.

Now that Sarai has thrown Hagar into the mix, Hagar will soon bear Abram's son Ishmael. This is what happens when we become disobedient and refuse to wait on God's perfect timing for what He promised He would do. A further look at this triangle reveals that Sarai is now at odds with her pregnant maid Hagar while blaming Abram for what has happened. Hagar decides that it is time to break camp, so she flees. God reenters the picture with His grace and mercy to bring some much needed relief and restoration. In Genesis 16:11 an angel of the Lord found Hagar. **"And the angel of the Lord said unto her** [Hagar]**, Behold, thou art with child, and shalt bear a son, and shalt call his name Ishmael; because the Lord hath heard thy affliction."**

In spite of their disobedience, which manufactured a delay in the perfect timing of God's plan, it still did not preclude God from keeping His promise to Abram. Twenty-five years later, God, being the kind-hearted, gracious, and forgiving God that He is, gave Abram and Sarai a son of their own named Isaac, so Sarai became pregnant at an old age.

Prior to the birth of Isaac, God also exceedingly multiplied Abram's son by Hagar (Ishmael). Our acts of disobedience will put a damper on the blessings that God has prepared for us, causing us to wait much longer for our breakthrough. Jesus says in Mark 13:31, **"Heaven and earth shall pass away: but my words shall not pass away."** That sounds like a rock solid promise to me. We need to understand from this point forward that God will do what He says in His Word. We simply need to be patient.

During the last five years, as lieutenant commander of the Homicide Unit with the Birmingham Police Department, I have reviewed over five hundred incident reports on deaths. Of these reports, some were natural deaths and some were undetermined deaths. Others were accidental deaths, suicides, and some were homicides. The most egregious of all crimes in nature, homicide is the killing of one human being by another. In the vast majority of these homicide cases, arrests have been made. We are always grateful when the responsible individuals are brought to justice. However, there are several open homicide cases where the suspects are still at large, as either a fugitive from justice or no suspect has been developed. While I bear no malice in my heart for any one subject to punishment, there are still consequences for the inappropriate actions for which the perpetrator must pay.

# Consider the Consequences of Disobedience
## (Simply Obey)

I commiserate with the families who are still perplexed as to how their lives were dramatically changed forever with one phone call or a knock on the door because of a thoughtless act committed by another. Some of the perpetrators responsible for committing these flagitious acts of disobedience are still at large and have shown no signs of regret or willingness to surrender.

Those of us who are saved by grace know that there is no such thing as a perfect crime. Regardless of some secular beliefs, Galatians 6:7 says, **"Be not deceived; God is not mocked: for whatsoever a man soweth, that shall he also reap."** There are consequences for disobedience in the earth that we must pay, notwithstanding our right to eternal life.

In Matthew 10:28 Jesus says, **"And fear not them which kill the body, but are not able to kill the soul: but rather fear him which is able to destroy both soul and body in hell."** We should not fear anyone or what they can do, will do, or have done. Instead, reverence God who has all power. In addition to being a good and merciful Father, He is also a just God. He will judge all of us accordingly.

Nahum 1:3 says, **"The Lord is slow to anger, and great in power, and will not at all acquit the wicked. . . ."** This is encouraging news for anyone who may still be struggling with being the victim or family of anyone who has suffered from any act of criminal violence. Regardless of whether an arrest and conviction have taken place, remain focused and steadfast in the Lord, etching only the promises of His Word in your heart as you remind Him daily of what He has said in His Word. Nahum 1:7 says, **"The Lord is good, a strong hold in the day of trouble; and he knoweth them that trust in him."** Continue in prayer and watch carefully as your life incrementally takes on a new dimension. Trust God daily and make Him the center of all you do in life as you vow to simply *love His way.*

Our actions or lack thereof will always yield results. If we do the right thing, we will, in God's time, always get favorable results. Patience is the order of the day. When we do the wrong thing, which also includes doing nothing, we will always get less than favorable results, sometimes encompassing the lives of others.

Go visit any city or county jails and then visit the state and federal penitentiaries. Start conducting random interviews with any inmates who are honest enough to tell you why they are incarcerated. Then witness for yourself as you immediately get firsthand information, and just as clear as the sun shines in the sky, you will know that *there are consequences for our acts of disobedience.* I am not advocating that every person in jail or everyone who has ever gone to jail was justly imprisoned. Mistakes and unfortunate incidents happen, and they too have consequences, regardless of how negligible they may be.

Romans 5:19 says, **"For as by one man's disobedience many were made sinners, so by the obedience of one shall many be made righteous."** Because of Adam's disobedience, which prompted mankind's exposure to evil, Jesus stepped down from royalty to walk the same path as Adam did. Satan also tempted Jesus as Adam was tempted. It is not a sin to be tempted. However, Jesus being God's very own precious jewel, withstood the test and did not fail as did Adam. He also left us with everything we need to live a victorious life through Him and to further enhance the Kingdom of His Father.

> **Jesus came to give us life
> And more abundant life,
> Through His death, burial, and resurrection.
> We now have the right to the tree of life.**

After completing His Father's earthly mission, according to Ephesians 1:20-21, God **"set him at his own right hand in the heavenly places, far above all principality, and power, and might, and dominion, and every name that is named, not only in this world, but also in that which is to come."**

# Consider the Consequences of Disobedience
## (Simply Obey)

Since the ascension of Jesus, we now have the ever-present power of the Holy Spirit, our Comforter, along with the living Word of God, as our guides to carry us through to complete our mission. Through His death on the cross, Jesus repurchased the world from the curse of the sin that was caused by the disobedience of Adam and Eve. If you are involved in any semblance of disobedience, cease from it. If you are not walking in disobedience, then don't start. If you spend your life in sin, you will spend eternity regretting it. We can no longer make excuses for not totally submitting ourselves to the obedience of God, walking in His perfect path for our life. We must, in an all-out effort, spread the Good News of salvation, as we inform unbelievers across the globe just how simple life is when we choose to *love God's way,* because we are all about His love.

# Chapter 8

# Choose To Be Happy (Happiness Is a Choice)

*E*verything we do in life is the product of a choice that we made. There are a myriad of choices, both significant and insignificant, that we make from day to day. Some of our choices, though not intended — whether they are perceived as good, bad, or evil — will invariably affect not only our life but could also impact millions of others.

The moment you begin your day, your never-ending list of choices immediately breaks ground. You can choose to get up and get started or you can choose to lie down and sleep longer. You can choose to go to work or you can simply choose not to. We make several of our daily choices with such regularity that a large percentage of them have become second nature.

Each day of our life we also choose whether or not we are going to be happy. Deciding to be happy is a choice that we should consciously make each morning. Whether or not you have a good day is predicated primarily on your mind-set as you open your eyes each morning.

It has been my experience that trying to decide at 1:00 p.m. to have a good day is a little bit late to get started, although you can still finish your day strong. David said in Psalm 118:24, **"This is the day which the Lord hath made; *we will rejoice and be glad in it.*"** We are not just simply to be glad. Instead, we are charged to "rejoice and be glad." The Lord loves us so much that He not only gives us the privilege and opportunity to enjoy another day. He also gives us another simple illustration of His love for us by using the personal pronoun "we" in this very unique passage of scripture.

Our salvation is so important to God that He chose to be very meticulous about even the simplest of words that He allowed these inspired writers to interpolate into His holy Word when it was written. He was personally concerned about each of us long before we ever knew what a personal pronoun was. That's because He wants us to realize that the significance of having a personal relationship with Jesus is of unrivaled importance and that His love is a very present love for all.

Moreover, God wants us to know that the choice of happiness David spoke of over two thousand years ago is still available to us today. Christians everywhere should rejoice every day, if only because of the assurance of our salvation, the larger than life gift of God that He so graciously gives to those of us who confess and believe in His Son Jesus. So all of the saints of God should be rejoicing right now, exploding with irrepressible exuberance!

In Exodus 18:9, **"Jethro rejoiced for all the goodness which the Lord had done to Israel, whom he had delivered out of the hand of the Egyptians."** In Acts 8:37-39, the eunuch who confessed to Philip that Jesus Christ is the Son of God, went away rejoicing after Philip water baptized him. Psalm 40:16 says, **"Let all those that seek thee rejoice and be glad in thee; let such as love thy salvation say continually, The Lord be magnified."** The *New International Version* reads, **"But may all who seek you rejoice and be glad in you; may those who love your salvation always say, 'The Lord be exalted!'"**

Matthew 5:12 says, **"Rejoice, and be exceeding glad: for great is your reward in heaven. . . ."** Those of us who truly seek the Lord first, understand the graphic representation of our salvation and know firsthand that we have every reason to continually magnify the name of Jesus, regardless of any drama, adventure, or complicated matters that try to press us into a quandary or any misfortunes that may surface and attempt to importune us on a daily basis.

It is obvious that when David arose on this particular morning, he had a made-up mind in spite of all that he had previously endured. He simply chose to make a conscious decision to rejoice and be happy in the Lord. Regardless of the hodgepodge of hurdles that you may presently be facing, God still wants us to trust His Word and to rejoice and be happy in Him. God did not make us simply to survive.

**He wants us to be active members
In the Body of Christ,
Carrying out His will in our life.**

Bear in mind, several people did not answer the bell as the alarm sounded this morning. But we have to trust and believe that our heavenly Father takes no pleasure in losing any sheep, whether they are securely in the fold or have gone astray.

In John 10:10 Jesus says, **"The thief cometh not, but for to steal, and to kill, and to destroy: I am come that they might have life, and that they might have it more abundantly."** Jesus not only reveals to us that He and His Father advocate long life, but He also infers that neither He nor His Father take life. Jesus advises us of our most formidable adversary, while giving us all of his job specs and attributes. Hopefully, you know by now that evil and death come from the author of destruction, Satan himself.

Note that Jesus has unmistakably tapped Satan as *universal enemy number one*. God simply does not remotely benefit when even one of His special creations is suddenly killed, saddened, or when we idly waste incalculable time complaining instead of being happy in Him.

First Chronicles 16:29 says, **"Give unto the Lord the glory due unto his name: bring an offering, and come before him: worship the Lord in the beauty of holiness."** We were made to worship Him and to make heart-giving contributions to the edification of His Kingdom. God has not and will not place any of us in violable situations or dilemmas, nor has He ever designed or sanctioned any blueprint or schematic for any obstacle to render us harm or to make us feel defeated in any zone of life. He certainly did not cause us to reap any unfortunate harvests that resulted from some of the bad choices we made.

First Corinthians 10:13 says, **"There hath no temptation taken you but such as is common to man: but God is faithful, who will not suffer you to be tempted above that ye are able; but will with the temptation also make a way to escape, that ye may be able to bear it."** Jesus also experienced temptation when He walked the face of this earth, yet He never sinned. We will experience temptation too in some form or another in this life.

We have a choice as to whether or not we will follow the footsteps of Christ and live, or continue in the footsteps of Adam in sin, eventually causing death. God has provided us with wisdom in His living Word and in the Holy Spirit to guide us. They place a path or avenue of escape at our disposal, designed exclusively to help us circumvent evil and to take an off route that will leave temptation standing at first base.

The best way to face a potentially evil or tempting situation is to make an about face, return to the Word, and review your orders from God. Whenever Satan dangles his plans in front of you, on the surface it may appear to be good. But shift your focus towards the guaranteed "very good" things that God has already provided for you in His Word. Remember, you have a choice. God has completed His work, and He simply will not choose for us. We have to be circumspect and follow the guidance of His Word and His Spirit in all that we do. Remember, there are consequences for every choice that we make.

First Samuel 15:22 says, **"To obey is better than sacrifice. . . ."** There is nothing in this world we can sacrifice or forfeit that is remotely equivalent to the gain that we will experience when we choose to be obedient to the Word of God. Once we choose to commit to study and meditate in His Word, utilizing the omnipresence of the Holy Spirit as our guide, we will find out that the righteousness of God is the pathway to success.

God included us as a part of it so we can promote enhancement towards His Kingdom and rejoice and be happy in the process. We paralyze ourselves on a daily basis, wasting invaluable time when we worry about certain issues and situations in this world that we have absolutely no control over except to pray. Secondly, being pessimistic about situations that may never come to fruition.

First Peter 5:7 says, **"Casting all your care upon him; for he careth for you."** Your cares include any and all of your concerns. God is concerned about the total you — your personal interests, your worries, or anything that is remotely capable of causing you anxiety regardless of the magnitude or the realistic value.

God has shown us through the sacrificial death of His only Son and in His holy Word that He loves us unconditionally and He is indeed a good parent. His goodness will continue to hover over those of us who choose to obey and abide in His Word. As a good parent, wouldn't you find it mysterious if your children continued to worry unnecessarily about anything that you have already taken care of for them? So it is with our heavenly Father. He does not want us to worry about anything. He wants us to be completely happy and dependent on Him.

Each morning we should get up with an attitude, *this is going to be the best day of the rest of my life*. But remember, it's a choice that we consciously make. If David could make this claim, then so can we. David says in Psalm 144:15, **"Happy is that people, whose God is the Lord."** Everlasting happiness can only be found in God through His Son Jesus. If Jesus is Lord of your life, you should not only be happy in Him, but you should be reaping all of the benefits that come with being His very own.

## Life Is So Simple When
## WE CHOOSE TO LOVE GOD'S WAY

Be honest with yourself. Are you happy? I mean, consistently happy, day in and day out? I'm sure you can find a mere semblance of happiness in anything that you want, but this is not true happiness. This type of happiness is short-lived at best, and it is just a matter of time before it will quickly diminish. I am not talking about an illusion or something of doubtful authenticity.

Looking for happiness from any source other than our Savior and Lord Jesus Christ will ultimately lead to disappointment and failure. Happiness is defined as prosperity, a state of well-being and contentment, or a pleasurable or satisfying experience. Take your pick, but if you want to know the truth about happiness, *to be happy is to be blessed,* and blessings come from God by way of people.

A happy person is:

1. A person who has chosen Jesus Christ as the Lord of his or her life and is committed to serving only Him no matter what — Peter — 1 Peter 4:12-14.
2. A person who has asked for and received wisdom, knowledge, and understanding from God — Solomon — 1 Kings 3.
3. A person who despises sin and obeys the Word of God — Joseph — Genesis 39.
4. A person who is determined to endure to the end, regardless of circumstances — the Apostle Paul — Philippians 1.

True happiness can only be found in obedience to God. John 13:15,17 says, **"For I have given you an example, that ye should do as I have done to you . . . If ye know these things, happy are ye if ye do them."** Happiness is not just knowing what God wants us to do, but it is doing as He has instructed us in His Word. Nothing pleases the Father as much as obedience, as Jesus clearly demonstrated.

James 5:11 says, **"Behold, we count them happy which endure. . . ."** God has already provided a perfect plan for our life, but we must choose to reach deep down inside, never wavering, and remain locked into His Word and simply endure to the end. We need to make up our minds to finish the race without compromising. Some of us lost our focus and got off course shortly after we were shown the way. It was only through God's grace that we found out quickly that not only is God's plan the easiest plan for us to follow, but it has also been constructed in our best interest and is guaranteed to see us through if we choose to remain loyal to it.

We are blessed in that through provisions in God's Word, we were allowed another opportunity, and with that opportunity we finally came to ourselves. This is reminiscent of the prodigal son choosing to go forward after hitting rock bottom (see Luke 15:11-32). There are certainly other criteria that one can add to his or her "happiness list," but you or anyone else will never truly be happy until you have accepted Jesus Christ as Savior and Lord of your life and are diligently seeking the Kingdom and righteousness of God.

If you choose to be happy in God, this means that you must first be happy in Jesus. In John 5:23 Jesus says, **"That all men should honour the Son, even as they honour the Father. He that honoureth not the Son honoureth not the Father which hath sent him."** The blood of Jesus Christ has redeemed us, and to please God we must walk and live by faith through His Son Jesus.

The primary reason, above all else, that you and I should choose to be happy in Jesus is simply because Jesus died for our sins, and by virtue of His death, burial, and supernatural resurrection, we now have a right to eternal life. As believers, the Holy Spirit indwells us, and as a result, we should be filled to repletion, undaunted, and unfazed no matter what the circumstances appear to suggest. We are convinced that through the strength of Christ, we can do all things (see Philippians 4:13).

To some it may appear that this is impractical or imperceptible or just a pipe dream. I can only tell you from the Word of God what is required of those of us who live in the Body of

Christ and those who are still roaming in the wilderness. Once you get revelation knowledge of what Jesus' death did for us out of perfect obedience to His Father, who loves you and me so much, your life will change dramatically and you will wonder why you did not believe and take hold of His redemption plan sooner.

When you receive the special blessing of salvation, expect change in your life. Second Corinthians 5:17 says, **"Therefore if any man be in Christ, he is a new creature: old things are passed away; behold, all things are become new."** In other words, once you have chosen Christ and made His Word the center of your life, you will have a changed heart and new mental software as the former things in your life which were not of God have been eradicated.

It is foolish for us to remotely say or think that we are in the Body of Christ if we are essentially doing the same things that we did before we gave our life to Him. We know that this Christian experience is not going to cause our outward physical appearance to suddenly change, but it is quite evident that our inner man must be completely made over with a totally new way of thinking. Does this mean that we will never be faced with conflict, confrontation, or mind battles? Of course not. According to Luke 4:13, **"When the devil had ended all temptation, he departed from him *for a season.*"** Even after tempting Jesus, the Word of God implies that Satan would eventually come back for an encore.

Remember, there is nothing that we can label "impossible" with the help of God. Jesus says in Matthew 19:26, **"With men this is impossible, but with God all things are possible."** We must remain steadfast and obedient as we walk by faith, trusting in God's Word that He will do whatever He has spoken. God's Word is true from the beginning to the end, and it simply cannot change. Jesus tells us in Matthew 24:35, **"Heaven and earth shall pass away, but my words shall not pass away."** Just in case you missed it, He repeats this

# Choose To Be Happy
## (Happiness Is a Choice)

passage of Scripture a second and a third time verbatim in Mark 13:31 and Luke 21:33, respectively.

My brothers and sisters, this is the only standard to finish your race that you will ever need. If it is stated in the Word of God, suffice it to say, *it's a done deal!*

We are the ones who often show signs of inconsistencies, even after we have made verbal commitments. Maintaining a close-knit relationship with God, through His Son Jesus, and being obedient to His Word, will cause us to take a huge leap towards revealing evidence of change and bringing real happiness in our life, without ever bringing attention to ourselves.

Romans 3:23 says, **"For all have sinned, and come short of the glory of God."** We were born in sin and will always need the love of God through the blood of Jesus to sustain us. If your resume of life subscribes to this, God will continue to bless you and supply your needs. So continue to lower your ego and look up to Him!

Think how successful athletes subscribe to a strict regiment and constantly practice to strengthen every area of their profession, even though they have already reached the pinnacle of their sport. We marvel at their ability to succeed to the acme of their positions as they perform on the field on game day. However, we only see them on game day. We are not privileged to see all of the painstaking efforts that they put into practice sessions, reviewing tapes, attending meetings, and all of the other mental and physical sacrifices they have made to get to that seemingly flawless level. Most of the athletes who stand out from the pack made a conscious decision to develop a strong work ethic and to go above and beyond the simple requirements.

As disciples of Jesus, we must make a conscious choice to be about God's business of praying, studying, and meditating in our Playroom (the Bible) so we can work towards perfecting His Kingdom and carrying out His will for our life here on earth while preparing for our judgment day or "game day," if you will.

## Life Is So Simple When
## WE CHOOSE TO LOVE GOD'S WAY

We must make a conscious decision as saints of God to stand out and not just simply fit in. Choosing to be happy in the Lord will go a long way toward honing your attitude and saying how your performance will measure up during your game day as you stand before the justice of God.

Another key component to happiness is attaining wisdom. The wisdom I am referring to can only come from God. I am not talking about erudition or man-made wisdom. In John, chapter 3, Nicodemus, a ruler of the Jews, found it incomprehensible that a man could be born again without entering his mother's womb a second time. It is evident that Nicodemus was an educated man. However, he did not possess the godly wisdom that Solomon was speaking of in Proverbs 4:7: **"Wisdom is the principal thing; therefore get wisdom: and with all thy getting get understanding."** The wisdom of God is invaluable and her benefits are unlimited. Having access to the intellect and discernment of Jesus are weapons that no Christian should be without. James, the brother of Jesus, says, **"If any of you lack wisdom, let him ask of God, that giveth to all men liberally, and upbraideth not; and it shall be given him"** (James 1:5). God will liberally and indiscriminately give wisdom to His children.

Knowledge from on high is the knowledge that we should aspire to attain. However, we must get comprehension and understanding along with our wisdom. Wisdom without the correct application or without understanding will not be retained and could easily lead to a downfall.

Solomon requested understanding and discernment, which pleased the Lord, who not only granted Solomon his desires but also gave him riches and honor. Colossians 2:3 says that Christ is the key to opening the hidden treasures of God's wisdom and knowledge. All things of God must come through His Son. To receive wisdom and supernatural blessings from God, we must simply ask. Just ensure that you have checked it with Jesus for life, as you diligently seek Him and expect a response. Make up your mind to choose Jesus for a lifetime and not for mere convenience.

## Choose To Be Happy
### (Happiness Is a Choice)

To leave God's ark of safety and go back to the world is nothing short of an ill-fated mission. No one should ever want to escape enemy soil and find peace, then arbitrarily reenter that battle, staged on enemy turf, with no weapon, allies, ambassadors, and without God. What a terrible disadvantage!

In reference to wisdom, Solomon says, **"She is a tree of life to them that lay hold upon her: and happy is every one that retaineth her"** (Proverbs 3:18). As a child, did you ever learn to do something that once seemed insurmountable, like learning to ride a bike, or learning to swim, or finally understanding and grasping the concept of geometry or algebra, after spending long, arduous hours of intense study? How could you ever forget those challenging steps of growth?

During those times, though you were not aware, you were using untapped wisdom by making a quality decision to persevere. You knew deep down inside that you could do it, and more importantly, you did not give up, because you realized early on that there are so many benefits to pressing forward and there are no rewards in quitting.

As children, we often use biblical principles, good judgment, and godly wisdom without fully comprehending the nature behind it. Then we grow up and mature, and after becoming adults, we often have the proclivity to confuse even the simple principles in life that we executed all too well as children. Choosing to be happy in the Lord comes with an abundance of benefits, but can only descend through Jesus Christ our Lord. You must not only make Him your choice, you must stick with Him no matter what.

Sin deprives us of true happiness in God. He detests sin and so should we. If you have confessed that Jesus Christ is your Lord and repented with a sincere change of heart, you should no longer be vacillating in sin. If you are still wavering after confessing Jesus Christ as your Lord, you have not cemented your choice in Jesus. If this is the case, the meager amount of happiness you are currently experiencing will eventually dissipate, and if you continue your course of action by living on the edge, you are doomed for failure and your ticket to hell will soon be punched.

Romans 6:14 says, **"For sin shall not have dominion over you: for ye are not under the law, but under grace."** To have dominion over sin is to possess the authority to govern or rule over it. Simply put, before we go against the grain, we have a choice. In Genesis 1:26-28, after God created the world, He said, **"Have dominion . . . over every living thing that moveth upon the earth"** (v. 28). God gave us dominion to rule in the earth, and if God has given us dominion to rule, it succinctly means that the only way we can lose this right is if we choose to do so.

It is obvious that God doesn't have dominion over these areas of our life because He has delegated this authority to us.

God, the Creator of the universe, chose to give us dominion over every living thing that moves on the face of the earth. And if we allow sin in any form to rule over our life, it is by our hands and not God's. Sin is dormant until we choose to give it life. The only choice we have to make is simply to choose to maintain the dominance that has been given to us by God.

We are subservient to whatever we are loyal to, whether it is sin or obedience to the Word of God. If you are still dabbling in sin, it simply means that sin has jurisdiction over your life. If you are obedient to the Word of God, you have chosen to exercise your issue of godly armor through the Word of God that gives you domination over sin. This is just another opportunity for us to make a choice between applying or not applying the Word that God has given to us. If you are presently overtaken in a fault, all is not lost because you can still overcome.

So what is this thing in your life that currently has dominion over you and is so good that it keeps you incessantly going from slavery to freedom and from freedom back to slavery? Is it worth jeopardizing your salvation? First Kings 18:21 says, **"How long halt ye between two opinions?"** Our earthly bodies, although designed to live according to Genesis 6:3

("a hundred and twenty years"), will eventually become beat down, and fail to completely do what they were designed to do, because of the wear and tear of sin and disobedience.

Choose to be happy in Jesus while there is still daylight! Psalm 90:10 says, **"The days of our years are threescore years and ten; and if by reason of strength they be fourscore years, yet is their strength labour and sorrow; for it is soon cut off, and we fly away."** In this life on earth, there will be occasional pain and issues that we will face. The Bible says so. Things are not going to always go our way. Invariably, all of us are going to die and spend eternity somewhere. We simply will not live here forever. So if you haven't done so already, abandon Satan's ship and switch over to God's side. Seek His plan to spend eternity with Jesus.

### The benefits in changing
### Will far exceed the pain in staying.

Hook up with Jesus and weather the storm! He has already handled our business for us and has made the journey so much easier to travel. In John 14, He has promised those of us who are believers that He is coming back to receive us so we may be with Him. This is the hope of every believer.

Remember how you kept getting up whenever you would fall off your bike and how you swallowed a little water as you fought with your fright, but finally you learned to swim? Your conditions in life will remain the same, but *only if you want them to*. We will pay for our bad decisions in life as well as our indecisions.

Hebrews 12:7 says, **"If ye endure chastening, God dealeth with you as with sons; for what son is he whom the father chasteneth not?"** God corrects those whom He loves. Make the choice to be happy in Jesus. Stay on board. Seek and find what the will of God is for your life. In your daily prayer, pray for God's will to be done in your life on earth as it is in heaven. Your mind must be renewed and spiritually tuned to grasp an understanding of the perfect will that God has in store for you when you find your path and stay the course.

Remember how God promised Abraham and Sarah a son, but they became impatient and tried to speed things up and made it happen on their clock? Our choice to meddle with God's plan will undoubtedly cause unforeseen problems as bad choices always do. Hebrews 6:15 says, **"And so, after he had patiently endured, he obtained the promise."** It was only after Abraham had regrouped from his derailment that he received what God had promised him from the outset, a son named Isaac.

The world has all kinds of traps designed to bamboozle you. But when you utilize the magnificence of the Holy Spirit to guide you through those pressing moments, He will never fail you. Everyone gets tempted at times, and temptation is here to stay. If we would only remember:

**To be patient just a little bit longer,
Confess the Word just a little bit harder,
Then we will view things
Just a little bit smarter!**

Before long, the appeal to make a knowingly bad choice will disappear like a puff of smoke. That's when that smile of happiness is shown from ear to ear as evidence that heeding the voice of the Spirit has paid big dividends. We should be elated anytime that because of our trust in God, we successfully manage to circumnavigate a choice that we knew would have eventually sailed back to haunt us. James 1:4 says, **"But let patience have her perfect work, that ye may be perfect and entire, wanting nothing."** Once you reach an upper level of spiritual maturity, you will be better equipped to deal with Satan's sleight of hand.

It is relatively easy to stand back and second-guess other sisters and brothers when they fail, especially if you have neither developed your own faith life nor had your character attacked, or if neither has been tested or placed on the line for anything. It may be easy for us to deal with a temptation when we are in the presence of others. But what will we do, or how will we respond when we are alone and the lights are out and we think no one sees us?

Regardless of what you have gone through in this life or what you may presently be experiencing, ignoring the Word of God will never make things better. Depression, suicide, seeking revenge, or vying to get even will not change matters. Contemplating or executing any of these things will only exacerbate your existing condition. When we make our choices in life, we should always consider, who else is my choice or decision going to affect? Sometimes in our selfish thinking we give very little thought or consideration to this question.

Remember, no storm in life will last forever, and nothing is ever as bad as when it first appears. We must learn to find solace and contentment within our circumstances, and we can only master this by knowing that Jesus Christ is Lord and Savior, and in Him alone you already have the victory. The Apostle Paul says in Philippians 4:13, **"I can do all things through Christ which strengtheneth me."**

There is not a prop in the world as strong as the love that Jesus showed for us on the cross, and we are privileged to share in the supernatural power that God used to raise Him from the dead. Neither the cross nor death nor the grave could hold Him. He is the best Team Leader in all of life, and there are no second-place finishers in His love. We were made to be happy and serve Him as our Lord. If you are not living a fulfilled, wholesome life on purpose, then right here and now is the time for you to start.

Answer this question: If you do not give your life to Jesus today, when will you do it? You will not live on earth forever! If you miss out on the opportunity to choose and serve Jesus and not fulfill your specially designed path for this life, you will not only fail in this world, but you will also fail in the hope of the world to come. There will be no make-up test, no work for extra credit, no special study sessions, and no summer school.

## *Life Is So Simple When*
## *WE CHOOSE TO LOVE GOD'S WAY*

Hebrews 9:27 says, **"And as it is appointed unto men once to die, but after this the judgment."** This life here on earth is not a practice run.

### This is the real deal,
### The finale if you will.

This is the only time that you will have to prepare for the coming of Jesus. He is going to return, whether you and I are prepared or not. Jesus has already done His thing for mankind, and at present, all of us are welcome to share in it. When He returns, and that is a mathematical certainty, He will be coming back for His team. I would not want to check out of earth's motel without **knowing** that I have my ticket punched to go meet Him.

You will simply never experience true love and happiness until you have chosen Jesus Christ as your personal Savior and you know beyond the shadow of a doubt that your ticket is stamped for heaven. When we close our eyes at night and go to sleep, we are comatose. We have no idea where we are or if we will ever return. If we are blessed to wake up the next morning in our own bed, we should be like David and make a conscious choice to rejoice and be happy in the Lord.

This world we live in is not new to us, we are conversant with it, and we are fully aware of the opposition. There is a tug-of-war that goes on inside of us practically each morning when we awake, and sometimes throughout the day. Others like you and me also go through the same battlefield of the mind. It does not matter who you are, what you do, or where you live. As you mature spiritually, you will get a better understanding of what is going on in your mind, and hopefully that wisdom will translate into making the right choices more easily.

Proverbs 2:6 says, **"For the Lord giveth wisdom: out of his mouth cometh knowledge and understanding."** With knowledge of the truth from the Word of God, you will become better equipped to face intricate situations in life.

## Choose To Be Happy
### (Happiness Is a Choice)

Choosing to be happy plays a key role in your well-being. I feel as though I am in the best of health and I do make a conscious effort to eat healthy and exercise regularly. You would think that represents being over the hump with struggles to exercise daily and to stay fit. However, that is far from the truth. We have to decide every day to make the best choices in every area of our life. Of course, the easy way out would be to simply say, "I'll exercise later," or "Maybe I'll do it tomorrow."

**God needs innovators,
Not procrastinators.**

Each time we procrastinate, the will for us to postpone can get stronger and stronger. It is very important that we exercise our bodies and make a conscious choice to live a healthy and wholesome life so that we can serve God in the most efficient and effective way possible. Third John 2 NIV says, **"I pray that you may enjoy good health and that all may go well with you, even as your soul is getting along well."** God wants us to make the intelligent decision to faithfully serve Him, while at the same time reap all the perks included in His benefit package. Good health happens to be one of them.

All of our choices in life are important, some perhaps more than others, but not many are as important as the daily company that we choose. Did you know that your friends help determine the choices that you make? The company that you keep can also play a role in the outcome of your long-term happiness. The choice of who we spend time with and what we spend time doing is vitally important to our growth and success.

Proverbs 14:16 says, **"A wise man feareth, and departeth from evil: but the fool rageth, and is confident."** Proverbs 4:14-15 NIV says, **"Do not set foot on the path of the wicked or walk in the way of evil men. Avoid it, do not travel on it; turn from it and go on your way."** Do you need to discard some of your company? Are you traveling the path of bad company? Bad company can drain you of energy and rub off on you in ways that you never thought possible.

I remember my mother saying, "If you spend enough time with a person, you will eventually start to favor them." Of course, Mother was right. You do begin to favor them, but more importantly, you can emulate their contrary ways and negative thinking.

Listen to what Solomon said in Proverbs 13:20: **"He that walketh with wise men shall be wise: but a companion of fools shall be destroyed."** Nothing positive will ever happen for you when you persistently hang out with people who wander aimlessly with no vision and bring absolutely nothing to the table. If you continue to lodge with the unwise, you will indeed mimic them and eventually perish with them. If you want to latch on to someone, get with someone who is going somewhere. Get in the Word of God and start to mimic Jesus and work towards finding your pathway in the will of God. Your success will be thorough when you follow God's plan for your life and not the advice of someone who is headed down a dead-end street. All of the nourishment and instruction that you need for this journey are in the Word of God.

At some point, all of us have made unwise decisions. Unfortunately, some of us are still reeling as we struggle to make sense of these negative reflections. On the other hand, some of us who made bad decisions rebounded and never looked back. But none of our seemingly insurmountable struggles can justify not regrouping and making the choice to join the success team of God the Father, the Son Jesus, and the Holy Spirit. This choice is not like the court of law where you are given the benefit of the doubt, ensuring that you have entered a plea of not guilty by simply remaining mute. Do not confuse this procedure with not making a conscious choice to confess to serve Jesus. Failure to unequivocally choose Jesus ensures that you have penciled in Satan as your choice.

Romans 10:10 says, **"And with the mouth confession is made unto salvation."** You have to let your choice be known, so vote your true conviction. Psalm 1:1-2 says, **"Blessed is the man that walketh not in the counsel of the ungodly, nor standeth in the way of sinners, nor sitteth in the seat of the scornful. But his delight is in the law of the Lord; and in his law doth he meditate day and night."**

When you detach from spending time with the ungodly and shift that dead time towards saturating your mind and infiltrating your soul with the Word of God, you can't go wrong and you are guaranteed to find true happiness and prosperity. Your leaves will not wither, and your fruit will not only be good, but it will always be in season. That's not magical, that's real.

You know if there are certain people and habits that should be eliminated from your circle of life. Listening and receiving counsel or advice from people whom you know do not have your best interest at heart is fatal. Get your wisdom from God. Choosing to clock out the people whom you know should be expelled from your circle of life is another choice that you alone will have to make.

Real happiness is solidifying a personal relationship with God and spending time meditating in His Word. I know there are some of us who feel as though we will miss out on too much and simply refuse to find the time to spend in the Word. The truth of the matter is that once you start to spend quality time daily in the Word of God and your spiritual ears and eyes are opened, you will realize just how much you have missed out on by being away from His Word. No price tag or time frame can measure up to the final analysis. It's a habit that all of us need to improve or develop.

That may sound challenging, but why don't you try it and simply hold God to His Word? Remember what I said about eliminating ungodly advice and *all* of the bad company that you keep. Some of us are in the midst of bad company on a daily basis and we know what we need to do. We need to eliminate these people from our life, whether they are saved or not. Just be man or woman enough to make these life-changing decisions if you need to. Hanging around bad company is a hindrance to

## LIFE IS SO SIMPLE WHEN
### WE CHOOSE TO LOVE GOD'S WAY

your spiritual and personal growth. I am not advocating that you discard all of your friends. We all need friends and we need to get them on their pathway to the Kingdom of God as well.

You will have to use your ingenuity about the people in your circle who may be stifling your growth. God did not create us to sit around all day and engage in idle gossip or put labels on others, while trying to cover our own faults. You can take all of that to the nearest bank and not get one penny for it!

Each day presents new challenges, but we do not have to fall prey to them. There is nothing new that Satan can present to us regardless of how persistent he is with his application. James 4:7 says, **"Submit yourselves therefore to God. Resist the devil, and he will flee from you."** It is a simple choice. All of the deceptively enticing or falsely alluring things that Satan presents to us will only lead to sin, destruction, and eventually death.

**Ignore Satan and he will depart.**
**Choose you this day**
**To be happy with God.**

God will give you true happiness for a lifetime. When you choose to follow God's simple plan for happiness in your life, you will be successful in clearing another hurdle towards *choosing to love God's way*.

# Chapter 9

# Always Give Thanks (Simply Thank God)

> God sent His Son Jesus
> Who laid down His life
> For an infested world filled with sin.
> He came with love and paid the price,
> So I thank You, God, for Jesus,
> With every fiber of my heart,
> And for Your gift of salvation
> And a God-quality start!

Each morning when we arise, we should flag God down. Not to necessarily ask Him for anything nor to make any special request or to hand Him a petition. Instead, we should simply seek His face just to give thanks to Him for what He has already done.

I can't help but get high in my spirit when I think about the gift of salvation, along with all of the goodness and mercy that God continues to extend to all of us, which are totally unmerited. Psalm 107:1 says, **"O give thanks unto the Lord, for he is good: for his mercy endureth for ever."** If you really stop to think about it, to receive His tender mercy alone is worthy of a lifetime of praise. After all, His mercy endures forever and the last time I checked, "forever" is still a very long time!

Let's back up for a moment. This verse says God is good. Notice, it did not say that God *was* good, even though He has always been more than good to us, nor did it say that God *will be good*, yet we know that this is also true because of our hope that lies in Jesus. Instead, it proclaims, "God is good," and that's because the Word of God operates in the present tense and because He is a very present help who is available to all. Psalm 46:1 says, **"God is our refuge and strength, a very present help in trouble."** God's love and mercy are available right now regardless where you may be or how deep you have fallen.

If you will get into the Word of God, you will find solace in the midst of your circumstances. God is a lenient Judge, who grants mercy every day to those who humbly come before His court of justice, seeking mercy and forgiveness for all of our sinful behavior. Not only for our deliberate acts of wrongdoing, but also for the deeds in life that we should have done but didn't.

During past times in our lives, while we were in the world willfully sinning, God had mercy on us in that after we repented, He still did not give us what we justly deserved. This is incredibly good news, especially to those whose lives are still inundated with sinful behavior. You need to realize that even in your existing condition, God is still waiting on the opportunity to be merciful to you, if you would simply repent, believe, and receive His Son Jesus. It will never get any easier for us to do the right thing. There is still hope for all, which is just another reason for concerned families around the world not to give up. Instead, simply stop and give thanks.

David said in Psalm 122:1, **"I was glad when they said unto me, Let us go into the house of the Lord."** You will find rest, peace, and security in the house of the Lord. The house of the Lord can be found in His Word, and it is filled to repletion with His coverage and protection. There is simply no better place to meet God and leave your heavy loads, while receiving His never-ending guidance, than in the house of the Lord. There is supreme safety in the house of the Lord, as the Lord offers a protection plan for His children.

Psalm 9:9 says, **"The Lord also will be a refuge for the oppressed, a refuge in times of trouble."** Problems are solved in the house of the Lord, peace is found in the house of the Lord, healing is found in the house of the Lord, and of course, you will find love in the house of the Lord. God is love and the presence of His love abides throughout His house. We should be thankful that we can go to the house of the Lord where the doors are always open. I simply cannot think of a better place to visit on a daily basis than the house of the Lord. Even as we leave church on Sundays or during the week, the house of the Lord should continue to reside within each of us as we saturate our communities with His presence. The Spirit of the Lord should be eminent in our lives as we bear witness everywhere we go. What a resplendent God we serve! It just does not get any better than having the love of God and knowing just how much He cares.

David says in Psalm 34:1, **"I will bless the Lord at all times: his praise shall continually be in my mouth."** We have several reasons to continually praise the Lord as He hears our cries and answers our prayers. Think about anytime in your life when you were disconsolate and God was the only Source you knew you could go to. How can we ever thank Him enough for what He has already done? Take it a step further and reflect back on some of the thoughtless things you have done, some of the clandestine places where you have gone, and some of the erroneous decisions that you have made. You can find innumerable reasons why you ought to give thanks incessantly to our heavenly Father.

Even if you have experienced aggravated circumstances at some point in life, bear in mind that had it not been for the mercy of God, they could have been worse. No, it's not necessary that every time you open your mouth you have to quote scriptures or pretend to be any more sanctimonious than you really are. However, when you do open your mouth, nothing should ever come out that will defile you or bring grief to the Spirit of God. Ephesians 4:29 says, **"Let no corrupt communication proceed out of your mouth, but that which is good to the use of edifying, that it may minister grace unto the hearers."**

## LIFE IS SO SIMPLE WHEN
### *WE CHOOSE TO LOVE GOD'S WAY*

Indeed we are responsible and accountable for the counter-productive words that come out of our mouth. Some people are not just silently observing you, but they invest plenty of stock in the things you say. Corrupt communication can cause unforeseen problems. Everything said, made, and done by God is "very good." His goodness is but a microcosm of what He is, because He is always good all the time!

The Psalmist says in Psalm 92:1-2, **"It is a good thing to give thanks unto the Lord, and to sing praises unto thy name, O most High: To shew forth thy loving-kindness in the morning, and thy faithfulness every night."** If your focus and attitude are such that you stop and give thanks to our Creator each morning before you begin to take on any major task or project, this pleases God, and you are on the right path to "diligently seeking Him" first. Your faithfulness should begin first thing in the morning as you allow the Spirit of God to become deeply engraved in all of your subconscious thoughts and guide you in your actions throughout the day.

However, it must not stop there. Your prayers of thanksgiving must continue as you give reverence to God before retiring for the night. God is faithful to His Word throughout the day, and He guards our hearts while we sleep.

Psalm 32:8 says, **"I will instruct thee and teach thee in the way which thou shalt go: I will guide thee with mine eye."** God's Word instructs and teaches His faithful children the correct way to handle any situation, regardless of how high the odds are stacked or how complex or distant the solution may seem to be.

The Psalmist also says that God will guide you with His eye. For God to guide us with His eye does not simply mean that He will protect us, but He will also *watch and direct our actions* during the course of our life. There is no better guidance to have than the eye of God. Who knows where we would be if we did not have the eye of God to give us the proper guidance? We can't always know what's going on around us, from which direction the enemy is approaching, or where the next sign of trouble is brewing. But as long as we are under the watchful eye of the Creator, it really doesn't matter. I can look back over my life from previous experiences and know that there is indeed no higher guidance than the eye of God.

You must remember that in all of your praises, *consistency* is the key to the Kingdom. There are not enough words in any modern-day language to fully describe the effectiveness of consistently seeking God first. Matthew 6:33 should be cratered in the face of all the earth for men around the world to see and grasp. It can never be overstated. Jesus said, **"But seek ye first the kingdom of God, and His righteousness; and all these things shall be added unto you."** Have you ever given serious thought as to what things He will add? He will add all of the things you desire that are in line with His Word when you choose to be faithful.

Numbers 23:19 says, **"God is not a man, that he should lie. . . ."** He is the Spirit who cannot change His mind. There is no lack and there are no limits to the benefits and blessings that God will add to your life when you consistently seek Him and His righteousness first.

What is "righteousness"? His righteousness would include His commandments, statutes, beliefs, and views. We cannot accomplish any of these outside of Jesus. In other words, it entails having the mind of Jesus, living by His example, and showing compassion for others while denying yourself.

Jesus constantly showed compassion for people during His earthly love walk. In Luke 17:12-19, Jesus had mercy on ten lepers and healed them all. But after they were cleansed, only one of the ten returned to praise and glorify God. That's right, only one! Ten percent of us praising and thanking God is not nearly enough. The other nine did not think enough of the Person in the forefront, who was responsible for their supernatural healing, to turn around and simply say, "Thank You, God!"

Do you know what leprosy looks like? Most of the people who were infected with this dreadful disease had bodies that were severely deformed and mutilated. For the most part, they were shunned and banished from the general population. Anyone who has ever been made whole from any exacerbating situation should be forever thankful to Jesus for any semblance of relief.

These lepers were just like some of us today. God heals or blesses us supernaturally, or even delivers us from a painful situation, and sooner or later we are right back to our old vain behavior, thinking it was owed to us. We need to count our blessings on an everyday basis and keep our faith on the line, even thanking God in advance for our blessings that are in the rough, and the ones that are just around the corner.

Take a sheet of paper and divide it in half. On one side quickly list only a few of the reasons for which you are thankful. A good starting point would be:

> **The air we breathe.**
> **Our blood that flows.**
> **The rain that falls.**
> **The wind that blows.**
> **The sun that shines.**
> **Family and friends.**
> **The Word of God,**
> **From "in the beginning" to "Amen."**

It does not take long to name a few. Now, on the other side of that same sheet of paper, if you feel that you have no reasons to be thankful, hold up! Before you allow that thought to be entertained in your mind, there are a couple of things you need to do:

1. Get dressed and go visit the nearest nursing home in your neighborhood.
2. Go to the nearest community hospital just to peer in on some of the patients.

In order to feel the full effect of my point, you must be true and play fair. Don't go visit anyone specifically, at least not this

## Always Give Thanks
### (Simply Thank God)

time. Just walk up and down the corridors and stop and say hello and give an encouraging word to the first person that you feel needs it most. When you leave the first room, go to another room and visit someone else. Keep doing this routine until you are fatigued, you have seen enough, or you are exhausted. Then go home, get on your knees, and tell God, "Thank You for my existing condition. I have no reason to complain or to be ungrateful."

What we need to do is take our minds off of our circumstances and ourselves and simply focus on God and doing His work in the earth through serving others. Start giving God more praises by spending quality time in His Word and by attempting to encourage others. You may not always succeed, but at least it will afford you an opportunity to see just how much you have to be thankful for.

Spend more time in the Word with your spouse, family, and friends. Try introducing some stranger to Jesus or give more of yourself away to others who may not be as strong as you. What about that elderly aunt or uncle or that elderly person in the community with failing health who knew you as a child? Maybe they nurtured you or your relatives with words of wisdom or godly advice and prayed for you too when you did not know how to pray for yourself. Now it's their turn to receive encouragement.

They may be alone and don't have the mental or physical capacity to tend to their personal needs. Perhaps they are longing for someone to simply stop by. Most of them are reluctant about leaving their homes and they just need someone to come and visit and tell them that God has not forgotten them and He will never stop loving them.

As you give encouragement to someone else, watch the reasons to give thanks to God soar. Life is supposed to be a journey, not a destination. This life is just a temporary stop sign and it should be enjoyable. The grand finale is yet to come, and what you do or refuse to do with your God-given time, talent, and finances will play a major role in determining where you will spend eternity.

Each of us has the same twenty-four hours at our disposal. What are you doing with your time? If you are too busy to give something back to the Creator of the universe, the One who made you, loved you first, and sacrificed the best of all that He had for you, then you are entirely too busy! And if you are too busy to show someone who is lost in the world the way to eternal life through Jesus, the Savior of the world, who died for you before you were ever conceived, then you are way too busy.

Remember, heaven and hell are real places. All of us need to look back over our life and thank God for where He has brought us. Then, we need to make a list of all the people who helped us along the way and thank them too.

You simply cannot make it in this world by yourself. Seek God by staying in His Word and sharing it with others. This is the best way to crystallize your relationship with God through Jesus as you learn to *love God's way*. Staying in His Word will help you to stay on all of the right highways and off the shoulders in life.

As important as the Word of God is to us, we take entirely too many shortcuts. Most of us refuse to read the instructions to anything. We want our finished product to look like the picture on the box, but we do not want to read the instructions prescribed by the manufacturer. We purchase products every day and try to assemble them without first reading the instructions. Then we get discombobulated, so we go back and find the instructions and haphazardly read them to seek some guidance to assemble the product correctly.

We use this very same unsatisfactory principle every day in the mainstream of life when we attempt to live a successful life without reading the Word of God. We vehemently refuse to walk in the righteousness of God, yet when signs of trouble come our way, the first words to leave our mouth are, "Oh, my God," or "Help me, Jesus." Or we open up the Bible and conduct a cursory search to try and locate a scripture or two that is tailored for dealing with our condition. That's why it is imperative that we establish an account with heaven and make some deposits while our standing is good. It is almost impossible to open an account when you are bankrupt. And when you are spiritually bankrupt, you do not have the wisdom, the rationale, or the inclination to comprehend. Therefore, the Word of God will appear null and void.

The Word of God is your road map to a successful life here on earth, and it will successfully navigate you to the highway that leads to eternal life when you study and spend quality time in it. Whenever tribulations arise, the Word should already be burned in your spirit so you won't have to search hard to find the right passages. There are no benefits in being spiritually bankrupt.

Hebrews 11:6 says, "[God] **is a rewarder of them that diligently seek him.**" Whenever I think about a reward, I think about finding something of value that is lost or missing and the owner or some other interested person is willing to pay anyone who finds it and returns it. God rewards us when we are found and returned to Him, acknowledging that we were lost in sin. By our belief and acceptance of the love shown by Jesus Christ on the cross, it is proof that we have been found, identified, and reconnected to God. So through Jesus, all we must do according to Romans 10:9 is, **"Confess with thy mouth the Lord Jesus, and shalt believe in thine heart that God hath raised him** [Jesus] **from the dead, thou shalt be saved."** We are rewarded with the gift of salvation by His grace and everlasting mercy and immediately returned to His fold. This process renders us a new creature in Christ, and our new beginning officially starts.

God values each of us more than we could ever imagine, and He wants us to establish a personal relationship with Him through His Son Jesus. You are given a chance to improve your personal relationship with God each morning by giving Him thanks before starting your day. Then, continue to build your relationship throughout the day by praying, studying, and meditating on His Word.

The redemptive blood of Jesus Christ within itself deserves a "Thank You, God" each morning ahead of anything else we do. I look at thanking God first thing in the morning as answering roll call in the school of life. When I tell God, "Thank You for another day," I am essentially saying, "Present, Lord. I am here, ready for You to guide my steps so I can properly serve You." You must have your spiritual ears turned on and tuned in so you will hear and know all of the instructions that God has for you for the day. If you do not answer "present" by giving thanks, then by all accounts you must be absent!

Psalm 37:23-24 says:

**The steps of a good man are ordered by the Lord: and he delighteth in his way.**
**Though he fall, he shall not be utterly cast down: for the Lord upholdeth him with his hand.**

In this life, all of us are going to stumble at some point and maybe even fall. But we know that falling is not designed to be permanent because each of us was born with a talent to show who God is and what He is doing in our lives as well as what He can do for others. God is concerned with every aspect of our life. When you allow God to order your steps, you permit Him to manage your moves. So if you are trusting God to do what He said in His Word and He is holding your hand and guiding you every step of the way, tell me, *how can you fall, let alone fail?*

With God holding your hand, you simply cannot fall. The only time we fall is when we choose to break away from God's Word and try to do things on our own. In doing so, we disregard the advice of the Spirit. We decide of our own volition to go "solo," abandoning God's unchanging Word. The Word of God challenges us to continue in righteousness by charging us in Galatians 6:9 to **"not be weary in well doing: for in due season we shall reap, if we faint not."** In a nutshell, if you give up, you won't get your harvest, irrespective of how close you may be to the finish line. You must endure to the end. Don't get tired and give up doing what you know is right.

Sometimes to continue in righteousness may appear cumbersome and may involve a great deal of patience and longsuffering, but you must continue to trust and believe that *God's Word is the only way.* So just do it because when it comes to doing right, there is no end.

Habakkuk 3:18 says, **"Yet I will rejoice in the Lord, I will joy in the God of my salvation."** We should continue to be grateful to the Lord regardless of the things that we have had to endure because of our disobedience and inept decisions. Learn to be thankful for what Jesus has already done and believe that God will do according to His Word to bring you relief from any existing condition.

God is a sovereign God who only knows truth. Whenever we get out of God's will, we invariably contaminate His purpose for our life. Stay in the Word and continue to trust the truth. Only then will you know that the voice of the Spirit is commensurate with the context of His holy Word. You must become conversant with the Holy Spirit. If you are not familiar with the voice of the Spirit, you will be inclined to listen to the wrong voice and follow the wrong instructions. Whenever we take heed to the wrong advice, essentially we break away from God's hand and proceed on a collision course with a vehicle called failure.

Jesus said in John 14:26, **"But the Comforter, which is the Holy Ghost, whom the Father will send in my name, he shall teach you all things, and bring all things to your remembrance, whatsoever I have said unto you."** The Holy Ghost confirms the Word of God. Without the guidance of God's Spirit hovering over our life, we are doomed to fail. With the Holy Spirit, we have a personal Tour Guide, a Teacher with a plan for our life. I am talking about a present-day help of wisdom and guidance from the Spirit of God, who will not lead us wrong. But we have to choose to activate Him in our life.

Proverbs 2:6 says, **"For the Lord giveth wisdom: out of his mouth cometh knowledge and understanding."** Disobedience and hardheadedness are what cause us to fall and eventually fail. If you manage to hold on to God's unchanging Word, it will give you the confidence and courage to know that with Him you are never alone and you are indeed on the right path, the one that He has designed specifically for your life. If you have fallen, but you have managed to get back up and you are now serious about doing things God's way, He is still willing to guide you. But you must continue to hold His hand and heed His Word even after you get back on your feet or unfortunately you will run the risk of failing for life. This is simply another reason to give thanks to God, just knowing that our God is a God of another chance.

Who is Lord over your life? Be honest. What do you think about first thing in the morning? It's just a rhetorical question. However, it has been my experience that whatever we start thinking about first thing in the morning will have profound impact on what we do throughout the day. It is also a known truth that whatever is in your life that you think about most will be unconsciously magnified in your actions.

Proverbs 3:5-6 says:

**Trust in the Lord with all thine heart; and lean not unto thine own understanding.**
**In all thy ways acknowledge him, and he shall direct thy paths.**

Whatever dominates your mind on any given morning and you have determined that it's a good thing, then it should automatically include God! God wants us to depend on Him totally. We should never limit our thanks to God based solely on what He did yesterday or even what He is presently doing, but thank Him also for the supernatural blessings that are on the way. It is simply impossible for us to importune God. He is never too tired or too busy to listen and receive His children.

# Always Give Thanks
## (Simply Thank God)

**Acknowledge God in *all* you do,**
**Giving Him the praise and the glory**
**And the entire honor too.**

Even when we sit down to eat, it's a good thing to give thanks to God for the food that He continues to provide for us. Besides, anytime we eat, even while sitting at our own dining table, we have no idea what may have accidentally or deliberately been placed in our food. And in most cases, we are not even familiar with the food preparers or what type of processes our food has undertaken. Jesus always gave thanks to the Father before He ate or served others.

In John 6:11, it was only after Jesus had given thanks to God that He fed more than five thousand men, plus women and children. Giving thanks to God for our food is a way of not only thanking God for providing nourishment for our bodies, but it also assures us that we are still under His watchful eye, even as He gives us our daily bread. Now we can relax and enjoy our food wherever we eat. Psalm 23:5 says God **"preparest a table before me in the presence of mine enemies. . . ."**

In today's world, all of us welcome the additional benefit of security for ourselves and our families. We need and relish protection at every turn in society. We are not clairvoyant enough, regardless of the advancement of technology, or who says, "They will be looking out for us," to always know what's on the horizon. So it behooves us to thank God in advance for watching our backs, because without His omnipresent nature, we are severely handicapped with limitations as to what we can see and what we can do on our own. The enemy is camped all around us whether we see them or not.

It is simply to our advantage to seek God first each day whether things are good or not so good. Goodness has the tendency to fade away from every good thing in this world, but it will never fade away from the love of God. For each moment that God extends our life, it is simply out of His goodness, and it is certainly another reason to give Him thanks.

## LIFE IS SO SIMPLE WHEN
## WE CHOOSE TO LOVE GOD'S WAY

We ought to take the time to thank God each day that we are able to serve Him in a free society, and pray for the people who reside in other parts of the world who are oppressed and not able to serve Him freely. David says in Psalm 136:1, **"O give thanks unto the Lord; for He is good: for his mercy endureth forever."** Don't be ashamed to give thanks to God. Instead, encourage people with the compassion of Jesus to also give thanks and let the world know what a great and mighty God we serve.

In Psalm 119:7 David says, **"I will praise thee with uprightness of heart, when I shall have learned thy righteous judgments."** My dad died in 1985. My success in life is due in large part to the godly foundation and value system that was instilled in me as a child. If my dad was around today, I would thank him again and let him know just how much I appreciate him and my mother for building the right foundation for me when I was too small to even pick up a brick.

In Psalm 119, David says that when we learn better, we should simply do better. After he had sinned, God forgave him but He also admonished him. Maybe it took a little while for him to fully understand and accept the discipline, but eventually David was grateful to God, and he shows how he benefitted from God's chastisement by living upright and doing what he knows is the righteousness of God.

As young children we do not always appreciate the discipline and criticisms leveled by our parents or authority figures in our lives. However, as we mature and begin to reap the benefits of a good foundation, it becomes salient to us as to why the discipline was necessary. The Christian model for showing appreciation for God's love and His benefits is to walk upright and obey His Word. God cares and knows what is best for us even when we do not know, do not agree, or don't quite comprehend. More importantly, we should be like David and exhibit our praise and thankfulness to God in our living and by not letting go of His Word.

## Always Give Thanks
## (Simply Thank God)

Why fall when we simply do not have to? Isn't it good to know that we can benefit from the experiences of others, all throughout the Word of God, pain free and without ever partaking in the same situations? That's simply another reason for us to be grateful.

Sometimes in falling or in failing, we inadvertently take others down with us, causing some of our close relationships to become estranged. And even though the scars will always be there as a reminder, God wants us to mend and reestablish our friendly and wholesome relationships. His love for us and His Word will serve as a starting point. We should do a self-assessment at the end of each day and make improvements wherever needed. I am not talking about New Year's resolutions or setting unattainable goals. I once heard that the only New Year's resolution you need is to ask God for help. That is the down-to-earth truth!

Let me ask you this: Are you a better person than you were a year ago? Are you kinder, gentler, and more understanding? Are you more grateful? I thank God that since I yielded my life to Him that I am a better person. I say this not to gloat or to be high-minded, but instead with all honesty, all sincerity, and without fear of contradiction. By choosing to love God's way, we exude Christ-like confidence. This does not mean that we are to be arrogant or condescending. It's just having an aura of unshakable confidence in all matters of concern.

A personal relationship with God, trusting in His Word, and acknowledging Jesus as our Savior and Lord, simply works wonders. Matthew 5:45 says, **"For he maketh his sun to rise on the evil and on the good, and sendeth rain on the just and on the unjust."** The sun and the rain are two of life's essentials that none of us can survive without. The sun is our main source for heat and light, while rain has an abundance of usages. God provides these godly benefits to all of His precious creations regardless whether we are saved or not. That's simply another reason for all of us to give thanks because God shows a certain measure of love to every member of our families, in spite of sin, differences of opinions, or discrepancies in our love walk. We should strive to emulate His model of excellence.

Each day that God gives us should serve as a reminder to us to give thanks unto the Creator. After all, even those who are lost in the world have been given another day and another chance to make it right with God, through the redemptive blood of His Son Jesus. Luke, chapter 15, tells of the prodigal son who went out and squandered his inheritance after he requested and received it from his father. He fell so low that he was about to settle in a pig sty before he finally came to himself and decided to go home.

Each day that we spend away from God's protection is another day spent squandering our inheritance. This young man got another chance to be redeemed. Some of us may be sitting on our last chance, and because of our continual refusal to obey God's Word, we may be running low on opportunities. Paul forewarns us in Second Corinthians 6:2, **"Behold, now is the accepted time; behold, now is the day of salvation."** Jesus warns us in Matthew 24:44, **"Therefore be ye also ready: for in such an hour as ye think not the Son of man cometh."** It's not like we are not privileged to this information. God wants us to prepare today. The death, burial, and resurrection of Jesus crushed every imaginable fault in our life. There were no stones left unturned and no excuses will be acceptable for rejecting Him and not preparing for His return.

God has other levels in this life on earth, notwithstanding eternal life, that He wants us to experience along with a manifold of missions that we need to accomplish. But we must first give our life to Him through Jesus. You can have abundant life here in the earth through Jesus, which includes a good life, a complete life, and a successful life, while you prepare for eternity with God. That's another reason to simply say, "Thank You, God!"

God does not want us to mire in mediocrity and settle for anything less than His best. God is prodigious and He wants bold soldiers to step forward to do what we were commissioned to do in order to win more souls for Jesus. He wants us to have plenty of the best so we will be able to bless others and share with them godly wisdom in our quest to help them make the right decisions for their lives. But the truth is, you will never get there if your present lifestyle does not change and your mind-set is not renewed. Philippians 2:5 says, **"Let this mind be in you, which was also in Christ Jesus."** If it were impossible for us to have the mind of Christ, then why would the Apostle Paul make this appeal? Why would God allow it to be promulgated in His living Word? We have got to think Christ-like, mimicking His ways with love and compassion that obviously was His trademark.

It makes no difference who brings the adversity. There is simply no other way for us or to get others into the fold than to consistently follow the written Word laid out by God, and the life that was lived and exemplified by Jesus during His completed work on earth. No other way will succeed.

If you haven't already done so, why not give your life to Jesus and give the Word of God a chance to work in your life? The world might then see Jesus in your life and come to you to inquire what they must do to be saved. I simply thank God every chance I get that He loved me enough to give me another chance to make it right. He has also given you another opportunity because He loves you too and relishes the chance to pencil you into the family. Don't squander this opportunity. Come aboard today and live for Jesus by choosing *to love God's way*. I thank God in advance for the choice that you have made to live for Jesus. It is simply the best choice that you will ever make in your life.

# Chapter 10

# Know Your Role in Society (Simply Win Souls for Jesus)

Your role in society as a born-again Christian is vitally important for the furtherance of the Kingdom of God. Once you are saved and your name is etched in the Lamb's book of life, your assignment as an ambassador to the Kingdom of God begins.

One of the first orders of business for Jesus, as He saturated the earth with His love — being a compassionate model of consistency and our perfect example in both life and death — was to establish His discipleship in the earth. He began this assembly during the infancy stages of His earthly mission shortly after John baptized Him.

In Matthew 4:19 Jesus commanded the first of His chosen ones, Peter and his brother Andrew, to **"follow me, and I will make you fishers of men."** Just as His disciples were commissioned, we too, as saints of God and followers of Jesus, have been charged with this great commission to be fishers of men.

> We are commissioned
> To be "fishers of men,"
> To reel in as many souls
> For Jesus as we can!

As believers and representatives of God's Kingdom, this is our primary function, our mission statement if you will — *to win lost souls for Jesus.* Matthew 28:19-20 says:

## LIFE IS SO SIMPLE WHEN
## WE CHOOSE TO LOVE GOD'S WAY

> **Go ye therefore, and teach all nations, baptizing them in the name of the Father, and of the Son, and of the Holy Ghost:**
>
> **Teaching them to observe all things whatsoever I have commanded you: and, lo, I am with you alway, even until the end of the world.**

It is good to know that we have a Supreme Leader who will back us to the hilt as long as we abide in His Word and follow His divine instructions, even if the going gets tough and the way seems dim.

In today's society, there are many people in leadership positions who equivocate and unfortunately will not back their loyal followers or subordinates to the end. Some followers are even blamed for unforeseen difficulty, when obviously the fault lies within the leader. However, Jesus promised us that He would be with us **"even until the end of the world."**

Life is all about serving others and meeting their needs. Not only did Jesus commission us to be fishers of men, He commanded us to **"go ye therefore, and teach . . ."** (Matthew 28:19). It makes no difference what your occupation is. You may be a carpenter, an engineer, a cook, a mechanic, a professional athlete, or a custodian. Regardless of what you do or wherever you go, you should be reeling in souls for Jesus with every fiber of your being! Why do you suppose Jesus used the word "fisher" when conveying assignments to Peter and Andrew? Was it simply because they were fishermen? As mentioned earlier, God is meticulous about every word that He permits to be used in His holy Word. He is concise and to the point and He is not prone to wordiness. He chose to use the word "fisher" because fishermen are:

- Active — not lazy.
- Not shy.
- Talkative.
- Creative.
- Patient.

# Know Your Role in Society
## (Simply Win Souls for Jesus)

Usually fishermen have a calm demeanor. They are also autonomous and self-motivated. But at the same time, they are also very capable of working with others or even with a group. They have a penchant for attracting people with their stories, whether they are high or low in rank.

Fishermen are active workers who get up early, yet they have no problem if they must stay a little late just to get a catch. There are no time constraints in the life of a fisherman. We are all blessed with the same twenty-four hours in a day, so we must be willing to cast out for Jesus anytime we are called.

First Peter 5:7 says, **"Casting all your care upon him; for he careth for you."** One definition of "cast" means to send forth by throwing. Have you ever noticed how fishermen relax after they have cast out? That's the way God wants us to give our worries and concerns to Him. Simply cast them at His feet and forget about them. Whenever God gets ready to answer us, there will be movement on the line, and sometimes it catches us by surprise.

God wants us to trust Him and to have the faith to expect Him to answer, but at the same time, He also wants us to relax in such a manner that we actually forget all about those concerns and worries that we previously cast at His feet. God's response to our petition should catch us by surprise in the same manner that a fish rattles the line, whether it's within the hour or a short time later. What an awesome and wonderful God we serve!

Fishermen are talkative, not shy. They never meet a stranger. They realize that every person in life is important and that it doesn't cost a thing, but rather it pays, to at least speak to people or simply acknowledge them. We should always present ourselves to others with an aura that says, "I am approachable!" You never know what person God will use to get a blessing through to you, or who you might be called on to minister to. Remember, the squeaky wheel always gets the grease!

Fishermen are well represented at both ends of the spectrum, and they are creative. Fishermen have the proclivity to always make something happen. They are patient like Simon. Sometimes they toil all night and catch nothing (see Luke 5:5), but they heed wisdom and they are optimistic as they know that tomorrow is a brand-new day and that things can suddenly change for the better.

This is the attitude that the saints of God must have if we are to fish successfully for the Kingdom of God. Thank God for His patience. When you look at the large picture of this world, you can easily discern that there are several people trapped in the belly of sin in the same sense that Jonah was trapped in the whale's belly on account of his disobedience.

Who better to respond to this calling to reel them in than followers of Jesus, possessing the true characteristics of fishermen? However, the lost will never be found and reeled into a safe haven if we continue to walk in disobedience and do not follow the commission given to us by Jesus. People everywhere need the love, grace, and mercy of God. They need to know that God loves them, regardless of where they have been or what they have done.

So now that you are saved and you have your set of orders, what are you doing? Are you reeling in souls for the Kingdom of God? He has guaranteed us security in that He will always be with us **"even unto the end of the world"** (Matthew 28:20). Jesus said, **"All power is given unto me in heaven and in earth"** (Matthew 28:18). There is no doubt about the commitment or surety in the Word of God, but what about us? What about the challenge that lies before us?

Jesus said in John 14:15, **"If ye love me, keep my commandments."** The word "commandment" is in plural form. This passage of Scripture is our mirror, designed as a looking glass for us to conduct a daily self-evaluation. Each of us probably looks in a mirror every day to see if we are presentable, making adjustments as needed. Each morning we should evaluate our love walk with the same emphasis, and again whenever we retire for the day, ensuring that we are loyal to the banner of our high calling.

Nothing should be misconstrued about our love for God. Quite simply, if we love God, Jesus has charged us to show our love, honor, and commitment to Him by simply obeying His Word and keeping His commandments. We are called to be men and women of God, representing and adhering to the highest principles and standards of Jesus, purposely doing well in all that we do as we minister to the needs of others. This is how Jesus lived His life, and we are to follow His lead.

We are not sedentary creatures, designed to sit around all day, leaving the Kingdom of God unattended or to simply work five days a week from 9:00 to 5:00 and live for the Kingdom of God on the weekends. As born-again Christians, we are members of the Body of Christ, an awesome membership that's afforded to all. But we must be about more than just membership. We need to be active members. Our full service is needed. You cannot serve God and help recruit for His Kingdom if you are not an active member in the Body of Christ. All parts of the Body are connected. Therefore, we must function together as one Spirit-filled muscle in order to do all of what we were designed to do. As members of the Body of Christ:

> **We are all different parts,**
> **Playing different roles.**
> **Blessed in different ways,**
> **But all winning souls.**

The Apostle Paul says in Romans 12:1, **"I beseech you therefore, brethren, by the mercies of God, that ye present your bodies a living sacrifice, holy, acceptable unto God, which is your reasonable service."** We are to present our bodies, not as dead sacrifices, but as living sacrifices. Everything living should be about God's business of representing His Kingdom in the earth, while everything dead ought to be buried. Psalm 150:6 says, **"Let every thing that hath breath praise the Lord. . . ."**

## Life Is So Simple When
### WE CHOOSE TO LOVE GOD'S WAY

The days of presenting dead animals as a sacrifice to God are over. Jesus made the ultimate sacrifice and cleared the way for us. If you are alive, that means you not only exist, but your existence should be active as you have been charged with presenting back to God a portion of whatever He has blessed you with in a manner that is befitting to your heavenly Father. Our bodies are whole and should be holy as God is holy. We can no longer say one thing and do another if we profess to live in Christ and are new creatures. Our bodies should represent the very core of righteousness as we offer every ounce of our being back to God. This would also include your talent! So whatever talent God has blessed you with, use it for His glory.

In Matthew 25:14-30, Jesus strongly advises us that we are to be more than perfunctory Christians who simply go through the motions to merely get results, never stepping outside of our comfort zones to give Him compounded interest on His investments in us. God wants us to use our talents to win souls for Jesus and to bring Him all the praise, glory, and honor. He wants us to be prolific in our endeavors and not to mire in mediocrity. You should never compare your reasonable service with that of someone else, because if each of us would utilize our talent to the full potential, we would be able to clearly see that one person's talent carries no more weight or value than the next.

If you have questions about an idea or a talent that you feel God has blessed you with, pray about it, talk to God, and listen to the Spirit as He gives you guidance. If necessary, share your concerns with a Christian friend, with your ministry, or with spiritual leadership in your local church to see in what way your talent can be utilized to bless the Kingdom of God. If you honestly do not know, you need to ask. Information and knowledge are power, and God requires that all of our talents be utilized. Give yourself away doing the works of God.

Many people in the Body of Christ are simply present, and they are not totally engaged in doing what they are called to do. They refuse to reach down inside and find that extra gear that will allow them to utilize their talent to an optimal level of potential, that will fully benefit the Kingdom of God while propelling themselves to another level.

Paul says that you should present your body, and this presentation is your reasonable service. Think about this for a moment. There is nothing spectacular about you presenting your reasonable service. Appreciation and thank you's are always great and wonderful. God wants us to encourage our sisters and brothers in the household of faith. However, your reasonable service is what God expects from you, what is generally required of you.

Your reasonable service is your fair or moderate service based on your God-given talent. It calls for using all that God has equipped and blessed you with for the edification and furtherance of His Kingdom. Through this simple act of obedience, your talent is given back to God as you magnify His name while engaged in serving others.

God is not pleased when we talk one way but live another. Hebrews 11:6 says, **"But without faith it is impossible to please him. . . ."** It is easy for us to talk faith, but what do you presently have your faith on the line for? We should not be satisfied with giving back only a smidgen of what God has blessed us with or to simply go through the motions. To give God only a fraction of what He has given us would be to sandbag God. The Word of God is not unreasonable. When you make a sacrifice or offering, you are simply giving up something good that has a far lesser value than what stands to be gained through your act of obedience.

The main sacrifice that we need to make for the furtherance of the Kingdom of God is to simply give Him more of our time. But regardless of how long you live on this earth, you and I could never sacrifice enough time to equate what Jesus did for us on the cross, nor is the sacrifice of any of our time or possessions commensurate to the eternal life that God has promised for those of us who love and live in Jesus.

## Life Is So Simple When
## WE CHOOSE TO LOVE GOD'S WAY

Jesus said in Matthew 9:37-38, **"The harvest is truly plenteous, but the labourers are few; pray ye therefore the Lord of the harvest, that he will send forth labourers into his harvest."** The *New International Version* says, **"The harvest is plentiful but the workers are few. Ask the Lord of the harvest, therefore, to send out workers into his harvest field."**

Jesus uses the adverb "truly" in the *King James Version* as an intensifier to describe to us the plenteous nature of the harvest. Jesus is talking to His followers of today. This is His State of the Universe message to us. He gives us the status of the universe, and he culminates by telling us what we can do to rectify the existing condition. We should simply pray to God and ask Him for additional workers.

Proverbs 15:29 says, **"The Lord is far from the wicked: but he heareth the prayer of the righteous."** There is an enormous harvest waiting for us. In other words, it is prime time for winning souls. We need some go-getters for God. There is so much work in the Kingdom of God that needs to be done and not nearly enough workers. Jesus is the One who is making this claim and delivering this heart-piercing message to us. Can you think of anyone else remotely qualified to give us a more accurate assessment of the existing condition, or to predict what is needed to carry out the will of His Father than Jesus Himself? We should never be satisfied in doing only what is expected of us. We need to pray early and pray often. Be obedient and reflect on Jesus' State of the Universe message. Pray for more laborers to be sent into the harvest.

When we fail to do what is expected of us, we not only fail God, but we fail the Body of Christ. There is no reason for us to experience failure in the Body of Christ, especially if we work and pray together. We must not permit dampers of any kind to be placed on the ministry of Jesus.

Second Timothy 1:7 says, **"For God hath not given us the spirit of fear; but of power, and of love, and of a sound mind."** To be equipped with these qualities means that we are spiritually, mentally, and physically qualified to do whatever God has sanctioned us to do. God is a God of excellence. Whatever your reasonable service or talent may be, it must be acceptable unto God. Your talent has to be a thing of acceptable quality, approbated by God Himself. God will not settle for anything other than your best.

If you have doubts about whether God values your offering, simply go back to Genesis, chapter 4, and read the story of Cain and Abel, the sons of Adam and Eve. Note with special attention the sequence of events that led Cain to commit one of the most heinous crimes in the history of mankind. In short, Cain offered God an unacceptable and faithless offering, going through the motions after his brother Abel had given God his best offering in faith.

Hebrews 11:4 says, **"By faith Abel offered unto God a more excellent sacrifice than Cain, by which he obtained witness that he was righteous, God testifying of his gifts: and by it he being dead yet speaketh."** Cain simply went through the motions. There was neither faith nor heart in his offering. Cain's less than satisfactory offering led him to kill his own brother.

Every week, countless incidents are reported from around the world as a result of some form of jealousy. It is mind-boggling as to how any saint in the Body of Christ could become jealous of another person, let alone another saint, when all we have to do is to ensure that we ourselves are giving God our best effort while standing on our faith and abiding in His Word. We all have the same rights in Christ.

I don't know about you, but it takes me all of my twenty-four hours to keep up with what I should be doing to ensure that what I do is acceptable unto God. The more you give back to God of what He has blessed you with, the more He will bless you in return. Jealousy is a pretext to many of our problems in society. Every day people become immensely covetous of others as they lunge with all their might to keep up with the Joneses. But when we keep our minds stayed on God, doing the things

## Life Is So Simple When
## WE CHOOSE TO LOVE GOD'S WAY

He requires us to do, we will be momentarily dazed at how God will move in this earthly realm, not just on our behalf but in the best interest of our neighborhoods as well. Every day we see how the character or behavior of one person can affect an entire community, state, or country.

Second Chronicles 7:14 says:

**If my people, which are called by my name, shall humble themselves, and pray, and seek my face, and turn from their wicked ways; then will I hear from heaven, and will forgive their sin, and will heal their land.**

This passage of Scripture is applicable to the problems in today's society. It cites three things that we, as children of God, need to do to hear from heaven and for the Word of God to work in bringing about relief for us in our social ills:

1. We must humble ourselves and pray.
2. We must seek the face of God.
3. We must turn from our wicked ways.

These are the results. God will:

1. Hear from heaven.
2. Forgive our sins.
3. Heal our land.

I am sure you will agree that the world in which we live needs healing that only heaven can bring. But until we are in compliance with the Word of God from His perspective, the healing process will not proceed. So first, according to this passage of Scripture, we need to *humble ourselves and pray*. If we are not humble, then we must be proud or haughty and perhaps we need to bring our attitudes down a peg or two! James 4:10 says, **"Humble yourselves in the sight of the Lord, and he shall lift you up."**

Before going to God for anything, make sure that your attitude has been adjusted, your ego has taken a vacation, and your self-importance has called in sick. In other words, take off your mask and just be you. The Lord already knows who you are and what things you have need of. Get your heart right as you approach His throne of mercy, and in due time He will lift you up.

God is not impressed with our ability to dramatize. We have of our own doing overpriced ourselves, having formed self-made assumptions based totally on our status symbol and what others are saying about us. When we put too much stock in these biodegradable values, it tends to make us look down upon others, perhaps thinking just a little bit more of ourselves than we should. These types of attitudes and dispositions do not please God. Obviously, it's okay to be happy with our accomplishments and achievements. There is nothing wrong with that. But don't overestimate yourself.

Every now and then go back to the yardstick of Calvary, and you will again see that none of us are remotely deserving of the unmerited favor that God has given to us through the death of His Son Jesus. So when you go to God, know who you are, but more importantly, know who He is. Allow God to exalt you through His Word. When He elevates you, you can be secure and never have to be concerned about failure. As long as you continue to abide in His Word, you won't take a fall.

There are hindrances that will keep our prayers from getting through to God: sin, disobedience, and doubt, to name a few. Of course, this list is not all-inclusive, but it's a good starting point.

There is no doubt that sin will keep the prayer line busy. Psalm 66:18 says, **"If I regard iniquity in my heart, the Lord will not hear me."** This passage of Scripture is terse and goes right to the subject matter. In other words, whenever we knowingly shelter evil in our hearts and delight ourselves in the pleasures of wickedness, God turns a deaf ear to our prayers. Consequently, our prayers will not have the velocity or the fuel to make it out of our prayer closets.

Proverbs 28:9 says, **"He that turneth away his ear from hearing the law, even his prayer shall be abomination."** Any person who deliberately disregards the law, or what is right, and has a penchant for disobedience, according to this passage, his prayers are detestable. If you turn a deaf ear to godly instructions, a deaf ear will be turned to your prayers.

The third hindrance to unanswered prayers is *doubt*. James 1:6-7 says, **"But let him ask in faith, nothing wavering. For he that wavereth is like a wave of the sea driven with the wind and tossed. For let not that man think that he shall receive any thing of the Lord."**

The cornerstone of our belief is the resurrection of Christ in that God supernaturally raised Him from the dead. This is where our faith starts. Remember, without faith it is impossible to please God. So if you go to God in prayer, weaving back and forth with a barrelful of doubt, don't expect any returns from Him! There can be no vacillating or wavering when we approach the throne of our heavenly Father for anything. James says this person will get absolutely nothing.

Matthew 6:7-8 says:

> **But when ye pray, use not vain repetitions, as the heathen do: for they think that they shall be heard for their much speaking.**
> **Be not ye therefore like unto them: for your Father knoweth what things ye have need of, before ye ask him.**

Neither your loftiness with words nor your ability to verbalize gives you a decisive edge when praying to God. He sees your heart and He does not give extra weight or head-of-the-line privileges simply because of the length of your prayers. Jesus never wasted words. He was always succinct and to the point. Our heavenly Father does not oppose a petition or a lengthy prayer for that matter. Occasionally, Jesus prayed for long periods of time. In Mark 14:37-39, Jesus prayed for an hour. Afterwards, according to verse 39, **"He went away, and** prayed, and spake the same words." Luke 6:12 says, **"And it came to pass in those days, that he went out into a mountain to pray, and continued all night in prayer to God."** Jesus prayed all night before choosing His twelve disciples the next day.

God sees your heart and He knows all about your concerns and your motives long before you ever prepare to pray. He is simply not impressed or additionally moved just because of the length of our prayers or the use of extravagantly colorful words that may only serve as an extension of arrogance. It's really okay to go boldly to the throne to tell your heavenly Father how you feel, what you want, or how much you hurt. Be mindful that God alone is sovereign and excellent, so be real when you pray to God about anything.

God wants us to seek His face, to seek His presence. When you seek God, that implies that you are really going after His presence because you want to saturate your life with Him. When you begin to rigorously search and investigate for God in His Word, you will find Him. You will find Him through His Son Jesus. Jesus said in Luke 10:22, **"All things are delivered to me of my Father: and no man knoweth who the Son is, but the Father. . . ."** The more you stay in His Word, the more He will reveal Himself to you. Moreover, when you seek the Lord and find Him, just delight yourself in Him. Then, as you delight in Him, **"He shall give thee the desires of thine heart"** — the desires that are consistent with His Word (Psalm 37:4). Seek God as though you are lost, left totally in the dark, and the outcome of your life is predicated on your finding Him. When you start your quest to seek God, simply:

**Search the Scriptures,**
**All of them.**
**Study and pray**
**And you'll find Him!**

The key is to seek Him on a *consistent basis*. I cannot overstate the importance of establishing a personal relationship with God through Jesus. He is indeed concerned about every subdivision of your life. The more you seek Him, the more salient His Spirit becomes.

The third thing that we must do is *turn from our wicked ways*. Simply put, some of us who profess to be saved are still flirting with disaster. "To turn" means to take another direction or to invert or change positions. It means, "I am not ever going back." "To go back" simply means that you did not complete your turn and you are all over the place. You still lack scruples and you are morally challenged. Your heart is not right in the sight of God. It does not matter who you are or what you have done. You have within your heart the God-given ability to make the change. You must give up your sinful ways. No habit of the world is worth your salvation.

Often, we see or hear about so-called incorrigible children who refuse to submit to what their parents or authoritative figures instruct them to do. Wrong is wrong and one wrong is never palliated by another wrong. But could it be that some parents and adults in authoritative positions are living double lives? In other words, they insist "do what I say, not what you see." As a result, some of our children refuse to obey or respect us or our advice because we are asking things of them that are incongruous or not in accordance with our own love walk.

And so it is with some of the people in the world that we are trying to win to Jesus. They see us being sanctimonious on Sundays and back to the world Monday through Saturday. Mark 7:15 says, **"There is nothing from without a man, that entering into him can defile him: but the things which come out of him, those are they that defile the man."**

People in the world are very judgmental of us. They place our lives under the scope as they climb their towers to watch our every action outside the walls of the church. Some people in the world have straddled the fence as they carefully watch to see if we are living examples of what we preach and what we teach before they commit to follow us. Even though we don't see them, they are seated in the round, watching us as they come to periscope depth to see whether we are walking the walk or just talking the talk.

As strange as it may sound, most people respect what we do in Christ even though they are not yet followers and have not been mentally transformed. It's just that they don't seem to like hypocrites! There is nothing out of character with checking out the behavior of leadership or the followers of an issue, organization, or a particular movement when considering becoming a member. Do your homework and seek the information and knowledge for yourself. Quite frankly, it is a sensible and intelligible thing to do. Some people are right in the midst of making the decision that will ultimately change the course of their life. They are in search of that model direction, so they understandably monitor us carefully.

As Christians, we should never be remotely connected to any knowingly unprincipled behavior, let alone bring dishonor or discredit to the Kingdom of God from our own misbehavior. Remember, we are connected and our performance should be united as one Body in Christ. One dishonorable act by any member of the Body will cause pain for the entire Body. We should strive to live for Jesus with ironclad minds that are:

**Fully persuaded
And totally committed
To work for His Kingdom
With integrity unlimited.**

When we humble ourselves, we become submissive to the will of God. We start by throwing arrogance and high-mindedness out the window. This affords us the opportunity to take on the mind of Jesus and to fill that void with the written Word of God, as His presence becomes evident that we have permitted the Holy Spirit to get involved in our life.

Romans 8:16 says, **"The Spirit itself beareth witness with our spirit, that we are the children of God."** In other words, the Holy Spirit supports and confirms us. But in order for the Spirit to confirm us, we must be able to communicate with Him. Praying in the Spirit is an important weapon for development in the life of a Christian as we build up our spirit man on the inside, preparing to worship God in spirit and in truth. Every Christian needs this powerful weapon.

Being raised in a traditional church setting, I was not taught nor was I conversant with the power of speaking in "unknown tongues." I was a member of the same church for many, many years. Today, I still consider it to be a loving church even though I have since moved to another church home. My aim in broaching this subject is not to denigrate any group of saints representing the Body of Christ. However, as children of God, we should all want the very best of whatever our heavenly Father has to offer.

I was totally in the dark and credulous concerning the knowledge and power of this spiritual weapon as it was never really discussed. This is a tremendously wonderful tool that no Christian should ever be without.

For training purposes only, imagine going hunting and being down to your last bullet, when suddenly you look up and see something coming your way that you know you cannot handle alone. You begin to pray to God with your understanding while at the same time taking aim to fire. That's okay if that's all you have at your disposal. But wouldn't it be to your advantage to know that you also have another weapon that is not only undeniably accurate but fully loaded and more than capable of taking care of that situation in a way that you could never do with all of your understanding and only one bullet?

I am sure there have been times when you have gone to God in prayer and prayed what you thought was a good prayer. You covered all your bases, but immediately you realize that there was someone or even another concern that totally escaped your mind that you forgot to include in your prayer. You will never have the manpower or the clairvoyance to pray the gambit or to pray for all of the things that you need at one prayer setting, let alone the unforeseen or the unexpected things that you may encounter by simply praying with your understanding. But to pray in unknown tongues, having the Holy Spirit intercede on your behalf, while building yourself up spiritually, is a benefit that is right at your fingertips.

If you are not in a Bible-based church that gives you this information and teaches the importance of the power of speaking in unknown tongues, seek the information for yourself and then make an intelligent decision on your own as to whether or not it is to your benefit to have it. It is advantageous and prudent to know that this information, knowledge, and wisdom from God are available to all saints the minute you give your life to Jesus. But the choice of whether or not to utilize it is yours and yours alone to make.

Romans 8:26-27 says:

> **Likewise the Spirit also helpeth our infirmities: for we know not what we should pray for as we ought: but the Spirit itself maketh intercession for us with groanings which cannot be uttered.**
> **And he that searcheth the hearts knoweth what is the mind of the Spirit, because he maketh intercession for the saints according to the will of God.**

The Holy Spirit validates us as children of God as He intercedes for us. He also aids us whenever we pray for others in the Spirit, because often we are not sure what is in the best interest of our friends or what they may need or desire at the time when we remember them in our prayers. Even when we pray with our understanding, we don't always know the ramifications of our answered prayers, even though our intentions are always good. But when you pray in the Spirit, you can rest assured that the Holy Spirit's intercessory prayers are always on the same page as the will of God. Our ever-present help in the Comforter not only validates us and watches our backs, but He also intercedes to God in our best interest.

Another benefit to praying in unknown tongues is that Satan is clueless regarding our spiritual lingo. He is not keen enough to figure out how to translate the utterances of unknown tongues to establish a new game plan. This is an incantation that he will never have!

Our cares are in the presence of God whenever the Spirit intercedes through our spiritual prayers. He represents our best interest in the will of God and through Him we get head-of-the-line privileges. God then faces us as He hears our prayer. When God is turned away from us, or rather when we have turned away from Him, it simply implies that our prayers are ineffective and God does not hear them. Therefore we can't hear from heaven. In other words, we do not meet the standards for our prayers to be maximized and expedited.

James 5:16 NIV says, **"The prayer of a righteous man is powerful and effective."** We should strive daily to model Jesus so we can communicate effectively with our heavenly Father at any time. Whenever we work the Word of God in our life, God hears from heaven and we will hear from Him.

As children of God, we ought to know and want to hear the voice of our heavenly Father as often as we can. Suffice it to say, we will never get to know His voice if we do not spend adequate time in His Word and foster a personal relationship with Him.

If it were possible for our heads to be unscrewed to pour wisdom from God into them to simplify the assimilation process, we could work around some of the redundancy. But since you and I both know that this is impossible, we must rely on repetition. *Repetition is the key to retention.* Only then will you begin to feel comfortable with approaching God to boldly tell Him what He said in His Word and all of the promises He included.

When we consistently seek His face, we delight in wanting to be in His presence, and we become eager to carry out His will for our life. I'm sure you have heard of professional athletes, namely basketball and baseball players, being in a zone or a level of completeness where there seems to be a period during a game, a tournament, or a series of games where they experience a seemingly never-ending streak of success.

Whenever I go into my prayer closet and pray and experience His presence, I feel like I'm in a zone too. By the way, professional athletes must wait until game day or they must go to an arena, their practice facilities, or a gymnasium to work out and find their zone. But as saints of God, our prayer closet can be in the car, at a restaurant, at work, or even in the presence of our enemies. Any Christian desiring to get into a zone with God can do so every day without working up a sweat! The feeling is one engrained with supernatural love, joy, and peace. The serenity is so evident that it almost feels like a dream, but it's not a dream. It's real! You will never experience the true presence of God or get into a zone with Him if you are not seeking Him diligently and learning His ways.

As children of God, it is a blessing to know that we are never at a disadvantage. You will find that you have at your disposal more than enough time to spend with God if you would only choose to turn your life from meaningless things and take aim at pleasing Him. Once we have accomplished this, God will tune His ear to hear our earnest petitions. In other words, we will be raised from among the living dead and become alive in our new life as a result of simply choosing to consistently stay lined up with His Word. Our sins will be forgiven and the consistency in our love walk will fare well for us in our recruitment effort in the world for the Kingdom of God. God's Word will go forward in our life and in society once we get into it, do what it says, and then execute in our life what we were created to do.

Think about it. Your body does not function fluently when its members do not perform in unison. So why on earth should we expect God to move on our behalf when the Body of Christ is not in one accord? Remember, we must go through Jesus to please the Father. We are the Body of Christ, and it is entirely our fault for any deficiencies that the Body may experience, simply because although connected, we are still not working together as all parts should to make the Body move correctly.

## LIFE IS SO SIMPLE WHEN
## WE CHOOSE TO LOVE GOD'S WAY

I am so glad that sending Jesus to die on the cross for our sins was not predicated on us utilizing our time and talents for God's Kingdom. As a matter of fact, Jesus had to reconnect us to God because through hardheadedness and disobedience, we lost our connection. Through His act of unselfish love, we were redeemed and are now able through Jesus to do all that we were called to do.

In Romans 12:2, Paul says, **"And be not conformed to this world: but be ye transformed by the renewing of your mind, that ye may prove what is that good, and acceptable, and perfect, will of God."** Why are we so into being like everyone else, rather than being like the only One who really matters? For Paul to say, **"Be not conformed to this world"** obviously means that there is another world that awaits us. Jesus said in John 8:23, **"Ye are from beneath; I am from above: ye are of this world; I am not of this world."** We cannot continue to mimic our present world and expect to reach the world for Jesus. He made it impressionably clear in Matthew 6:24 when He said, **"No man can serve two masters: for either he will hate the one, and love the other; or else he will hold to the one, and despise the other...."**

As born-again Christians, our main focus must be on God's Kingdom and not on the world in which we live. God knew that our minds would have to be retooled. This is why Paul emphatically reminds us to renew our mind. Our minds must be made over by rooting out the old and planting His Word in its place. But we cannot renew our minds if we have not accepted Jesus and if we are not in the Word of God, adhering to the wisdom that He prescribes for our life on a daily basis.

John 1:1 says, **"In the beginning was the Word, and the Word was with God, and the Word was God."** Between the times Jesus ascended to the Father and our present-day status, a drastic transformation has taken place in this world. Over a period of time, society has gradually removed the **Word** from the world. The w-o-r-l-d minus the Word leaves us with an "l."

# Know Your Role in Society
## (Simply Win Souls for Jesus)

This pernicious transition left us with the small letter "l," which symbolizes **lost.** Simply put, we are taking the Word out of the world, and consequently, we are lost in the world without the Word. We are permitting Satan to steal the Word out of this world. This is the simple unadulterated truth about what we are allowing to take place in our homeland. The world is the place where we should absolutely saturate and act out the Word of God on a daily basis.

Without the saints of God taking on our roles of filling the world everywhere we go with God's presence through His Word and by living out His example, some people may never hear or know the truth about Christ and may never become knowledgeable enough to experience a Spirit-filled, God-quality lifestyle, full of the love that He created in each of us. In other words, they will remain lost. To them, the road to eternal life will remain a mystery.

The light to life is found in the Word of God. And now that we have found it through Jesus, we must become the lights to lead others to Him. Failure to use our light to lead others out of the wilderness simply means that they will continue to stumble in darkness. And regardless of how successful they think they are, their life on earth will continue to be dominated by struggles until their spirits, bodies, and souls (the soul includes the mind, will, emotions, and intellect) are permeated with the Word of God. This permeation translates into them, joining us in refurbishing the world with the Word.

Remember, we are the Body of Christ, moving and working together to carry out the works of the Lord. All it takes is for one member to fail to do his or her part and we will have a less than positive effect on the expansion of God's Kingdom. The converse is a united stand for the Kingdom of God that will invigorate a hope in Christ for the lost. Each of us has an incomparably different talent, yet all of our roles are critical and designed to work dependently for the advancement of the Kingdom of God.

## LIFE IS SO SIMPLE WHEN
## WE CHOOSE TO LOVE GOD'S WAY

Jesus said in Matthew 12:30, **"He that is not with me is against me; and he that gathered not with me scattereth abroad."** In essence, if you are not helping, you are hurting. Not helping also includes doing nothing. Only when your mind is renewed will you be receptive toward receiving your divine orders for your life in the will of God. Whenever this is executed, the world sees more of the wondrous works of God and begins to glorify Him through Jesus. We seem to find time to do everything that we want to do, yet out of the twenty-four hours in a day, most of us profess to be too busy to find one uninterrupted hour a day to study the Word of God. Yet the Word can give us specifics as to what is required to be successful in this life and in the world to come.

Whenever we delight ourselves in God, Psalm 37:4 says, **"He shall give thee the desires of thine heart."** "Shall" implies a mandatory action. Simply put, when we exhibit great pleasure in pleasing God, He takes pleasure in accommodating our desires. He will give us what we want just because we are His obedient children, looking out for His best interests.

God's Word does not put a limit on what He can or will do for us when we remain indomitable in our faith. Our limits are hatched when we refuse to monitor what we say and what we allow to ruminate in our minds. How many tricks does Satan need to show us before we realize what his game plan is? It's simple" Steal, kill, and destroy (see John 10:10). That's all we need to know about him. He represents nothing good. We should all be conversant about his modus operandi (M.O.). If we would just peer in at the world, we can surmise how Satan uses people every day to keep us at bay and at odds with one another.

We need to keep our radar locked in on Jesus and what He did for all of mankind. God wants His special creations to have every available benefit in His package. He wants to heal our land, and He wants us to experience a spirit of abundance in every area of our life. Essentially, what each one of us needs to do to help make this a reality is:

## Know Your Role in Society
### (Simply Win Souls for Jesus)

1. Spend time studying the Word of God.
2. Pray always.
3. Spend time ministering the Word of God to unbelievers.

The abundant life and eternal life that God promises are to be shared. We should want our families, friends, and enemies as well to enjoy this complete life benefit package. Remind them that while there are no limits or shortages in God, any further delay to choose Jesus as Savior and Lord may prove costly.

Acts 5:27-29 says:

**And when they had brought them, they set them before the council: and the high priest asked them,**

**Saying, Did not we straitly command you that ye should not teach in this name? and, behold, ye have filled Jerusalem with your doctrine, and intend to bring this man's blood upon us.**

**Then Peter and the other apostles answered and said, We ought to obey God rather than men.**

Every born-again child of God should take time out from our jobs and demanding schedules, and grab as many unsaved hands as we can lay hold of and lead them to the Word of God in an all-hands evolution to *simply love God's way*. We must do as Peter and the other disciples did and choose to obey the Word of God by spreading the love and compassion of Jesus throughout the world, regardless of the opposition. We must take a bold stand for God promulgating the Good News of salvation as we campaign to win back what is rightfully His and put an end to this downward spiral of people headed for eternal damnation.

Have you won any souls for Jesus lately? As saints of God, we must start an all-out war that stretches to all corners of the globe with a universal motive: *To win souls for Jesus!* Jesus stresses in John 14:12, **"Verily, verily, I say unto you, He that believeth on me, the works that I do shall he do**

## LIFE IS SO SIMPLE WHEN
## WE CHOOSE TO LOVE GOD'S WAY

**also; and greater works than these shall he do; because I go to my Father."** Now that Jesus has ascended to the Father and is seated at **"his own right hand in heavenly places"** (Ephesians 1:20), what are you doing? Jesus incontestably states that we are to do **greater works** than He did (John 14:12). *Simply loving God's way* is a great way to start.

Most of us will live much longer than Jesus lived on earth. He could only travel by foot, horseback, or by ship. Our modes of transportation are unlimited and we certainly are advanced with cars not to mention planes and trains. So what are we waiting for? Who among us can afford to wait another day to share Jesus with someone? While Jesus was in the world, He worked the field for His Father until the very end. His work is completed. Now we must be about the business of spreading the Word and expanding the Kingdom of God to every living soul.

Jesus said in John 9:5, **"As long as I am in the world, I am the light of the world."** We are now the light of the world, ambassadors for the Kingdom of God. We must be on our jobs reminding the world to change their course of travel while visibility exists. John 9:4 says, **"The night cometh, when no man can work."** How many people have you led to Jesus today? Have you led anyone to Jesus? No one needs to be caught dead without knowing who Jesus is and what is available in and through Him. Let's get busy!

### Daily Prayer

Dear God, thank You for a revelation of You through Your Son Jesus Christ, through Your living Word, and through Your Holy Spirit. Forgive us of our sins and forgive those who sin against us. Help us to develop our ability to bring others to an intimate relationship with our Lord and Savior Jesus Christ, and to be kind, courteous, and understanding in all of our doings.

Father, we thank You for revealing our actions to us in a timely manner as we act out Your works in Your name. Thank

You for blessing us supernaturally as we continue to bless others.

We also thank You that we are able to sow abundantly in Your Kingdom on a continuous basis, magnifying Your name and winning a myriad of souls through You.

We know that there are no limits to what You can do, Lord, and through You there are no limits to what we can do.

Continue to bless the nations around the world, especially where people are oppressed and are not able to serve You freely. We pray for peace in Jerusalem and for peace in our homes and that Your Kingdom will come and Your will be done on earth as it is in heaven.

We will always be careful to give You all the praise, the glory, and the honor as we expand Your Kingdom in the name of Jesus. Amen.

# About the Author

Born on June 7, 1953, in Birmingham, Alabama, Herman Lee Hinton currently resides in Trussville, Alabama. He is married and the father of four children.

At present, Lieutenant Hinton is a twenty-two-year veteran with the City of Birmingham, employed as a police captain in the Crimes Against Persons Unit.

His education includes a Bachelor of Science in criminal justice from Miles College in Fairfield, Alabama.

In addition to overseeing the Homicide Unit, he also commands the Sex Crimes and Family Services Units. His work detail includes overseeing the work of over thirty investigators who conduct death investigations and other crimes against persons. He is responsible for submitting a variety of updates on daily activities, monthly and yearly reports, and vital information to other unit commanders and other agencies.